# BEING GEOFFREY BOYCOTT

BY GEOFFREY BOYCOTT
AND JON HOTTEN

fairfield books

First published by Fairfield Books in 2022

**fairfield books**

Fairfield Books
Bedser Stand
Kia Oval
London
SE11 5SS

Typeset in Garamond
Typesetting by Rob Whitehouse
Photography by Getty Images unless stated

© 2022 Sir Geoffrey Boycott and Jon Hotten
ISBN 978-1-915237-06-4; 978-1-915237-18-7 (special edition)

A CIP catalogue record for is available from the British Library

Printed and bound by CPI Group (UK) Ltd, Croydon, CR0 4YY

# BEING GEOFFREY BOYCOTT

BY GEOFFREY BOYCOTT
AND JON HOTTEN

# Contents

# Co-Author's note

During the pandemic's first phase, Geoffrey Boycott sat down and wrote what I would call a retrospective diary of his Test match career, which began in 1964, when he was 23 years old and still batting in his glasses, and ended in 1982, when he became Test cricket's greatest run-scorer. In all he played 108 times, and missed another 30 possible appearances during an exile that began in 1974 and lasted until 1977.

A lot of things happened in his career: being dropped after scoring 246 not out; captaining for four Tests; making a century in the first innings of his comeback match; scoring his hundredth first-class hundred during a Test against Australia at his spiritual home of Headingley; facing perhaps the fastest single over ever bowled, from Michael Holding in Barbados in 1981.

In undertaking to write something about each of the Tests, the least memorable and the most eventful, he had created something unusual and strikingly original. It was illuminating and forthright, done in that oh so familiar voice and characterised by his unvarnished, sometimes lacerating honesty. The diary conveyed the relentlessness of his professional life and his extrovert/introvert character. It had a direct objectivity and a high level of detail. Boycott has an astonishing memory, because I think the experience of playing cricket was for him the great love of his life. It took all of his physical and mental energy and it left a very deep imprint on him, one that he can tap back into.

As a raw document, exactly as he typed it, I think the diary will be a valuable resource for historians of the game in years to come. He hadn't begun with the idea of publishing, and at first, he just sent chunks of it to his wife Rachael to read. The fact that it's here now is a story in its own right, but a copy found its way to Matt Thacker at Fairfield Books, and he sent it to me, partly because he knew I was desperate to see it.

As soon as I started, the book's first line came into my head:
*'You hear it on the radio...'*
Who knows how or why these things happen, but then and there, I began to write it down. It became a sort of second-person response to what was in the diary, a way of contextualising what

was happening in Geoffrey's life around the matches, and also a way of reflecting his thoughts back at him. I used parts of the diary that weren't directly about the Tests. I researched old matches and read all of Geoffrey's books, and those of his team-mates and opponents. Sometimes my questions would prompt Geoffrey to recall things he had felt or said, or that people had said to him. We had one (for me) amazing 90-minute conversation about his routines and rituals around batting and preparing to bat. I scoured YouTube for videos of innings played long ago, and listened to clips and interviews, including his spiky appearance on *In The Psychiatrist's Chair* with the late Anthony Clare. From those elements, the voice came.

It says a lot about Geoffrey that he was open-minded enough to read it and consider the idea for what became this book, and then later to significantly add to it. In doing so, it became a book that's also about the internal and external forces that propelled him from a pit village in Yorkshire to the pinnacle of the world game – what it gave him, and also what it took out of him to reach a place that very few cricketers do.

**Jon Hotten**

# CHAPTER ONE

# 1964

*You hear it on the radio.*

*That's how they tell you. No phone call from the Chairman of Selectors. No conversation with the captain.*

*The 1pm news. BBC Light Radio.*

*Sunday 31 May, 1964.*

*That's how you'll hear…*

*You start the season of 1964 with runs: half centuries against Essex at Hull and Kent at Bradford, then 151 against Middlesex at Headingley and 131 against Lancashire at Old Trafford. Through the mail you receive an invitation to play for MCC against the Australians at Lord's. The newspapers are calling it a Test trial. Maybe it is. But before you travel to London you go to New Road, Worcester to play in the County Championship for Yorkshire.*

\* \* \*

Every winter at Worcester the Severn burst its banks and as the water receded it spilled its silt onto the square at New Road. The silt got rolled into the pitch and turned it hard, like concrete. So the story went, anyway. It sounded like an old wives' tale, but maybe it was true. It certainly felt true as Jack Flavell bowled me for nought in the first innings and Len Coldwell bowled me for seven in the second.

I'd never seen Flavell before in my life. I had never seen Coldwell, but they were brisk and aggressive and they knew how to use that new ball. Between them they sent down 2,000 overs a season. They didn't know it yet, but they were on their way to bowling Worcestershire to the 1964 County Championship title.

They hit that silty Worcester deck hard. That silty deck, faster than anything I'd ever played on. At Yorkshire, we had pitches that seamed or turned, that were way slower than New Road because of the amount of rain and the type of soil.

0 and 7.

Getting out was always failure and it hurt. Sometimes it hurt for a couple of days. It stayed in my head. When you fail as an opening batsman, you get plenty of time to think about it… My team-mates out there in the middle, making runs that I could be making. I detested failure, right from the first time I failed, right from the start.

\* \* \*

*Park Avenue, Bradford 16 June 1962. Yorkshire versus Pakistan, your first-class debut. You open the batting and hit your first delivery to the boundary, an auspicious start, but are then dismissed for four in each innings. A day later you bat at number four in the County Championship match against Northamptonshire and make scores of six and 21 not out. Against Derbyshire you open the batting and get 47 and 30. You drop back to the second XI while the first team go on to become county champions.*

*You are 22 years old and your future is uncertain. You don't drink, you don't smoke, play cricket in your glasses. You don't quite fit. In the handful of matches given to you, you have made 150 runs at 21.42. Vic Wilson, the club captain, recommends to the Committee that you should not be retained but then Wilson announces his retirement and Brian Close is appointed in his place.*

*Close sees something in you, how dedicated you are, how well you concentrate. He tells the Committee that he will sort you out. You spend the winter at Johnny Lawrence's indoor school and when you get back into the Yorkshire side you play the innings that changes everything for you, that changes your life. In the Roses match at Bramall Lane you go in at number five and on an awkward pitch against a bowling attack that features four England internationals make 145, your maiden first-class century, a knock so good that it is compared to some of Hutton's.*

*In July you give up your job at the Ministry of Pensions in Barnsley to play cricket full time. You have no contract with Yorkshire and your only income is a match fee for each appearance, a precarious existence dependent upon keeping your place in the team. Your life is in your hands.*

*Brian Close asks you to open the batting and you fail four times in a row. Close leaves the team soon afterwards to play for England against West Indies, and you ask stand-in captain Jimmy Binks if you can go back down the order – who wouldn't after scores like those? – and he agrees. You return to number five and make 80 against Glamorgan and 32 and 37 against Worcestershire.*

*You have just finished breakfast at the Salisbury Hotel in Scarborough before the match against Warwickshire at North Marine Road when Brian Close, back from England duty, finds you and says he wants you to open the batting.*

*'No thank you, captain,' you tell Brian Close.*

*'Well you have a choice,' Close says. 'You can either open the batting or not play. I have taken the decision to make you into an opening batsman because your technique, temperament and approach to batting fits it. Now go and do your best.'*

*You do. You always do. You finish the 1963 season third in the national batting averages.*

*You have opened the batting for many teams, but you have never liked opening the batting. You do now. Brian Close is right. It suits your game, that immaculate technique, and it suits your temperament. You like the certainty of knowing when you will bat, and who you will face. You can prepare for certainties. You can structure a life around 11.30am on the first morning of a game.*

* * *

Raymond Illingworth pulled me aside before I left for London.

'It might be a blessing, those two failures,' he said.

'I can't see how...'

'You're in great nick. And when that happens, sometimes we get overconfident without realising it. Those two low scores might just really make you watch the ball.'

I thought about what Raymond had said on the way to Lord's. I watched that ball. I watched that ball hard and I got 63 in the first innings and 17 in the second.

But Brian Bolus played and he made runs. John Edrich played, and he made runs, too.

I got no telephone call from the Chairman of Selectors. I heard nothing from the captain. I knew I hadn't done enough. I went from Lord's to Grace Road, Leicester, where we bowled Leicester out cheaply on the first morning. Yorkshire went in and I was undefeated on 70 at the close. In 1964, no professional cricket was played on

Sundays in England, and so Alan Thompson, the Northern cricket correspondent of the *Daily Express*, offered me a lift back home to mum's in Fitzwilliam.

'No point in staying in a strange city all day when you can have a night in your own bed, Geoffrey.'

On the journey he said, 'Why don't I pick you up tomorrow. Come for lunch with the family and we'll head back to Leicester late afternoon?'

'Alright…'

'I think you might get selected for the first Test, Geoffrey. Announcement tomorrow on the lunchtime news…'

'I'll bet you five pounds I don't.'

That's how certain I was – willing to bet my own money. Bolus and Edrich making runs. Cowdrey and Dexter available again after missing the winter tour of India.

'You're on,' he said, and shook my hand.

The next morning Alan Thompson arrived in Fitzwilliam with a photographer in tow and took me, mum and my brother Tony into the back yard. He turned mum's washtub upside down for the wickets and got me to bat in front of it. Alan drove us to his place in Huddersfield for lunch. At 1pm he turned on the radio for the afternoon news. The bulletin seemed to drag on and on before the announcer said:

'And finally, here is the England team to play in the first Test match against the Australians at Trent Bridge on Thursday:

'Ted Dexter, Sussex, captain; David Allen, Gloucestershire; Ken Barrington, Surrey; Geoff Boycott, Yorkshire; Len Coldwell, Worcestershire; Colin Cowdrey, Kent; John Edrich, Surrey; Jack Flavell, Worcestershire; Jim Parks, Sussex; Phil Sharpe, Yorkshire; Fred Titmus, Middlesex; Fred Trueman, Yorkshire.'

'Yes!' Alan shouted. 'That's a fiver you owe me, Geoffrey. Congratulations! Bloody well done, son!'

Days later I discovered that reporters from every other national newspaper were trying to find me, but Alan had spirited me away for his exclusive.

His exclusive and my fiver, that's what Alan got…

'They've taken the word naïve out of the dictionary, Geoffrey,' he said.

\* \* \*

*The official invitation to play for England comes through the post. It requests that you telephone the secretary of MCC to accept the offer. It tells you that your match fee will be £100. It tells you to arrive for net practice at 3pm on the day before the match and then at 7pm to attend dinner with the selectors, jacket and tie required...*

*At Grace Road, Leicester, you take your score to 151 not out. You finish on the Tuesday and on the Wednesday go to Nottingham and you present yourself at the Trent Bridge Nets.*

*There is Cowdrey. There is Barrington. There is Titmus. There is Ted Dexter, captain of England.*

*There is Jack Flavell. There is Len Coldwell. What are they thinking? 0 and 7.*

*During practice, John Edrich, your opening partner, steps on a ball and turns his ankle.*

*At the pre-match dinner, Walter Robins comes over to introduce himself. Walter Robins is the Chairman of Selectors.*

*'I will try my best to give you three Test matches to prove yourself,' he says. 'But we have got a series to win. So it might only be two...'*

*Walter disappears and leaves you to your dinner...*

*After you have eaten, Ted Dexter stands up to address the team:*

*'Our Fred,' he says, smiling across the table at Trueman. 'Our Fred here has a magic ball for all of the Australians, don't you Fred... A couple of outswingers and then an inswinger... that was Ian Redpath done and dusted last time, wasn't it Fred... A couple of short ones and a yorker and it was goodbye Bob Simpson... Another wicket for Trueman...'*

*Ted Dexter runs through the Australian batting, reminding each of the bowlers of their successes. Reminding each of the bowlers of what is required in an England shirt.*

*You sit back in your chair and soak it up, drink it in.*

*This is the night you have dreamed of.*

*The night before your first Test innings.*

*In the quiet of your hotel room, you lie on the bed.*

*You go through each of the Australian bowlers in your head, making your plans, hatching your plots, constructing your defence, even before the game has started.*

*And then you sleep, eight hours straight through, and you do not dream of cricket, because you have never dreamt of cricket, and you never do.*

## First Test, England versus Australia,
## Trent Bridge, Nottingham, 4-9 June, 1964

### *Debut*

The fourth of June 1964 dawned grey and wet. The nerves were waiting for me when I woke. The nerves were always there for every game I ever played, from benefit match to Ashes decider. It would worry me deeply if they weren't. The nerves prove that you care, they switch you on, make you ready to face what you have to face.

I always scored runs, every season, every team, every level from Barnsley seconds to Yorkshire. But all the same, you don't know you can do it until you do it. June 4, an auspicious day… the biggest of my life.

The cloud hung low over Trent Bridge with no wind to move it. At the Radcliffe Road end, the floodlight pylons of the Nottingham Forest football ground disappeared into the grey. On the benches and in the pavilion the crowd were in early, the men in hats, the women under umbrellas. John Edrich had woken to find that the foot he turned on a ball at nets had swollen overnight. When the rain let up and I walked out to open the batting for England against Australia, it was not John Edrich but Fred Titmus who walked out with me. Fred was usually a lower order player, a number seven or eight, but he was tough and knew how to handle a bat.

I didn't need to worry about Fred.

I had plenty of worries of my own in the poor light and the dicey pitch, and Garth McKenzie making the ball leap from a length at the Radcliffe Road End. He bowled with three slips and a gully, a leg gully and a man right under my nose at short square-leg, a field to match the weather on a bowler's day.

One lifter from McKenzie smacked into my bottom hand and did some damage. Then he knocked Fred off his feet with a short one. Corling was less of a problem from the Pavilion End, but things soon changed when Neil Hawke replaced him. Hawke had this bounding run and a wide, slinging action that banged the ball hard into the pitch. He was a big strong guy.

The score had ticked up to 30-odd when I pushed Hawke into the leg side and called Fred through for a single. Now, Fred was deaf in one ear, and he responded late. Hawke twisted athletically out of his follow through to chase the ball but before he could get there he and Fred collided and Fred hit the deck. Hawke grabbed the ball and lobbed it to Wally Grout who held it over the stumps with Fred still flat on his back and miles from home.

Without a word to anybody or a look at his captain, Wally Grout, this hard old bastard of an Aussie, threw the ball back to Hawke without removing the bails. Who said you can't be tough and a great sportsman?

And it was hard cricket on that uncovered pitch. Between the rain and the teams being introduced to the Duke of Edinburgh, there was time for one hour and fifty minutes of batting, and I made my way to 23 not out at the close of day one. The rain-soaked pitch was covered for the night, but only once the play was called off – a crazy rule.

* * *

*You sleep for eight hours in your hotel bed, return to Trent Bridge and take your score on to 48 before you edge Grahame Corling to Ian Redpath at second slip. Redpath misses the ball but Bob Simpson dives with lightning speed from first slip and scoops it up, a brilliant catch from the best slip fielder you will ever see.*

*Your first Test innings and Grahame Corling's first Test wicket.*

*This is how it goes. England make 216-8 declared, Australia are bowled out for 168 by Fred Trueman and Len Coldwell, who take three wickets each, but a whole day's play is washed away and the game ends in a draw. While you are fielding, you jam the finger that McKenzie damaged into the grass and have to go off. After the game you discover that it is broken and you will miss the second Test. Walter Robins calls and promises to keep a place open for you.*

*Even so, at Lord's, when Ted Dexter becomes a makeshift opener and is bowled fourth ball by McKenzie, you almost give a little cheer of relief.*

*On the television highlights, you see yourself bat for the first time. Until those grainy black and white images, you do not know how you appear to the rest of the world. It's a strange experience and you notice how obvious your glasses look and how low you keep your hands when you play forwards. The glasses are for eyesight so poor you once feared that you would never be able to play professional cricket. The low hands come from the rubber flooring at the Johnny Lawrence indoor school where you practise each winter, and from the uncovered pitches that you must make your runs on.*

*You realise that both of these things will have to change.*

48 and DNB

\* \* \*

### Third Test, England versus Australia, Headingley, Leeds, 2-6 July, 1964

*Second cap*

Walter Robins kept his word. I came back at Headingley for the third Test. From a rain-ruined draw at Lord's, where the first two days were a wash-out, Colin Cowdrey, Phil Sharpe and Len Coldwell were out. Jack Flavell, Ken Taylor and me were back. For Australia, Norm O'Neill was out and Bob Cowper was in.

The Yorkshire weather played ball, of course. The sun was out, the ground was full, the Headingley pitch perfect for batting. It was one of those days, those perfect days, when everything clicked and I played beautifully, eight boundaries in my 38, until Bobby Simpson brought Grahame Corling on first change, and I was immediately out, caught at first slip by Bobby.

We made 268 and then Norman Gifford and Fred Titmus got to work, sending the Aussies from 124-1 to 178-7 on the second afternoon. Ted Dexter took the new ball and handed it to Fred Trueman, told him to finish Australia off. But the pitch was dry, there was no great pace in it, not much grass, and Peter Burge, with Neil Hawke for company, smacked it around, hit Fred all over Headingley. Fred got Hawke in the end, but not until Burge had an unbeaten hundred to his name.

Next morning, he carried on, this time with Wally Grout at the other end, carried on until he hit Fred to Alan Rees, the substitute fielder. Australia were now in the lead by 121 runs...

...And when we got back in, Bob Simpson called on Grahame Corling to take the new ball. Bobby had seen me play well twice now, but he had seen Grahame Corling dismiss me twice, too, and now, after 20 minutes of batting and four runs from 14 deliveries, Corling jumped a little wider on the bowling crease, just a tiny variation that meant the ball he sent down looked as though it was coming in at me until it pitched and held its line. My feet didn't move but my hands did, following that ball until it took the edge of my bat and flew low past the glove of Wally Grout and into the left hand of Bobby Simpson, inches above the ground.

Ct Simpson b Corling.

Again.

Three times now. Three times in three innings.

England's second innings folded around Ken Barrington, who made 85 while it all burned down around him: three wickets for Corling, three for McKenzie, three for Veivers. Under the hot Yorkshire sun, with Headingley full and with people watching from the roofs of houses that overlook the ground, Neil Hawke swung the bowling of Fred Titmus to the legside boundary to win the game.

One nil. My first defeat in an England shirt.

As the two teams chatted in the Aussie dressing room, I walked over to Bobby Simpson.

'Well caught...' I said.

Bobby Simpson smiled.

'You nick 'em and I'll catch 'em, Geoffrey...'

I said: 'Well, I'd better learn not to nick 'em, then...'

**38** and **4**

\* \* \*

*You know you have a problem against Grahame Corling, and you know that Bobby Simpson knows. Bobby Simpson will have Grahame Corling opening the bowling against you whenever he can. You have to solve it. No-one else will.*

*You don't wait for someone to tell you how. You already know what to do. You find Bill Bowes at the team hotel. You know Bill from your time as a youngster, going to Yorkshire nets. You know that bowlers have insight into batsmen and batting, and bowlers don't come much better than Bill Bowes, with his 1,639 first-class wickets.*

*You tell Bill about the line that Grahame Corling is bowling to you. Many years later you will come up with a name for it: the Corridor of Uncertainty, but for now it is an unnamed, fearful place. Bill tells you that Herbert Sutcliffe would go back and across his stumps just before the bowler delivered the ball and his judgement of what to play and what to leave was excellent. You know that Herbert Sutcliffe had a Test match batting average of more than 60 and was one of the greatest openers ever.*

*You thank Bill for his time and at the nets before the next Test you try out Sutcliffe's method. Right away it feels good, feels right, a little press onto the ball of your right foot that lets you move further back to the short ball and, most importantly, get forward when you need to.*

*No-one tells you to do this. No captain, no coach, no chairman of selectors. They don't have to. From defeat, in failure, you learn.*

\* \* \*

## Fourth Test, England versus Australia, Old Trafford, Manchester, 23-28 July, 1964

### Third cap

Our Fred copped the blame for the defeat at Leeds, for not ending the Australian innings with the new ball when they were seven wickets down. But the pitch was dry, the sun was out, there was no seam, no swing. Fred Titmus was causing Australia all the problems, tying them down, and the captain took him off. On reflection, he made a choice and should have accepted some of the responsibility. He took a chance and it didn't work out.

But Fred bore the brunt. With his total standing at 297 Test match wickets, his name was not on the team sheet for the Manchester Test. Out too went Ken Taylor, Norman Gifford and Jack Flavell. In came Fred Rumsey, John Mortimore, Tom Cartwright and John Price.

Ken Taylor was another to get the wrong end of the stick.

When Yorkshire had played the Australians at Sheffield early in the tour, Ken scored 160 runs as an opener, but he was selected to bat at number six at Headingley. Anyone who has played cricket at a decent level knows that a guy who has opened the innings for years and is suddenly asked to bat down the order has a big problem. An opener never has to wait around, so when a guy is not used to it his nerves can become shredded. Some players become like jelly before they even take strike and are mentally shot before they get in.

Here he was having to deal with batting down the order in his first Test match for five years. Crazy! Ken was a nervous batsman. Collectively the selectors had played in 134 Test matches and they all had years of county cricket experience. It was mind-blowing how former cricketers could just forget all that they had seen and experienced in dressing rooms.

Ken scored nine in the first innings, and in the second innings he batted at number eight and scored 15.

What a waste.

At Old Trafford, Bob Simpson won the toss and batted us out of the Ashes. The first Australian wicket came deep into the afternoon, Bill Lawry out for 106. A run-out, too. Bob Simpson seemed to bat forever, right through days one and two and into the third morning, finally out for 311. Bob had made more than 40 first-class centuries but that was his first Test ton. It seemed amazing that he'd never done it before… he just batted and batted and batted… I knew that Ted Dexter had reached his wits' end when he handed me the ball: Boycott 1-0-3-0, Australia 656-8 declared, the Ashes far out of our reach. After two days in the field I was so tired, but when McKenzie and Corling took the new ball I used my new technique and it worked. I made 58 before McKenzie knocked back my off stump. I was glad of the rest day, and when we returned on Monday, the pitch was still flat, flat, flat and Ted Dexter and Ken Barrington filled their boots. England 611 all out.

The papers called it the most boring Test match ever played.

58 and DNB

* * *

*Alan Thompson of the Daily Express finds you in the dressing room while Dexter and Barrington bat and bat.*

*'Can you get away for an hour?' He says.*

*Alan takes you across the road to the Old Trafford football ground – the real Old Trafford, the Theatre of Dreams.*

*He leads you under the main stand, where the Manchester United first team are playing a game of cricket with a tennis ball.*

*Your footballing idol Denis Law steps forward and shakes your hand. Denis has just scored 46 goals in a single season, a Manchester United record. When the new season begins in a few weeks' time, United will take their first title since the Munich air crash. Denis will be the League's top-scorer and win the Ballon d'Or.*

*Denis is just eight months older than you, but already a star. You are still a kid with glasses, barely out of Yorkshire, but the world is slowly becoming interested in you. The papers run stories about where you grew up, your mum and your dad, your brothers... They write about how you came up through the Yorkshire system, about your batting and what makes you tick...*

*Bob Simpson and his team have been reading about you too. They have read that you like to sit quietly before you bat and contemplate the bowlers you are about to face. Before the final Test at The Oval, the Australians travel to Bradford Park Avenue to play Yorkshire. As you pad up, the Yorkshire dressing room is visited by Bob, Bill Lawry and a stream of Aussie players trying to talk to you, banter with you, upset your preparation. It is instantly forgettable rubbish, your first lesson in Australian gamesmanship.*

*You could have told them they were wasting their breath. You go out there and you make 54 in the first innings and 122 in the second. Bob Simpson does everything he can, he even brings up the field, every man around the bat, and so you hit Tom Veivers over the top, hook Neil Hawke for six and then drive him for four.*

*Bobby Simpson tells the papers that 'Boycott plays cricket the Australian way'.*

\* \* \*

## Fifth Test, England versus Australia, The Oval, London, 13-18 August, 1964

*Fourth cap*

The Ashes were done, gone. The final Test opened in the gloom of low cloud, setting the mood. Trueman was back and so was Cowdrey. Edrich was out and I was to open with Bob Barber, a third partner in four matches.

It was a swinging morning but a good pitch for batting. Ted Dexter won the toss, but Neil Hawke bowled us out. He clean bowled Bob Barber for 24, then he clean bowled me for 30. He got Dexter caught by Booth for 23 and Barrington caught by Bobby Simpson for 47. He got Fred Titmus caught by Wally Grout and wrapped up the innings before close of play by getting Fred Trueman caught by Ian Redpath. England all out 182 in 74.1 overs. All of us in the top order got a start. No-one went on. Australia had an over or two before the close, and then they batted all day on Friday, used the wicket that we couldn't, losing only five wickets and not a single one of those to Fred.

We all knew that Fred needed three more to become the first man in history to 300 Test match wickets. His first spell was still quick but his later ones not as fast as before. How could they be, in his 34th year, after all of those thousands of overs for Yorkshire and England? But he still had that perfect sideways on action, a great outswinger and a deadly, outswinging yorker, a fierce determination and a big heart.

The Saturday would be a red-letter day for us both. Just before lunchtime, Fred clean bowled Ian Redpath for number 298, and then with his very next ball had Garth McKenzie caught by Colin Cowdrey for number 299.

Fred on a hat-trick for the 300th!

What a fairy tale it would be. I watched from fine leg as Fred came in to Neil Hawke, who survived the hat-trick ball but not for much longer. Soon he edged to Colin Cowdrey too, and Fred had done it, become the first man up the mountain. I ran in from the deep to congratulate my idol.

By the close of play I was 70-odd not out, with the rest day on Sunday to think about those 30 more runs. Harry Secombe had invited both teams to see the musical *Pickwick* at the Saville Theatre and afterwards we all went backstage to shake his hand and meet the cast for drinks.

Monday morning inched around. The nerves were there but the nerves were good. I could handle them. I batted through the first hour or so and as lunch approached, I went into the nineties for the first time in Test match cricket.

Bob Simpson made sure that Grahame Corling was back on to bowl, coming in from the Pavilion End, but this time he was just a little too wide, just a fraction too short and I was into my favourite shot off the back foot through square cover to the rope.

It was a great feeling, a wonderful feeling for a kid in glasses from a village in Yorkshire, but it was all over soon afterwards, caught by Ian Redpath at slip from a Bob Simpson leg-break for 113.

That afternoon in the dressing room a crate of champagne arrived addressed to me, courtesy of Harry Secombe. He was one of the biggest stars in Britain and I'm a new, unknown boy. How generous, thoughtful and amazing was that?

**30** and **113**

\* \* \*

*The final day is a wash-out. The end of your first series as an international cricketer comes in the South London rain, the Ashes on their way back to a land of sun and dust, a place that you have never seen, that you can only imagine.*

*The Times points out that England have won just two of the last 20 Tests against Australia. Amid a gloomy post-mortem, the cricket correspondent writes: 'Boycott scored what I'm sure will be the first of many Test match hundreds. In him, England have introduced a batsman of quality.' In The Cricketer, John Woodcock writes that you were 'the real find of the series. To say that he has something of Herbert Sutcliffe's phlegmatic temperament is to pay him a high compliment.'*

*291 runs at 48.50 is your return.*

*The season is not over. In September you go to Bristol to play Gloucestershire. On a turning pitch you hit 177. You go past 2,000 runs for the season. You finish top of the Yorkshire averages and fifth in the national averages. The Wisden Almanack of 1965 will name you one of its five Cricketers of the Year.*

*None of this matters at home. Your brother Tony loves to get hold of the early paper when you're playing.*

*'How many did you get today, then?' He'll say, as soon as you're through the door.*

*Tony already knows. And he never asks when it's a hundred...*

*But he and your other brother Peter are always out in the field behind the house with you, out there while you work on your throwing arm, Peter keeping wicket behind a single stump and Tony hitting the ball to all corners for you to chase. Out there because Willie Watson, one of the England selectors, has told you that your fielding is not up to international standard...*

*And your mum, keeping the home together, keeping you fed and watered, caring for your dad, caring for you all.*

*Her three lads.*

*Your family, your mum.*

*Your heart bursts.*

*This is where it comes from, the love, the determination, the overwhelming fear of failure... of failing them. Failing yourself.*

*This is where it's from.*

*The selectors meet to choose a touring party to go to South Africa. This time there is no doubt when the announcement is made on BBC radio on a Sunday morning in September. Your name is one of the first on the list. But there are no places for the old guard. There is no place for Colin Cowdrey. The selectors pick Mike Brearley of Cambridge University, instead. There is no place for Fred Trueman. The selectors pick Tony Nicholson of Yorkshire instead. The selectors pick MJK Smith of Warwickshire to captain the tour and appoint Donald Carr, assistant secretary of MCC, as tour manager. They pick John Price, Tom Cartwright and David Brown. They pick Bob Barber, Peter Parfitt, Jim Parks, David Allen and Ken Barrington. They pick Ted Dexter, but Ted is standing for the Tories at Cardiff South East in the General Election. He will join the tour if he loses the vote.*

*The plane will leave for Salisbury, Rhodesia, on 15 October, 1964. You will be gone for four months. You have never left England. There are no nets, no training days, just a gathering at which the President of MCC tells the squad not to get involved in the politics of South Africa.*

*It is exciting, a thrill, a new life. You go to London for a medical and visit Simpson's of Piccadilly to be measured for your blazer with the red and yellow braid of MCC, Jaeger sweaters and lightweight grey trousers and also, as a gift from Simpson's, the most beautiful pair of cream trousers you'll ever own. You like clothes, like to dress well. It appeals to your immaculate nature.*

*15 October 1964. Off you go.*

\* \* \*

On the plane, MJK Smith looked up from the newspaper and said, 'Ted will be with us shortly.'

'Why's that,' I asked.

'He's just told some dockers in Wales that some people are more fit to rule than others...'

We were handed embarkation cards to fill in. It was all new to me. I'd never been on a plane before. Donald Carr came around to collect them and make sure we'd filled everything out correctly. I gave Donald my card. He looked at it for a moment.

'Geoffrey...'

'Yes manager...'

'Under occupation, you have written, 'making runs...''

'Yes manager.'

'Well what about when you are fielding?'

'That's what I do while I'm waiting to bat...'

\* \* \*

*The tour begins with a number of first-class matches. You find the fast, bouncy pitches hard to adjust to. You don't make many runs. It's those low hands again, the low hands from the Rothwell Indoor Cricket School with Johnny Lawrence and his rubber mats. Every Saturday of every winter from the age of ten, you make the trip: two buses and a long walk through the rain or snow with your cricket bag, never missing a session, loving every minute. But the ball stays low on those rubber mats and it stays low on the uncovered Yorkshire pitches and your hands stay low to cope. You are a product of your environment: everyone in cricket is.*

*In Rhodesia and South Africa, the ball comes on a bit quicker. Your favourite back foot shot, where you punch or force the ball from just short of length through square cover now goes straight to point or flies to gully. It slides off the face of the bat because you are a fraction late. You're middling the ball and still getting caught, and it is hard to adapt.*

*Two hundred runs in ten innings is nothing to rave about, but then you get to Port Elizabeth to play Eastern Province and you solve the problem, because that is what you do. You get to 197, and as lunch approaches on the second day, Mike Smith sends a message to say that he will declare at the interval, so now is the chance to make your double ton. Peter Pollock works out what is happening and takes forever to bowl the final over, and when he finally does, he bowls you two bouncers that you can't reach and two beamers that only just miss you, and he laughs at you while he does it.*

\* \* \*

## First Test, South Africa v England, Durban, Natal 4-8 December, 1964

### *Fifth cap*

Humid, hot as hell but we won the toss and were glad to bat. Bob Barber and I put on 120 for the first wicket, so we were off to a flyer. Bob played cricket with a smile on his face, treated batting like it was fun.

After a while, Trevor Goddard brought his off-spinner Kelly Seymour on. Bob came down the pitch to me.

'This guy can't bowl,' he said.

'Oh can't he,' I thought... 'Let's at least have a look at him first...'

But Bob whacked him over midwicket and chirruped:

'You can't bowl to me without a fielder there...'

Goddard put a man out at cow corner. Bob launched the next one over mid-on.

'You'll need a fielder there, too...'

Goddard didn't react, so Bob kept doing it until he moved a man there, too. Bob was having a great time, laughing away, coming down the pitch to chat to me. The South Africans didn't know what to make of him, and they were not the only ones... As a young kid at Yorkshire if I tried to hit a spinner over the top the coaches would say 'keep it on the floor lad .... tha' can't get out there...'When South Africa batted, a couple of early wickets by our seamers put them under huge pressure to avoid the follow on. They seemed to be stuck, mesmerised by our two off-spinners, and as the game progressed the ball started to turn. In two innings David Allen took seven wickets, Fred Titmus took six and Bob Barber came on with his leg-spinners and got a couple more.

The South Africans lost 15 wickets to spin at Durban, but I reckon we actually got about 30. Only half were given. There were so many inside edges, bat-pads that the umpires didn't see or didn't have the courage to give against their star players.

Graeme Pollock, who was to become a truly great player, was baffled by Fred Titmus's flight and guile and made nought and five. South Africa were big favourites and when they lost by an innings and 104 to go one-nil down, it was a huge shock to the country.

`73` and `DNB`

\* \* \*

*In Cardiff South East, James Callaghan wins a majority of 7,841 over Ted Dexter, and becomes Chancellor of the Exchequer in Harold Wilson's new government. Ted takes defeat hard. Interviewed by Kenneth Morgan immediately after the count, he says, 'it was all my fault'. He is shaking and close to tears. He arrives in South Africa late and then misses a tour game to visit the Kruger National Park with his wife, Susan. A slow day for the press and anything for a good headline, he gets it in the neck once again.*

*Politics is not confined to the UK General Election. It is the era of Apartheid under its architect, Prime Minister Hendrik Verwoerd.*

*The UK Government has just discontinued its arms trade with South Africa. The grounds are full of white people. There are fenced-off areas for Cape Coloureds and fenced-off areas for blacks. You have never seen anything like it, especially at the Wanderers, where the second and fourth Tests are played. It is a deeply conflicting experience. The people are wonderful and welcoming. You go into their homes for meals. The South African cricket board lay on Ford Zephyr cars with drivers to take the team to play golf or to the beach. The sightseeing is spectacular. You have a 16mm Bolex camera loaned to you by Harry Secombe that you take to Victoria Falls, up Table Mountain, around the Cape of Good Hope, to Kirstenbosch Gardens, to the Cecil Rhodes Memorial, for an overnight stay in the Kruger National Park. You and Bob Barber visit a rhino game reserve called Hluhluwe. You get up in the middle of the night to be driven from Durban so that you can meet the head ranger just as dawn comes up. The head ranger is Ian Player, brother of Gary Player, the champion golfer. Ian takes you deep into the bush where you see white and black rhino. Ian tells you that the white rhino are bigger but the black rhino are more aggressive. They have poor eyesight and only see shapes so you must stand still and keep quiet if one looks directly at you. You creep towards a black rhino as it feeds on grass, and you're 15 yards away when it stops eating, looks up and gets ready to charge. You and Ian are rooted to the spot, terrified, and when the rhino finally decides to ignore you and start eating again, you turn around to see that Bob is halfway up a tree.*

* * *

*Donald Carr and MJK Smith invite Wally Hammond to watch the first Test from England's dressing room. You are in awe of one of the greatest batsmen to have played the game. He has scored more Test match runs than any man in history, including his great rival Bradman. He moved to Durban after his retirement and began working at the University of Natal as a sports administrator, but in 1960 he was involved in a serious car accident which has left him much frailer than he once was. In spite of his reputation as a difficult team-mate he is immediately popular with the squad. You meet him, but you're young, just 24 and still in your glasses and you don't have the confidence or the maturity to ask him about batting despite all of the questions that crowd your head. Seven months later he will be dead.*

\* \* \*

## Second Test, South Africa versus England, The Wanderers, Johannesburg, 23-29 December, 1964

### *Sixth cap*

Throughout the tour, no cricket of any kind was played on a Sunday. Everything closed, shut down. It was church, rest, no television, go to bed early. The second Test had two rest days as a result – hard to imagine now. The game stopped on Christmas Day and then again on Sunday 27.

That wasn't all that took getting used to. At nearly 6,000 feet above sea level, in the thin air of the Highveld, the ball flew through much faster than I'd ever experienced before. Catching was difficult because the ball hit you before you were set and ready to take it. The pitch was excellent, but faster and bouncier than anything I'd ever seen before. The carry was amazing – it just seemed to keep coming at me.

I was out early and cheaply to fast bowler Peter Pollock. Ted Dexter passed me as I was coming back to the dressing room. He looked so determined after everything he'd been through. A dazzling 172 was his answer to the criticism. Could he bat when in the mood… courage, technique, strokeplay, Ted had the lot. If I was to pick my best England Xl from the players I have played with or seen he would be my number three every time.

Bob Barber set the tone as Peter Pollock bowled genuinely fast. Bob would duck his bouncer before pretending to play a sweep shot and laugh after the ball was in the keeper's gloves. When Pollock pitched it up, Bob drove him superbly through the offside. Great theatre. He was finally bowled off an inside edge for 97. For all Bob's appearance of a cavalier approach, he was upset at getting out. Behind that outward fun-loving exterior, he was a committed cricketer, a fine batsman and a great guy. He was fantastic to me, like an older brother. When Peter Pollock had bowled those beamers at me in Port Elizabeth in the game with Eastern Province, Bob told him afterwards that he'd better not try it again, or he'd have trouble…

On the fourth day of the match we had thunder, lightning and torrential rain. The ground was flooded. Not just puddles or pools of water: the ground was a lake. We got showered and changed into our going home clothes. The South Africans didn't, and told us not to go home yet. We thought they were mad – you could have floated a boat out there.

And then, amazingly, the water disappeared. Where to, I have no idea, but with 40 minutes to the close, we were back out there. Graeme Pollock had just come in and still looked uncomfortable against the off-spinners. Titmus and Allen tried to keep Graeme under pressure, but the ball got wet as soon as it went into the outfield and they couldn't grip it. There were a number of loose deliveries. Graeme got away and was 37 not out when play ended. Next morning with a dry ball, sun out, the spinners got into their rhythm and David Allen bowled Graeme for 55. Too late, the spell we had on him was broken and his escape to a half-century would lift his confidence. Colin Bland batted superbly for 144 not out to save the match with rain and bad light at teatime finishing the day's play.

**4** and **DNB**

CHAPTER TWO

# 1965

*You open with Mike Brearley for the first time at a two-day tour game in Salisbury. You're walking off for tea when Brearley catches you up near the boundary and says: 'Are we going to the same place?'*

*'None of your egghead intellectual stuff,' you tell him.*

*Brearley never forgets the exchange. He writes about it many years later in his book 'On Cricket'. It seems to say something to him. He wants to understand you as a player and as a person.*

*He is just a year and a half younger, but your lives are very different. He has a first in Classics and 2:1 in Moral Sciences from St John's College Cambridge, and is about to undertake another four years of postgraduate study. He plays the first half of each summer for the University and the second half for Middlesex. He's good and scores lots of runs (not as many as you score) and in the cloistered world of cricket, where the Gentlemen versus Players fixture ended just two years ago and where, in 1964, Cambridge University play ten first-class matches against county teams and one against the touring Australians, being a gentleman and a Blue still carry weight.*

*Brearley takes an interest in the South African policy of Apartheid. He wants to visit the townships. After the President of MCC told you all not to get involved, Mike Brearley ruffles feathers. It doesn't do him much good on the field, where he is not yet ready for Test match cricket and does not play. But he is ahead of the curve. Your paths will cross again.*

\* \* \*

### Third Test, South Africa versus England, Newlands, Cape Town, 1-6 January, 1965

*Seventh cap*

Two days to fly a thousand miles and rest ready for back-to-back Tests in searing heat. We had bowled and fielded for three days trying to get a win in Johannesburg, so we were desperate to bat first. Mike lost the toss and now we were going to get another two days' bowling and fielding.

Five days out of seven. Phew!

And then Ian Thomson had Eddie Barlow caught behind first ball. The umpire didn't give it and our players were staggered. It was so obvious – he pushed at the ball away from his body and the ball couldn't have hit anything but his bat.

Later on in his innings, Fred Titmus and the lads around the bat felt he was caught bat and pad and got away with another. Nobody clapped when Eddie got his century.

At the end of play when he was interviewed by the press, he didn't pretend he hadn't hit it or make excuses. He just said, 'I hit it. I wait for the umpire's decision. The umpire didn't give me out. Simple.' Later on, I saw when he was given out and he thought he wasn't out he didn't complain. He just accepted it.

Ken Barrington was our most consistent batsman on the whole tour. He hardly missed a ball and looked impregnable in making back-to-back centuries in the first two Tests. At Newlands, Ken was playing another good innings when, on 49, the home team went up for him caught behind off Peter Pollock. The umpire gave him not out. Ken waited a few seconds then walked off. That caused a stir, but he had made his point about walking.

I've always had mixed feelings about it. It's easy to be a walker when you have scored some runs and you can return to the dressing room a success. The real test about walking is can you or will you walk when you are on nought or single figures…

By the time South Africa batted again, our bowlers were knackered. In the space of seven days, Ian Thomson and John Price had bowled 54 and 81 overs. Our two off-spinners, Fred Titmus and David Allen, had tired fingers from having to bowl 135 overs and 128 overs respectively. The big danger was that they would split their spinning fingers and be unavailable for the last two games.

Ten of our guys bowled in the second innings with only the captain not turning his arm over. I was asked to help out by bowling my medium slow rubbish. And that turned out to be very rewarding. In 20 overs I snared three wickets for 47 runs. Graeme Pollock was batting well against this collection of liquorice all sorts and I bowled him out for 73. I bowled out Colin Bland for 64 with an inswinger and Sydney Burke, a seam bowler tailender, tried to slog me and holed out.

**15** and **1 not out**

\* \* \*

## Fourth Test, South Africa versus England, The Wanderers, Johannesburg, 22-27 January, 1965

*Eighth cap*

Mike Smith won the toss and put South Africa in. I was too young to be part of the decision-making but both teams had been queuing up to bat first. I listened to conversations between many of the team who were beginning to believe that our batting was so strong that the home side could not bowl us out twice.

I was the only batsman not making many runs. Maybe putting them in was a tactic to make South Africa do all the running, as they had to win one of the last two Tests and we had already experienced Johannesburg's famous late afternoon electrical storms. Sure enough, rain came after tea the first two days and they had to declare and try get us out. England matched them with runs from Bob Barber, Ken Barrington and a not out century by Peter Parfitt.

South Africa chased quick runs and Bob Barber took a boundary catch, but in doing so broke a finger. He had to go off and would be unable to bat unless there were exceptional circumstances. After the match he went home, his tour finished.

Trying to bat out any last day to save a Test match is more about strength of mind than technique. There is usually wear and tear on the pitch and the opposition bowlers add a little extra to their efforts. By this fifth day huge cracks had appeared so there was the occasional steepler and the odd low ball. Up and down irregular bounce can be as disconcerting as sideways movement, especially facing fast bowlers. South Africa declared at lunch and raced through their overs with very attacking fields as time was the enemy and there were no limitation on overs in a day. You could bowl as many as you could send down. We kept losing wickets, which kept South Africa in with a sniff of victory. I played one of my best innings at a crucial time, seeing out 87 overs of pressure bowling in exactly four hours. So 21.75 overs per hour. It takes six-and-a-half hours to bowl that many these days.

**5** and **76 not out**

\* \* \*

*You bat like your life depends on it, because it does. This life, the only life you have ever wanted. South Africa toil and work and you resist them. You go deep into yourself, to that state of concentration so fierce that the world shrinks down to these twenty-two yards, twenty-two yards where it becomes you versus Peter Pollock [you win], you versus Atholl Mckinnon [you win], you versus Harry Bromfield [you win], you versus Joe Partridge, Graeme Pollock and Trevor Goddard [you win].*

*You versus South Africa for 87 overs.*

*You win.*

*You win, and England draw. England draw and remain one-nil up with one game to play.*

*You get to know a girl in Johannesburg. She has an apartment in the city and so when Ian Thomson turns 36 years old on the second day of the game, you organise a Saturday night party where everyone can celebrate with the rest day to follow. Thomson, the last-minute replacement, the old man who had never won a cap and once the tour is over never will again, has bowled his guts out on those flat pitches, kept going when everyone around him couldn't.*

*By the time you reach Port Elizabeth for the final Test, John Price goes down with an injured side, David Brown with an injured heel, Tom Cartright with an injured shoulder. MJK Smith and Donald Carr call up the Somerset medium-pacer Ken Palmer, who is coaching in Johannesburg, to open the bowling. They ask you to bowl first change.*

\* \* \*

32

## Fifth Test, South Africa versus England,
## St George's Park, Port Elizabeth, 12-17 February, 1965

### *Ninth cap*

What a mess. When I'm your third seamer then you have hit rock bottom. We were in trouble as we lost the toss and I had to bowl 26 overs for 69 runs and one wicket. Eddie Barlow must have been kicking himself getting out to me caught Parfitt at slip. Ian Thomson bowled 47 overs, Kenny Palmer 35 overs.

When we took the second new ball, I walked up to Mike Smith.

'I will bowl first with the new cherry, as I'm quicker than those two…'

Gallows humour. The pitch was a shirtfront, the African sun was out and Ian and Kenny were fed up and bushed.

Graeme Pollock grew up in Port Elizabeth. He batted like it was his front room. He had found his mojo and by this time in the series our bowling wouldn't have troubled my mum! He got 137, South Africa 502 and by the time Fred Titmus bowled Mike Macaulay to end the innings, we'd sent down 189 overs.

It was really about whether we could save the match and finish with a 1-0 series win.

South Africa gave us the usual awkward bit of batting on the second evening after two long days in the field. Bob Barber had gone home and Mike Brearley was not selected so John Murray was my partner. He got out and Titmus came in as nightwatchman. Our top three wouldn't have frightened club bowlers.

A long rearguard innings was required from everyone and we were up for it. I stuck it out through the third day, and no matter what they did I was comfortable until near the very end I edged the off cutter/spinner Bromfield to a close fielder on the offside for 117.

I'd never got out there before. A bit of tiredness, I think, after three long days on the field plus the overs I had bowled. But we kept them out there for 207 overs and got 400-odd before Ian Thomson sent down another 25 overs and Kenny Palmer 28 as South Africa crawled towards a declaration at three runs per over. I got another wicket when Trevor Goddard sent Mike Macaulay up the order to slog. The South Africans gave us a few overs at the end, and I got out, probably because I was shattered, caught Waite bowled Macaulay 7.

I was to be wicket-keeper Johnny Waite's last catch in Test cricket as he retired after the game. He came to tell me he was happy because his first had been Len Hutton, caught off Atholl Rowan for 63, during the first Test of the 1951 series at Trent Bridge.

**117** and **7**

\* \* \*

*England win the series but the press talk about the run-out of Ted Dexter in the first innings. You and Ted, batting together, putting on 63 of which Ted makes 40, you calling Ted through for a single from the last ball of the over...*

*[looking to keep the strike, they whisper...]*

*... You see the danger and send Ted back but he keeps coming and you're both at the one end when the wicket is broken at the other. Your call, your fault, they say. Selfish, and self-interested.*

*But what they don't see is that you are out there batting for your life and Ted, for all of his brilliance, could grow bored easily – sometimes you'd see he was miles away, leaning on his bat, practising his golf swing, having a doze, nodding off when you call him for a single...*

*That's the difference between you and him, between you and all of them. To you, it means everything, all the time. You don't have the innate brilliance of a Dexter, the dominance of Barrington, the elegant shot-making of Graveney or Cowdrey, but you do have this: you are made of steel. You are unbreakable.*

*The tour ends, but you don't want it to, you're not ready for this to end and so you book a flight back to Johannesburg while the rest of the party fly home, and then you go back to Victoria Falls, and this time it is low water and the rainbow seems endlessly wide.*

*You fly home to Fitzwilliam, where you show your family the films you took and tell them about the Falls and the rhino and the wonders that you have seen, you the kid in glasses from a pit village, England's opening bat.*

\* \* \*

*'Brighter Cricket' is the watchword for the 1965 season in England. A new vision of the game to combat the falling crowds and the attritional nature of a contest played on uncovered pitches. The authorities want action and results. Doug Insole is appointed Chairman of Selectors and demands it of the England team when, for the first time, they host twin Test series, first against New Zealand and then South Africa. Back at Yorkshire, the only aim is to regain the County Championship from Worcestershire. Brian Close believes that winning matches is the key – it's ten points for a win, two for a first-innings lead in a drawn game – and that draws and losses are more or less the same thing. He orders a batch of balls with an extra row of stitching on them, and the first game, at Middlesbrough versus Hampshire, is over by lunch on day two. Yorkshire all out 23, you and the rest of the batsmen imploring Closey to chuck those bloody balls in the bin!*

*You are one of Wisden's Five Cricketers of the Year, but the award follows you like a curse. You pull a muscle and miss two games. You run yourself out against Gloucester at Harrogate and then even more stupidly, do it twice against the touring New Zealanders at Bramall Lane, injuring your shoulder diving for your ground in the second innings. You miss another two weeks. When you do get back, you play on poor pitches and your form is patchy and it's stop-start no matter how hard you try, no matter how much you work.*

*You will not make a first-class hundred all summer.*

\* \* \*

## First Test, England versus New Zealand, Edgbaston, Birmingham, 27 May – 1 June, 1965

### *Tenth cap*

Fred was back. So why did MCC not pick him for the winter tour? If the England selectors were of the opinion that once Fred had achieved his world record number of Test wickets he was past it and it was time to move on to younger people, that was fine. But to then select a nearly 36-year-old Ian Thomson as a replacement for Tony

Nicholson and who had never played in a Test match before was baffling. If Fred was now considered good enough to be chosen again, it didn't make any sense not to take him on the tour to South Africa. It had no logic.

We batted first in the miserable weather. It was cold and dark, so cold that hot drinks were served on the field during the second day's play. It was all about Ken Barrington scoring 137 runs in just over seven hours. It may have been slow and boring but Ken put us in a position to win the Test. Nobody else. Him. All of that was forgotten or deliberately avoided because the Chairman of Selectors decided that England had to play brighter cricket. It would have been nice if he had told us players.

Insole made his views known to the newspaper writers after Ken's innings and it was a great story for them. Much better than England having beaten New Zealand. Barrington was dropped, omitted or left out, however you wished to see it, for the next Test match as a punishment for not scoring quicker. If all countries followed Doug Insole's view and judged their own batsmen by his standards, players all over the world would have been punished and dropped. As Chairman, Doug had so much influence so why not inform us players of what he expected and how he wished us to bat before the Test series began? Not once did he call us together as a group or individually. Surely the first thing any leader should do is to let his team know exactly what he expects.

Fred was still fast enough to hit the left-handed Bert Sutcliffe up the ear 'ole. Bert had to go off and came back later on only to have to retire again still a bit wobbly. Thankfully he was fine for the second innings and batted nicely to score 53. Very few people will remember that the new left-arm fast bowler Fred Rumsey didn't take a wicket in the match and Fred took four. New Zealand had never beaten England in a Test match, and they didn't look likely to here, either. We won by nine wickets having made them follow on, and I was there at the end.

**23** and **44***

\* \* \*

## Second Test, England versus New Zealand, Lord's London, 17-22 June, 1965

### *Eleventh cap*

We didn't know it at the time, but this would be Fred's last Test match.

Two for 40 and nought for 69. Nothing special. Nothing bad about his bowling. We would all like to go out with a bang, just like in the comic books, scoring an unbeaten ton or bowling the opposition's last man out to win by one run. Not many get an exit like that, however great they have been.

The records of Frederick Sewards Trueman will stand the test of time against any fast bowler in history, but most of all it's the memories of him cricket lovers will cherish.

307 Test match wickets at 21.6 and a wicket every 49.4 balls.

And as Fred noted, he didn't get a chance to bowl at Sri Lanka in their infancy or Zimbabwe and Bangladesh: 'Try bowling at Conrad Hunte, Rohan Kanhai, Everton Weekes, Frank Worrell, Clyde Walcott and Garfield Sobers on a flat West Indies pitch,' he used to say!

I got out to Dick Motz twice for 14 and 76. He was a big, strong, bustling, in-your-face fast bowler. When he came in from the Pavilion End, I felt a little intimidated as I could see the ridge on the pitch right in front of me. You couldn't miss it. MCC officials would try to tell you there was no such thing, all in the imagination. Let me tell you, there was a hump or mound there when you took guard. And looking at where a length ball would pitch from the faster bowlers, you suddenly felt about five feet four inches tall. When a bowler hit the seam sometimes it would leap up at you. Not funny.

Motz's partner at the other end was an even bigger guy, a young left-arm over-the-wicket fast bowler called Richard Collinge. Lord's has this huge eight-feet two-inch slope across the ground from cover to mid-wicket. When you first see this Mecca of cricket you just cannot believe it slopes that much. It really is amazing. No other major cricket ground in the world is like it. It is unique. Bowlers love it because that slope gives them something to work with.

My abiding memory was the pleasure I had batting with Ted Dexter in our second innings. Ted stood so upright, tall, elegant, imposing, technically sound, played the short ball well either getting right behind it or avoiding it. He made 80 not out and it was a treat for me to be at the other end. In the end, another good win for us.

**14** and **76**

\* \* \*

*This blighted year takes a further twist when you pick up another injury and miss the third Test, this one on your home ground, too. England bat first. In a summer where you can't make a ton, your replacement John Edrich scores 310 not out and Ken Barrington, forgiven now by Doug Insole, 163, as England lose just four wickets in the match and win by an innings and 187 runs.*

*Now there is some pressure on your place, a place you have held for 11 matches. For the first Test against the South Africans, Doug Insole retains John Edrich but moves him down to number three so that you can return and open the batting with Bob Barber, return to Lord's, to that ridge and to that slope…*

\* \* \*

### First Test, England versus South Africa, Lord's, London, 22-27 July, 1965

*Twelfth cap*

A game that will forever be remembered for the fielding of Colin Bland. Tall, very athletic and with an enormous reach, he ran out Ken Barrington for 91 and Jim Parks for 32 with direct hits from midwicket. Both were so far out the umpire wasn't required to make a decision.

I'd first seen him in July 1961 when a young South African Xl called The Fezelas played a Yorkshire 2nd Xl at Scarborough. At the end of the first day, Colin put on an exhibition of fielding, throwing down a single stump and finishing by hurling a ball from the corner of the ground near the main entrance to the scoreboard in the opposite corner. One bounce into the seats. Very slightly downhill but an enormous distance. I would need a bicycle to get the ball that far! He was a phenomenon. Best outfielder I have ever seen.

In the England second innings, I was at the non-striker's end when Peter Pollock, bowling fast from the Pavilion End, hit John Edrich on the head. John didn't seem to pick the ball up and just froze. It hit him full on the side of his head near the temple and he went down like a sack of potatoes. Horrible. No helmets at the time. Hell, we all know there is aggression in sport and understand there is danger, but when you see someone go down like that, you fear for his life. You sense immediately when it is serious, and I ran up the pitch to him. He was groggy as you would expect, and he tried to say he was alright to carry on. He wasn't, and many people surrounding him encouraged John to go off as there was no way he could continue.

31 and 28

\* \* \*

*The cricket wasn't interesting enough for some newspapers who tried to say you took too long over your 28 runs and as Ken Barrington was dropped for batting slowly you should be dropped too. They do not know that Mike Smith had told you to stay in and seal up one end. You tell the Daily Express: 'If the selectors want to drop me, that's their business... If I am to go on playing for England, my attitude to opening the innings will not change.'*

*Tough words, fighting talk, not really. You're on the defensive because you are short of runs, too tense and the rhythm isn't there but you travel to Trent Bridge for the next game, your confidence low, your place hanging by a thread, your future in your own hands.*

\* \* \*

### Second Test, England versus South Africa, Trent Bridge, Nottingham, 5-9 August, 1965

*Thirteenth cap*

The abiding memory for anyone at the game was a superb first innings hundred by Graeme Pollock. His driving through the offside was sensational and he made almost half the South Africans total of 269. With Colin Cowdrey making a splendid hundred in reply, England were still in the game only 29 runs behind. The problem was Tom Cartwright, who had taken six wickets but fractured the thumb on his bowling hand. He was a workhorse and a wicket-taker and I had to fill in for him with 26 overs for 60 runs. Not bad as a stop-gap but I was never going to be as penetrating. Wickets are always the key.

I was out first innings caught at slip for nought off Peter Pollock, and not for the first time sweated on making a pair. In the second innings, I missed an arm ball by the left-arm spinner Atholl McKinnon. I saw it the moment he started his run-up: his action and delivery was so obviously different. Yet I couldn't move. I was frozen like a boxer who sees the sucker punch coming and can't get out of the way. Down went my stumps with a clatter.

Out bowled for 16 and out of the England team.

As I was being driven home by a friend, I was in tears because I knew I would be dropped for the last Test Match at The Oval. I was 24 years old and feeling at rock bottom.

`0` and `16`

\* \* \*

*The great ones don't cry for long. The great ones dry their eyes and wipe their tears even as Eric Russell of Middlesex is recalled for his first Test match appearance in four years and makes 0 and 70 in your place as England draw the match and lose the series.*

*Yorkshire have no chance of winning the County Championship in this rain-ruined summer. You rejoin the side at Headingley for the game with Leicestershire. At the end of day one, Brian Sellers, captain of six title-winning sides and Chairman of Yorkshire cricket, comes into the dressing room.*

*'Right you lot,' says Sellers. 'I want you all here to see me before the start of play tomorrow.'*

*Next morning, Secretary John Nash calls you in one by one to see Mr Sellers. Richard Hutton, fresh into the Yorkshire side from Cambridge University, comes out looking as pale as death.*

*'What did he say?'*

'He said, 'You call yourself a fast bowler. If you are going to be a fast bowler, there are three things you need. Length, line and pace. And you've got fuck all. If it doesn't improve, I'll sack thee… Now bugger off!"

You are saved until last, and after Hutton, you're not looking forward to it.

You stand at attention until Mr Sellers says, 'Sit down and tell me what's the matter…'

You say: 'I practise and try like hell, but the feel and the rhythm just won't come…'

'I think you are too tense and trying too hard,' he tells you. 'Here's what I want you to do… I want you to play yourself in for 40 minutes to an hour and then whatever your score, relax and look to play some shots. Doesn't matter if you get out. You will be selected for every match until the end of the season.'

Everyone else gets a rocket. You get an arm around your shoulder, some wisdom in your ear. You go out to bat in Yorkshire's second innings and make 84. The weight lifts. Your mind clears. Your body responds. You bat ten times and make 500 runs.

Then it happens. The first of those magical days when everything comes together, a confluence of ability, dedication and opportunity, a day that no-one that sees it will ever forget.

The team drive from Scarborough to London on the Friday night through torrential rain to play Surrey at Lord's in the Gillette Cup Final. The talk amongst you is that the game will be abandoned, but the rain stops and the match begins just 90 minutes late. The pitch is a pudding, the outfield is soaked. Surrey win the toss and put you in, sure that they've already won the trophy.

You pass John Edrich on the outfield during the knock-up. You have agreed that whichever of you finishes on the losing side will travel up to Scarborough to open the batting in a festival game.

'Enjoy your drive,' John says, and smiles.

Brian Close shuts the dressing room door and says that 170 will be a winning score. It looks like he's right, too, as you and Ken Taylor make 20 runs from the first 12 overs before Ken is dismissed and Close walks to the wicket to join you.

The Surrey fans joke that all their team needs to do is keep Boycott in and they will win, but Closey gives you a few words of encouragement and the next over you straight drive Geoff Arnold for two boundaries and pull him for three. You hit David Sydenham over square-leg. You take three boundaries in an over from Ron Tindall.

The score mounts. At halfway, it's 109-1. You hit Geoff Arnold high over his head and into the pavilion seats for six. No-one has seen you play that shot before. You do it again, and when Arnold tries to bounce you, you hook him into the Tavern for six more.

You and Close put on 192, of which his share is 79. Fred Trueman, your cricketing hero, joins you and together you add another 34 in no time.

What joy these moments are. What a game it can be.

You finally fall to Ken Barrington's leg-breaks, but you have made 146 with 19 fours and three sixes. Lord's stands to you.

Surrey have no chance once you've finished with their bowlers, and after Fred takes three and Illy takes five, they are shot out for 142 and Brian Close is holding the trophy above his head.

The worst season of your life ends with the gold medal for man of the match in your pocket, your name in the history books. You are 25 years old.

When you hear that Doug Insole has selected you for the winter tour to Sri Lanka and Australia, you feel nothing but relief. Doug Insole has been all over the newspapers talking about 'brighter cricket' and 'attacking batting.' You get the message. A new adventure begins. But this one begins badly. In Ceylon you stay at the Galle Face Hotel, a great colonial pile overlooking the sea. You play in a one-day game and score three. On the flight to Singapore you fall ill with a high temperature, and when you land you are admitted to hospital, where you remain for eight days, suffering from severe gastroenteritis. As a child you had your spleen removed and you are ill and vulnerable, miles from home.

You meet up with the team in Perth still in pain: an aching back and painful left thigh. You miss two warm-up games but play the third, on a sticky dog in Adelaide. The native bulli soil is drying after heavy rain, the South Australians are bowled out just after lunch. You catch a break with the heavy roller and the heat, the pitch loses its venom, and you bat like you're still at Lord's, making 94 before you're caught trying to whack spinner David Sincock.

*In the field the next day, the pain in your leg becomes unbearable. You're helped from the arena and sent to see Dr Donald Beard, who has you admitted to hospital. He runs some tests and determines that when you'd had an injection in Singapore the needle narrowly missed your sciatic nerve. Exercise has inflamed the injury. Rest is prescribed.*

*You look up one day to see Donald Bradman sitting on the end of your bed. He stays for 30 minutes, but you are so awestruck that your mind goes blank and you forget all of the things you wanted to ask him. He gives you a signed copy of a book, 'The Changing Face Of Cricket', written by his friend Johnny Moyes and completed by himself. You keep it forever.*

*You recuperate at Donald Beard's house. One afternoon you go to the nets and test out your back. Donald is the worst chucker you've ever faced. You have batted once in 12 weeks when you are picked to face Queensland in the tour match. You score 30 and nought, feeling unfit, tired and short of practice. You do not want or expect to play in the first Test, but Peter Parfitt has lost form so you are selected to bat at number six.*

* * *

## First Test Match Australia v England,
## The Gabba, Brisbane, 10-15 December, 1965

### Fourteenth cap

When we fielded, Eric Russell split the webbing on his hand so I moved up to open. I scored 45, and we followed on with no chance of losing as there was only three hours of play left.

As we walked out in the second innings Bob Barber said: ' I fancy a bit of sunbathing today, Geoffrey...'

I never knew what the hell Bob was going to say or do, and he started slogging the new ball bowlers. One big six had him trying to hit it so hard and so far that he fell over. He was out for a rapid and entertaining 34 and departed to change into his trunks.

When I had scored 23 I played back to a delivery from leg-spinner Peter Philpott. The ball bounced up off the hard pitch and I was concerned it might spin back on to my stumps so I brushed it away with my right glove.

'Don't do that, son,' said Wally Grout.

I didn't know the Law. I could have been given out handled the ball. After the game I went and apologised to the bowler, stand-in captain Brian Booth and the umpire.

**45** and **63 not out**

# CHAPTER THREE

# 1966

*Mr Billy Griffith, the tour manager, comes to tell you that you are in a squad of 13 for the second Test. Eric Russell is fit again and he will play if Ken Higgs, who is suffering from a stomach bug, is also fit to play. But if Ken does not recover in time, you will play and Eric Russell will not, because you can fill in by bowling some overs.*

*You lose your rag with Billy Griffith. You tell him: 'If Eric Russell gets anywhere near me at the top of some stairs, I'll push him down...'*

*Billy Griffith says, 'I'll pretend I didn't hear that...'*

*'Well I will,' you tell the all-powerful Billy Griffith. 'I haven't come here to watch him bat...'*

\* \* \*

## Second Test, Australia v England, MCG, Melbourne, 30 December 1965-4 January, 1966

### *Fifteenth cap*

By chance, I was rooming with Ken Higgs. In the practice days before the Test I kept telling him it was as hot as hell out there.

'If you have to bowl, Ken, you might collapse and die. And if you do I'll put white roses of Yorkshire on your coffin!'

To a true man of Lancashire like Ken, that really would be the end...

Ken stayed ill and I played. Australia made 358 and after fielding for a day and-a-half, I was walking out to bat with Bob Barber when he said, "No singles today or you are running on your own...'

You never knew whether to take Bob seriously or not. We raced away to a partnership of 98 in 77 minutes scoring at six an over. Bob made 48 and me 51 with very few quick singles.

Mr Billy Griffith must have been in Heaven. And Doug Insole, too. As the match was petering out to a draw, I bowled nine eight-ball overs and got the wickets of Peter Burge, caught for 120, and Tom Veivers stumped for three.

The new wonder boy Doug Walters, not yet 20, was being labelled the next Bradman after he got 155 on his debut at Brisbane. He was now going for two in consecutive Tests, and just after tea, when he was in his eighties, he drove the ball back to me. We all believed he was out, but he stood his ground and finished with 115.

For years afterwards, whenever I went to Lord's for a match with Yorkshire or England, Mr Griffith would come up: 'do you remember that time in Melbourne when I told you Eric Russell was going to play, and you said…'

It obviously made an impression.

51 and 5 not out

\* \* \*

### Third Test, Australia v England, SCG, Sydney, 7-11 January, 1966

*Sixteenth cap*

A good toss to win. A bit lively first morning, but a nice pitch to bat on, with the likelihood it would turn later in the match. Garth McKenzie flicked my left ear with one sharp bouncer, but very quickly Bob was in full flow. His front foot driving was reminiscent of Graeme Pollock at his best – and Graeme was the best cover driver I ever saw. Half volleys or on the up the ball just sped through the gaps and the score galloped along at an amazing rate.

An Ashes contest was supposed to be hard-fought cricket with both sides manoeuvring for an opening. Not today, because no Australian bowler could contain Bob Barber. No luck involved, just beautiful strokeplay, and the only time he slogged was when David Sincock came on with his left-arm wrist-spin.

They called Sincock 'Evil Dick' – for the obvious reason, yes, but also because he spun the ball enormously and if you read him wrong or he thought he nearly had you, he would fix you with a murderous stare. Bob didn't take too well to that sort of gamesmanship.

He came down the pitch between overs, and I'm thinking. 'Jesus what now!'

'I don't think this chap can bowl. I'm going to slog him, Geoffrey…'

And he did. I was some guy just making up the numbers at the other end. I was caught and bowled off the seventh ball of the 55th eight-ball over for 84, and the umpires called tea. The England total was 234 for 1, and my partner was 147 not out. Sensational. He was finally dismissed to the second new ball for 185. Can you believe Bob's dad had arrived to watch the Test match that morning and Bob had picked him up at the airport… His father wanted to experience the infamous SCG Hill with its notorious barrackers, so he sat on the grass up there and watched his son play the innings of his life.

As the day came to an end, Neil Hawke nearly spoilt the party, making the second new ball swing and seam to take out the cream of English batting in Barrington, Cowdrey and Mike Smith as well as Bob.

On 328 for five at the close of day one, no side should lose a Test, but our jubilation was tempered slightly by the dramatic fall of wickets. We should have known not to worry as John Edrich was still there. What an amazing temperament he had. Nothing seemed to bother him. Even when he occasionally played and missed, he put it out of his mind and faced the next ball as if it never happened. Terrific guy, great to bat with, and he made a century to put us in the driving seat.

Then it was about our seamers getting early wickets with the new ball. Bill Lawry went in the first over of the Aussie innings, and despite one scrapping partnership for the second wicket from Graeme Thomas and Bob Cowper, we skittled the rest and forced the follow-on. With more than 200 to bowl at, our spinners Fred Titmus and David Allen did the rest, sharing eight second innings wickets for a big win that got our noses in front for the series.

**84** and **DNB**

\* \* \*

*You are invited on a fishing trip in Sydney Harbour. The water is a mill pond in the Aussie sun, the light bouncing from it, and you want to see more of the great steel bridge built by Dorman and Long, two lads from up the road in Middlesbrough.*

*Now another Yorkshireman is here to conquer the waves.*

*You set sail in a boat with Jim Parks and his girlfriend and the team physio Jack Jennings. Out in the Heads, where the harbour ends and the Pacific Ocean begins, things get choppy. Beyond the Heads the waves are all of a sudden the size of cars, lifting the boat's nose almost to the vertical before dropping it into the void. Jim Parks' girlfriend is on the cabin's only bed, being sick into a bucket. Jack Jennings has his glasses in one hand, his false teeth in the other and is vomiting over the side. You hold onto your breakfast until that moment, but seeing everyone else losing theirs is too much. By the time the skipper finds shelter in one of the bays along the coast, you have vowed never to sail again...*

*...Thankfully the trip to Tasmania across the notorious Bass Strait is by air rather than sea. You have a chipped bone in your finger after the Sydney Test and miss the first game in Launceston, but when the team travel to the other end of the island to play the State side in a three-day game at Hobart, it finally happens – you get past three figures for the first time in god knows how long. It felt like forever. You make 156, but then it hits you – the realisation that the game may not have first-class status. All of the other matches against state sides have been over four days...*

*You ask some of the senior players. They tell you that an MCC Committee will decide whether to give the game first-class status and that the Captain's Report will go a long way to making up their minds. Mike Smith is resting, so Colin Cowdrey has the reins for the Hobart match. You ask Colin. You practically bloody beg Colin. He smiles and says he'll do his best for you.*

*On the final day, Tasmania are batting and Colin needs to rest his bowlers for the next Test, so you volunteer to help him out. Anything to be in the captain's good books and have that century declared first-class! You get through seven eight-ball overs and give it all you've got. You would have bowled at both ends if he'd asked you to.*

*When the match ends the lads fall about laughing when they tell you that the game has always been a first-class fixture. You've been well and truly had...*

*Back on the mainland you head for Adelaide and the best batting pitch in Australia. The papers are full of Barber and Boycott's partnership, John Edrich's century, England's new Brighter Cricket that has them 1-0 up in the Ashes series. Doug Insole and his MCC friends must be preening themselves in the committee rooms of Lord's.*

*Everyone is on a high, on top of the world, getting sucked into believing that every day should be like the first day in Sydney... Mike Smith wins the toss on a flat pitch. Bob Barber goes for a big drive at Neil Hawke's third delivery and is bowled off his inside edge for nought. You smack 22 from 18 deliveries with four boundaries before driving extravagantly at Hawke and are taken brilliantly at third slip by Ian Chappell. John Edrich goes for five, nicking Garth McKenzie to Bobby Simpson, the big three from Sydney already back in the hutch with 33 on the board.*

*Brighter Cricket...*

* * *

## Fourth Test, Australia v England, Adelaide Oval, Adelaide, 28 January – 1 February, 1966

### Seventeenth cap

All we had to do was win the toss and bat sensibly. Not defensively, but bat with a bit of care and attention and certainly not go gung-ho after the bowling.

It got worse. Cowdrey ran himself out for 38. We dug a grave for ourselves which we couldn't find a way out of.

I believe cricket mirrors life, and in life you have to be able to adapt, and much more importantly, know when to adapt. We had got our share of good fortune with winning the toss at Sydney on a result pitch and one of our guys playing the innings of his life. That ain't going to happen all the time. Their captain and best batsman Bobby Simpson had missed a Test with a broken arm and another Test with chicken pox, but he was back now.

England 241 all out on an Adelaide belter was pathetic.

Australia didn't need any heroics. They didn't need to score fast or smash quick runs. They had four days to put us to the sword, and they toyed with us. Bob Simpson and Bill Lawry extracted the full cost of our folly with the bat during a first wicket stand of 244, and from there we had beaten ourselves. All we had to do was bat with common sense and professionally and Australia would have had to chase the game.

In a crusade for brighter cricket, the Ashes were gone. Why? When you have got the Aussies down... keep them down. If they get up and get their confidence back, they are insufferable.

**22** and **12**

\* \* \*

*In the dressing room, Ken Barrington can't sit down, he can't sit still. He is muttering about how you have handed it on a plate to the Aussies...*

*'On a fucking plate, lads...'*

*You look at Ken and you feel it too. The lack of care and respect for the game. Chucking away your own wicket for a quick 20.*

*Chucking away the form you fought so hard to regain.*

*Things can turn quickly on a tour. Small things become big things.*

*Billy Griffith can't say no to an invitation. After hours in the field, you put on your fancy blazer and attend this function, that cocktail party, another governor's welcome... too many nights you stand around for an hour and a half answering the same questions, making the same small talk, wishing you were somewhere else. Anywhere else.*

*One evening, you're so bushed at another of these things, you find a chair and sit down.*

*Gubby Allen, the most influential man at the MCC, more powerful even than Doug Insole, stares over at you.*

*'Are you tired, Boycott?'*

*'Yes Mr Allen,' you tell him. 'I've been fielding all day while you've been sat in the committee room.'*

*He glares and walks away.*

*As the final Test approaches it all catches up with you: your long weeks of being ill at the start of the tour, in and out of the hospital.*

*The needles and the pain.*

*The sickness and the worry.*

*The lost fitness you never really get back.*

*Giving your wicket away playing Brighter Cricket, not stupid shots but the wrong shots... the wrong shots at the wrong time, played because your mind was not clear, your body was not right.*

* * *

## Fifth Test, Australia v England,
## MCG, Melbourne, 11-16 February 1966

*Eighteenth cap*

*The final Test is back in Melbourne, at the MCG.*

*The MCG is huge and hot. An unforgiving place. A brutal arena where weakness is fatal.*

*Australia only need to draw to retain the Ashes. England bat first, but you make just 17, caught by Keith Stackpole from Garth McKenzie's bowling. Thanks to a ton from Ken Barrington, England declare on 485, but Australia go in and bat forever on that huge, hot field. Bill Lawry makes 108 and Bob Cowper gets 307, the wicket flat, the ball soft, the bowlers flogged, the fielders knackered, the Ashes going... going... gone. On and on they bat, on and on to 543-8 from 154 eight-ball overs.*

*To twist the knife, they declare and stick you in again. The pitch is no longer flat. Now it has big cracks running along it opened by the sun, and the ball is no longer old and soft but new and hard.*

*It is brutal, this game, this country.*

*You are out for one, leg before to a Garth McKenzie shooter.*

*It is done, over, and you want to go home. Except you can't, not yet...*

* * *

So many weeks ill at the beginning of the tour and visits in and out of hospital had caught up with me. Also I was frustrated having recently got myself out playing attacking shots I would not normally have tried... but this wasn't a normal tour.

**17** and **1**

* * *

*The difference a year makes... This is not South Africa, where you didn't want it to end, could not get enough, stayed on after the others had gone home. Now you watch Bob Barber and Fred Titmus leave for England you travel to New Zealand for three Test matches and then to Hong Kong for two hit-and-giggle games, the next month stretching out in front of you like a prison sentence...*

* * *

## First Test, New Zealand v England,
## Lancaster Park, Christchurch, 25 February – 1 March, 1966

*Nineteenth cap*

These matches were scheduled for four days not five, and the weather was cold, overcast and dull, like England in April. The AMI Stadium was a rugby ground and we changed in rugby dressing rooms where we couldn't see a thing. Dark and claustrophobic and very uninviting after hot sunshine in Australia.

The pitch was grassy and juicy and if you were a seam bowler, you were happy. We won the toss and batted, and it wasn't surprising that us openers were despatched quickly. My nemesis Dick Motz dismissed me cheaply, and then Eric Russell ran me out in the second innings.

New Zealand collapsed in the second innings to pressure but just held on for a draw.

**4** and **4**

* * *

## Second Test, New Zealand v England,
## Carisbrook, Dunedin, 4-8 March, 1966

*Twentieth cap*

The southernmost Test venue on Earth was cold and gloomy like Christchurch, but this time with a wet pitch to add to the fun. New

52

Zealand batted, and I can't think why? The pitch was never going to dry or get any better in that weather.

When we batted I got a throat ball from Gary Bartlett that I gloved onto my stumps for another failure. He was so obviously a chucker, but the umpires and officials weren't interested. Plenty of rain over the first two days made it difficult to get a result. Another draw.

**5** and **DNB**

\* \* \*

*There is one more Test to go and for the first time in your life, you pray to be dropped. The Times correspondent writes: 'The Yorkshireman has looked stale and out of touch since leaving Australia,' and he is right.*

*Your prayer is answered. They pick your room-mate John Edrich to open and maybe the curse reaches him, too, because he wakes you in the middle of the night with pains in his stomach and he is taken to hospital to have his appendix removed, so Peter Parfitt plays instead. You fly to Hong Kong, and then, finally, home to England, touching down five-and-a-half months later having played eight Tests, 15 first-class matches and 27 sundry games. MCC make a profit of $37,500.*

*You need an omen, a sign that the winter will leave you.*

*You need some runs. Runs make everything alright. They always have. When you're scoring runs, all of the other rubbish that crowds your head becomes white noise.*

*Yorkshire go to Lord's to play MCC, first game of the 1966 season. You make 123 and 68 and you think, okay, this is it, this is going to be a good summer.*

*But you are left out of the first Test against the West Indies in favour of the new pairing of Colin Milburn and Eric Russell.*

*Twenty Tests ago, you were the new thing. Four Tests ago, you and Bob Barber were hitting Australia all around the SCG. But now it's Colin Milburn who is the new thing, Colin Milburn who is run out for a duck in his debut innings but in the second who brings Old Trafford alive with a knock of 94 with 12 fours and two sixes, Colin Milburn who is the new golden boy of English batting, belting Wes Hall, Charlie Griffith and Garfield Sobers all over Manchester.*

*...Ollie, the press christen him, delightedly. Ollie Milburn, the 18-stone everyman who likes a ciggie and a drink, who'd rather stand in the pub with the supporters than the Long Room with the committee men...*

*But England lose heavily, by an innings, and Doug Insole and his selection panel drop Eric Russell and recall you. Mike Smith makes way for 39 year-old Tom Graveney, playing his first Test for three years. Colin Cowdrey is the new captain. The selectors drop David Allen and David Brown and bring in Basil D'Oliveira and Barry Knight. You go to Lord's no longer the new light of English batting. You go to Lord's to fight for your place, to start again after 20 Test caps...*

\* \* \*

## Second Test, England versus West Indies, Lord's, London, 16-21 June, 1966

### *Twenty-first cap*

West Indies batted fairly well and when they were all out on the second day, I was changing into my batting gear when Peter May sort of sidled up to me and said:

'Geoffrey. You won't try any quick singles will you?'

I said, 'why?'

'Because Ollie won't make it...'

Jesus, what a thing to say to me when I am rushing to get my batting gear on and just trying to concentrate on the bowlers I am going to have to face.

Colin got out early, and I did OK, making 60 before trying to club Lance Gibbs over midwicket and mishitting it for an easy catch.

I was at the other end for Tom Graveney's first ball from Charlie Griffith. It was fast and short, at the ribs, and Tom gloved it just wide of their keeper David Allan. He survived and I had the pleasure of batting with my hero for a time until I got out. Tom went on to score 96.

With a rest day on Sunday, Colin Milburn insisted he would take me out on Saturday night. He took me to Raymond's Revue Bar in Soho, which had naked women dancing and climbing up and around these poles. There was a nearly naked girl swimming in a tank full of water.

I said, 'Ollie, what the hell are we doing here? There's some funny guys about and I am dying for something to eat...'

Not a place I was used to, but it must have done Ollie some good because in the second innings he batted splendidly to score 126 not out, while I only made 25.

The most memorable part of the match was the fantastic partnership between Garry Sobers' with 163 not out and his cousin David Holford with 105. Holford was an unknown and not someone we expected to make big runs. Sobers was majestic, the best batsman in the world.

**60** and **25**

\* \* \*

### Third Test, England versus West Indies, Trent Bridge, Nottingham, 30 June – 5 July, 1966

*Twenty-second cap*

A Test match we could and probably should have won. A 90-run lead on first innings usually gives you a huge advantage, but Basil Butcher made an outstanding double hundred under pressure in the second innings.

Colin Cowdrey and Tom Graveney scored excellent centuries in our first innings to set us up, and even when Sobers was able to declare, we only had to bat out a full day on a good pitch to make a draw. We couldn't do it.

In the first innings, Sobers bowled me a magic ball. I was aware from left-arm over at a brisk to sharp pace, he could swing it prodigiously into the right-hander and then seam one away. I have always believed to play swing well you need to see it early but play it late.

I was looking to get forward to try to counteract the swing, holding my hands back so as not to go at the ball hard. Just as I felt the point had passed where it could swing back into me, I relaxed. Just a fraction, but enough. At that moment, it swung like a banana and I was absolutely plumb.

Gone second ball. I sweated for two playing days and a rest day on getting a queen pair! Not much fun.

And I nearly got one. Sobers bowled me a similar delivery second innings and I just got an inside edge onto my pad that saved me. I went on to 71, which was the highest score in the England second innings. I was playing well when it got very dark and overcast and difficult to pick up the ball.

I nicked one from Charlie Griffith that went at a perfect height and not too quick to Sobers at second slip. Maybe he didn't pick it up either, because it was a cuckoo and he dropped it. Next ball I nicked it again and Garry caught it. Then the umpires came off for bad light.

England lost again.

`0` and `71`

\* \* \*

### Fourth Test, England versus West Indies, Headingley, Leeds, 4-8 August, 1966

*Twenty-third cap*

Not much fun on my home ground. A juicy pitch and poor weather made batting against the new ball tough. Once again, Sobers got me with a beauty that seamed away and I nicked it to the keeper. If he had bowled it to me again I probably would have nicked it again, too. When we started our second innings, the light was murky and soon got worse, so as West Indies were pushing for victory, Sobers took off his quick bowlers. Most of the English umpires were former county pros and they were not easily persuaded to go off for bad light. The light quality and the speed of the bowler had to be a danger to the batsmen for them to consider halting play.

So on comes batsman Peter Lashley, an occasional bowler at medium, very medium, to slow pace. The ball nips away and I nick it to the keeper. What a death! This guy played four Test matches, averaged 22 with the bat and bowled three overs, yet his claim to fame was me. I was his only wicket.

When he batted, he was so crouched over that I nicknamed him the Crab. For years and years later when I toured the Caribbean to play or commentate, Peter somehow always found me, and came to greet me with a huge smile on his face. I'm thinking oh no, not the Crab and Headingley…

England lost again easily.

**12** and **14**

\* \* \*

*England's football team have won the World Cup. On top of the world, that's where Alf Ramsey's men are. That's not where you are. Not where Doug Insole's England cricket team are. You are losing heavily to West Indies, 3-0 down after four games, two of those defeats by an innings.*

*Once the papers have stopped eulogising Bobby Moore and his team, they turn on the cricketers. Colin Cowdrey is sacked as captain and Brian Close is appointed in his place. Bob Barber returns to open the batting. Dennis Amiss is picked for a debut in the middle order. Close tells the selectors he wants Ray Illingworth for Fred Titmus and John Murray for Jim Parks. The new captain gets his way.*

*Despite making 245 runs at 40.83 with one century and one fifty, Colin Milburn is dropped. Despite making 182 runs at 30.33 with no centuries and two fifties, you are retained.*

*Perhaps it's because Brian Close knows what you can do.*

*Perhaps it's because those deliveries from Sobers would have got anyone out.*

*Either way, you don't feel good, don't feel right. The nerves, always there, always present, have become harder to control. You have gone deeper into yourself, searching for answers, but sometimes, the more you look, the less you see…*

*Close tells his team, 'We can beat this lot.' You know that he believes it, even though the summer so far says otherwise. Maybe it's blind faith or maybe it's because you've seen him at Yorkshire, but you believe him too.*

*In the team meeting on the eve of the game, Close tells John Snow to bowl fast into the ribs of Garry Sobers, and he will stand at short leg and catch him. You know better than to question the courage of your captain, but you have been watching Sobers bat all summer – 671 runs with three huge hundreds – and you've seen how clean and hard he hits that ball...*

*'I wouldn't stand there to Garry Sobers,' you think.*

*'Believe...' says Brian Close. 'Believe...'*

\* \* \*

## Fifth Test, England versus West Indies, The Oval, London, 18-22 August, 1966

### *Twenty-fourth cap*

The first thing I noticed was that we were only playing two out-and-out seamers, John Snow and Ken Higgs. Fast bowlers and fast medium bowlers are usually crucial when playing in English conditions. We would have spin from Illy, Closey and Bob Barber, with military medium back up from Basil D'Oliveira. Wow!

Anyhow it worked. Closey swapped the bowlers around, the wickets were shared and West Indies were never allowed to dominate or get a big partnership going. But when we batted, Wes Hall knocked my off and middle stumps back straight away. It was a case of here we go again, West Indies strangling us.

At 166-7 we were in a hole when John Murray played the innings of his life. He scored 112 and put on 217 with Tom Graveney to change the course of the match. Everyone knew Tom could bat, he had scored runs against all sorts of bowlers in all sorts of pressure moments, but John Murray in a Test with England in trouble?

It was fantastic, and the defining period of this match. I hardly missed a ball, sat on the balcony thrilled to watch my boyhood hero Tom cream the bowlers around for a magnificent 165. We would have settled for that, but then there was the icing on the cake. A crazy, unexpected last wicket partnership of 128 from our only two fast bowlers Ken Higgs, 63, and John Snow, 59.

Game over. So demoralising for any team. Snow got two early wickets to put the skids under them, and the coup de grace was

Garry Sobers, so often the saviour for West Indies, who got a first-ball duck. John put it into his ribs and guess who was at short leg... captain Brian Close.

His prophecy was complete.

**4** and **DNB**

# CHAPTER FOUR

# **1967**

*You are ten years old and at home when you hear the knock on the door and a man's voice saying to your mum: 'Jenny, I'm sorry, Tom's been hurt...'*

*Your dad had been in the pit laying rails for the coal tubs to run on when he was dragged along by some empties. He broke his back and his legs, his body damaged so badly that his health is ruined and he never fully recovers.*

*Even so, it is a terrible shock when he passes.*

*1967. The year you will lose your dad.*

*But first...Rain sweeps across the country as the season begins. Yorkshire's fixtures against Leicestershire at Headingley and the Roses match at Old Trafford are abandoned without a ball bowled. When you do play, uncovered pitches are damp and treacherous. You cop your first ever pair at Bradford when Kent's Norman Graham bowls you via your arm as the ball rears up and then has you caught behind gloving one from in front of your face.*

*Your first 12 scores go: 45, 9, 102, 0, 0, 6, 4, 0, 24, 60, 24, and 6... No form. No form and no confidence, and the Test match team soon to be announced...*

\* \* \*

I don't think the modern-day cricketer has any idea of what it was like batting on uncovered pitches in April and May in England. Cold and wet on uninviting, juicy bowling surfaces, and with bats weighing around 2lb 4ozs. All of the grounds in Yorkshire were club pitches with club ground staff preparing pitches for matches on a Saturday lasting around 90 overs. Yorkshire didn't own a ground, and some other counties were the same. Kent, Essex and Yorkshire each used about seven grounds for first-class matches. With games set over three days, those same pitches which were prepared for around 90 overs on weekends were then required to last around 300 overs with far better bowlers exploiting them.

\* \* \*

*You are not certain that you will be selected for the first Test against India at Headingley, not certain at all. You can't argue if they pick someone else, not with the trot you are on, but they don't and you are in.*

*In for a Test match that will cause you more pain and more hurt than any other in your career. In for a Test match that will shape your reputation forever.*

*You are about to play the most infamous innings of your life, an innings that will shadow you down the years.*

\* \* \*

## First Test, England versus India, Headingley, Leeds, 8-13 June, 1967

### *Twenty-fifth cap*

The facts are that I scored 106 runs having batted through the first day, and England were in a strong position at 281 for three. After a night's sleep and with the confidence of runs on the board, I was able to bat with a weight off me and score another 140 runs in three-and-a-half hours. England could declare and make India follow on, and ultimately win by six wickets.

I was dropped from the next Test as a disciplinary measure. The precedent had been set by Doug Insole nearly two years previously when he did the same to Ken Barrington. The newspaper writers knew it was a better story than the cricket, and ran with it for days putting pressure on our selectors. Insole was never going to miss out on any opportunity to bang his drum re 'Brighter Cricket'. He put a stain on my character and my cricket I could never get rid of.

Being dropped this way was the deepest wound, and I knew it would label me for life. Wherever I went and whatever I did, that disciplinary measure would follow me. That is why I have no time for Insole. It's common for some people to say you should never speak ill of the dead. That sounds fine if it's not you that has been criticised and condemned. What should I do? Lie or avoid the subject? I won't do either to save his memory. He did and said plenty at the time when as a player I was tied under Cricket Board Rules and not allowed to defend myself. Even if I had been allowed to say anything in my defence would I have dared disagree or complain? He was influential at MCC and as Chairman of Selectors in a position to never select me again.

I try to be frank, forthright and truthful, and I am aware it has got me into trouble in the past. I have to live with that but I won't try to hide the fact I was hurt at the time and the pain of that decision has never gone away.

**246 not out** and **DNB**

* * *

*This is how it happens: 8 June, 1967. Brian Close wins the toss and elects to bat first. There are fewer than 5,000 people in the ground to watch England play a poor India team. You open with John Edrich, who soon feathers one to Farokh Engineer from the bowling of Rusi Surti, dismissed for one. You and Ken Barrington survive the next hour. If India bowl a half volley, it seems to always be at Ken. If you play an attacking shot, it always seems to find the fielder. All you can do is hang in, fight, and you do… Even when you go scoreless for 45 minutes and it would be easier to play a daft shot and sit in the pavilion. That's not you, never has been. You fight. Fight the bowlers. Fight yourself.*

*Fight until lunch. 25 not out.*

*After the interval, Rusi Surti gets hit on the knee and can't bowl. Bishan Bedi pulls a thigh muscle and can't bowl. India's captain Tiger Pataudi leans on his spinners Chandrasekhar and Prasanna, who will send down more than 100 overs across England's innings.*

*Between lunch and tea, you add another 50 runs to your score. Ken is run out for 93. Tom Graveney joins you. The hours as you approach your century become tortuous, you have to tear every run from the bowler's hand.*

*Cricket as battle... Batting as war...*

*But you win this siege, win this battle with the game and with yourself. You win, undefeated at the close and you sleep well with those three figures next to your name.*

*You wake up and you don't look at the Daily Mirror, which runs the headline: 'Sling Boycott Out! After this Test crawl, he deserves the Barrington treatment'. You don't read correspondent Brian Chapman: 'Cricket could not afford to put a joyless effort of this sort in the shop window'. You don't read Ian Wooldridge in the Daily Mail, who writes that the slow progress towards a century 'could not be excused by his nearest and dearest relations'.*

*You don't read it, but you feel it, feel what people are saying about you.*

*These people who don't understand batting, or the game.*

*Doug Insole comes to the dressing room before play to read the riot act. You hold your tongue and put on your pads. As Basil D'Oliveira leaves the dressing room, Closey grabs him by the arm and says, 'Tell Boycs to take no notice, just play his natural game.'*

*What was lost is back, and in the next three-and-a-half hours you score 140 more runs, batting through to England's declaration at 550-4. Close is the other not out batsman, and he puts an arm around your shoulders as you walk off, 'making it obvious,' The Sun newspaper writes, 'that he was not dissatisfied with either his team or his number one batsman'.*

*You have a couple of days in the field while the storm gathers. India are rolled in their first innings but when they follow on, Tiger Pataudi makes big runs and England are required to bat again, to score 125 to win. You've turned an ankle and so Closey asks Ken Barrington to open and you sit and watch as England win by six wickets, all of those runs you scored key to the result, a victory that comes with hours of play to spare.*

*The selectors meet. Doug Insole, Peter May, Don Kenyon and Alec Bedser all vote to drop you. Brian Close tells them he'll give you a right bollocking and make sure it doesn't happen again, but he is outvoted.*

*You are in Abergavenny playing for the International Cavaliers when the team is announced. You sit at lunch, speaking to no-one, no-one speaking to you, feeling like a leper until Lance Gibbs takes you to a quiet corner and says: 'Hold your head up. You have nothing to be ashamed of. The selectors must be crazy. If you made those sort of runs for West Indies, you'd be a hero.'*

*It's a PR move from Insole. You know it. Lance Gibbs knows it. Both teams know it. Closey knows it, too. Many years later he will write about how much he admires the resilience you show in the days that follow.*

*But Doug Insole has put this stain upon you.*
*Selfish player, selfish man.*

*Not true. Not true at all, but you are stained. Marked. Humiliated and dropped. Hung out to dry by Doug Insole and his Brighter Cricket.*
*You will never forget it.*

*They think you are a machine, just because you don't show your emotions out on the field. But you don't eat, don't sleep. It gets inside your head, makes you question everything about who you are, the way that you play. England win the second Test inside four days, Ken Barrington moving up to open with John Edrich (the irony, the irony... Ken the last player dropped by Doug Insole for slow scoring), but for whatever reason, the selectors drop John and recall you, move Ken down to number three and recall Colin Milburn to open with you.*

\* \* \*

## Third Test, England versus India, Edgbaston, Birmingham, 13-15 July, 1967

### *Twenty-sixth cap*

I had never been so ill at ease, awkward and unsure of myself. So conscious that every minute I spent at the crease would be dissected by the media and selectors.

I was terrified to block a ball, and God forbid play out a maiden over. Looking back, I realise India were not a great bowling side in English conditions, but batting is about form and confidence and most of all, it's about what is going on in your head. My mind was not in a good place. I couldn't think straight and on the first morning, I jumped down the pitch to Bedi and was officially stumped, but I was so far down it was more like a run-out.

It was a poor pitch and our bowlers got stuck into India and fired them out for 92.

India were so poor we could have bowled them out again and beaten them in two days, but Brian Close decided to bat again. At the end of the day, he told the press that he'd done it because our bowlers were tired. It was a ridiculous lie. Four bowlers had shared 33.3 overs, so they had hardly broken sweat!

In my opinion, Brian stretched the match to three days so the TCCB would get a bumper Saturday revenue. Gate revenue was everything in 1967. TV income was comparatively low.

I saw the repercussions of my innings in everything. I think Brian was under pressure from the selectors for not being firmer with me on the first day at Headingley. He had never told me to get on with it, and at the end of the first day there were photographs of him with his arm around my shoulders.

It was obvious that he wasn't dissatisfied with my batting. Anyone who played with Brian knew that if you disobeyed him you were liable to get a very angry skipper grabbing you by the throat, sometimes worse. He was all smiles with me, and later said he defended me with the selectors. Doug Insole and his committee would have marked that down.

To me, Brian was on a charm offensive to keep his job as captain. Who wouldn't? If you do things for the wrong reasons though, somehow it comes back to bite you.

Doug Insole never spoke to me about the disciplinary measure he and his Committee had taken. He didn't have the balls or the decency to sit me down for a few minutes. Doug played for England in nine Tests and captained Essex for 10 years. He was no fool, and should have had some idea of the turmoil I was in. From then on, we were courteous and polite with each other but never anything else. I despised how he worked behind the scenes. His eyes never fixed you. He was a sly one, for me he was always Dangerous Doug…

*  *  *

*A week later you are at The Oval, Yorkshire versus Surrey, when the phone call comes from John Nash.*

*This is how you hear that your father has died. The Club Secretary on the phone from Yorkshire.*

*The shock and the grief. Worst thing you ever felt.*

*'Stay,' Closey says. 'Stay and bat for us. There's nothing you can do until the funeral.'*

*He's right. Nothing you or anyone can do now. Your dad gone. You get out there and bat for Yorkshire, your father's son. Somehow you make 74, but it passes in a haze that you barely remember.*

*You go home to bury your dad. You pick up an injury and miss the first Test against Pakistan.*

*This blighted summer. This dreadful year.*

*1967.*

\* \* \*

## Second Test, England versus Pakistan, Trent Bridge, Nottingham, 10-15 August, 1967

### *Twenty-seventh cap*

For the life of me, I don't remember much about my innings or the match. I do have a recollection of Asif Iqbal bowling me out with a nip back ball that skidded onto me a bit quicker than I expected for 15 and England won easily.

My mind was in a whirl with my father passing away, the funeral, my mum being very upset, and still feeling the effects of the huge publicity generated by my one Test match ban. I missed the Third Test match v Pakistan as I was injured again.

After the Nottingham Test, Yorkshire played Warwickshire at Edgbaston. It was a game-changing match for cricket. Brian Close was reported by the umpires for his team 'deliberately wasting time' to stop Warwickshire winning. I was mainly fielding on the boundary so I was never close enough to the action to hear what the umpires said to Brian.

When we left the field there were many Warwickshire supporters very angry with Yorkshire's tactics. Some members were shouting and swearing abuse at Brian for what they considered unfairly slow over rates and timewasting tactics like constantly fiddling with his fields. Brian jumped into the members' seats and grabbed one guy around his throat. He dragged the guy out of his seat, held him up against a wall threatening to punch him. The member was screaming it wasn't him that had slagged off Brian and in the heat of the moment with so many shouting at him, he may have got the wrong man!

Brian had to appear before a disciplinary hearing in London. He didn't help his cause by arriving late, saying he had car trouble. He was found guilty of time-wasting and unacceptable gamesmanship. Yorkshire accepted the decision, but that decision had huge ramifications. At the end of the Pakistan series, the selectors recommended Brian to MCC as their choice of captain to lead the tour of the West Indies. The MCC Committee refused to accept the nomination. They argued that Brian's temperament had been shown to be lacking, and appointed Colin Cowdrey as their captain instead.

It was a mind-blowing decision. It had never happened before and what's more very few people were aware that MCC could veto the selectors' choice and effectively sack the England captain. But cricket people knew that on winter tours, the players wore MCC blazers with red and yellow braid and on the blazer pocket was the MCC badge of St George slaying the dragon, not the three lions and a crown of England. The team toured as MCC and were only referred to as England when Test matches were on.

There was shock and outrage. Some were saying it was the old boy network at MCC sticking their nose up at a tough Northern professional. All hell broke loose in the media, but it didn't get Brian reinstated. Nonetheless, there was so much anger and bitterness that ramifications followed swiftly. From the following English cricket season the counties decided to form the Test and County Cricket Board to run cricket, reducing the power of MCC. In effect, MCC had shot itself in the foot. Reform was needed, but Brian paid the price for it.

**15** and **1 not out**

* * *

*The season of 1967 comes to its end.*

*Your 246 not out is the highest score made in professional cricket in England this year. You win all four Test matches you play. You head the Yorkshire averages with 1,260 runs at 48.46. Yorkshire win the County Championship.*

*Once, nothing else mattered. But now...*

*...You visit your doctor. You tell him that you're not eating, not sleeping, take no pleasure in cricket.*

*He lets you talk, about your dad, about your cricket. He tells you to drink a bottle of Guinness a day and play lots of golf. It seems like odd advice, but you do what he says and it works.*

*By mid-November, you're feeling like yourself again. You are selected for the winter tour to West Indies. Early evenings you pull on your football boots, your tracksuit, your hat and your gloves and go to the cricket ground where the parade of shops along one side throw enough light for you to do your warm-ups and your sprints. At weekends you go and join in the football matches local kids and teens play because it's more fun than running on your own.*

*The kids start calling round to your house, knocking on your door.*

*'Mrs Boycott, is your Geoff coming out to play football?'*

*You pick up a bat again. You go back into the past, back to Johnny Lawrence's school on weekday afternoons. Johnny rolls up the rubber mats and polishes the floorboards until they are slick and fast. You invite bowlers from the local clubs and give them a rock-hard Chingford composition ball, a solid lump of cork and rubber that flies from those polished floors. You have the bowlers deliver from 20 yards rather than 22 and tell them to try and hit you, knock your block off. You have Johnny bowl his leg-spinners, top spinners and googlies.*

*Four or five times a week you'll have three 50-minute sessions per day. You concentrate like mad. You get sore, tired. Sweat drips off you. You swap gloves, swap bats and keep going.*

*Johnny knows your game inside out. He pauses the sessions for long discussions of technique, honing every detail, until you shine.*

*You practise on Christmas Eve. You run on Christmas morning, even though it's snowed. Even though you hate running. On Boxing Day 1967, you fly to Barbados. Captain Colin Cowdrey takes you aside at the airport and tells you that he wants you to play your own way throughout the tour, and to ignore any instructions he gives the team as a whole.*

*He says: 'If I want you to bat outside of your normal style, I will tell you personally.'*

## CHAPTER FIVE

# 1968

*The first game is against a President's XI and you get off to the flyer that you have worked for – 135 as reward for all of the training, in the dark and the cold. But in the second game against Trinidad at Port Of Spain Wes Hall breaks the top digit of the ring finger on your right hand. The right hand you keep low because of the low, uncovered pitches. The doctors tell you a break takes six weeks to heal.*

*Tour over before it's begun!*

*All of that training, in the dark and in the cold, for this...*

*But the pain dies down and the doctors give you an aluminium splint to protect the break. You pull on a batting glove and you find a way to play by keeping the tip of the finger just off the bat handle.*

\* \* \*

### First Test, West Indies versus England,
### Port of Spain, Trinidad, 19-24 January, 1968

*Twenty-eighth cap*

I batted well for 68, but the best was to come. Colin Cowdrey looked a portly, unathletic cricketer, but boy, could he bat. He had no flaws and it didn't matter what type of bowling, his timing was superb and effortless. He made 72. Ken Barrington and Tom Graveney got hundreds. Our total was so big we were able to ask West Indies to follow on. Our bowlers had persevered on a pretty flat pitch and shared the wickets. No-one was expecting it. We almost forced an unlikely win, but Garry Sobers was there to the end and he was able to give confidence and shepherd Wes Hall to hang on. Just one of those two would have done it for us because West Indies had only Lance Gibbs to come, and he was so bad with a bat in hand that my mum could have bowled him out.

Unfortunately, 'nearlies' don't count, do they...

68 and DNB

*** 

*With the splint on your finger, you hit Wes Hall for four boundaries in his first two overs of the match. You forget about the pain and discomfort, forget it's even there, and focus on Wes Hall... Focus on Garry Sobers and Charlie Griffith... Focus on Lance Gibbs and David Holford...*

*A stellar attack taken for almost six hundred runs and England well on top, but then, as you push for victory, you come out after tea on day five with West Indies on 180-8. Colin Cowdrey puts you at short leg, somewhere you never field, especially with a broken hand, and when Wes Hall offers a sharp chance, you can't hold it. Wes Hall survives. Garry Sobers survives. West Indies survive.*

*This is the game. It is capricious. It gives with one hand and it takes away with the other...*

*You fly to Jamaica and then travel by road from Kingston to Montego Bay to play a Jamaica Colts XI. You stop for afternoon tea in Runaway Bay, 50 miles from Montego on the North coast. At the golf course, Colin Cowdrey introduces you to Fred Perry, Britain's greatest ever tennis player, champion of Wimbledon for three years in a row, winner of the Grand Slam and the Davis Cup.*

*Fred takes you aside. He tells you, 'You will be a star. And remember, stars have to be lonely.'*

*** 

## Second Test, West Indies versus England, Sabina Park, Jamaica, 8-14 February, 1968

### *Twenty-ninth cap*

A very hard, bouncy pitch for the fast bowlers. Wes Hall was a thrilling sight for any cricket lover. What a specimen of a man he was. Very tall, athletic and with a great smile, it was hard not to like him even when he was trying to knock your block off.

Wes had boundless energy, and a run-up that got longer and longer the faster he bowled. At either end of Sabina Park, the sightscreens were huge white concrete walls, and very soon I swear he was pushing off from one of them. He had this gold cross on a chain around his neck, and as he raced in, it bounced from side to side. It was hard not to get mesmerised by it.

Every so often he got so excited that in the middle of his approach he would literally have to slow down a bit and then go again. One time, he was running in so fast that the gold cross flew up and hit him in the eye, stopping him in his tracks.

I thought I was handling his pace alright until I got an inside edge that spread-eagled my stumps. Colin Cowdrey made a superb century that held the innings together, along with John Edrich's knock of 96. They got us through the new ball and were top class.

The real fireworks came when West Indies batted. John Snow had been left out of the Trinidad Test and he was not happy about it. He didn't say much, but underneath he was seething. He bowled fantastically, with pace, movement, carry, accuracy and hostility.

He was a handful, and getting Garry Sobers lbw for nought was the icing on the cake. John had 7-49 and we had bowled West Indies out in only 48 overs. Colin was able to make them follow on 233 runs behind. You expect it to be harder to bowl a side out second time when they follow on. Pride is at stake and they have seen and experienced your bowlers on that surface. The pitch had started to open up, with big cracks running along it on a fast bowler's length.

It was deadly. Some balls hit a crack and kept low, while others lifted past your nose. You never knew when you were going to get the shooter or the lifter. Batting was no fun on that. Clive Lloyd decided to play a few shots before he got an unplayable ball.

I was the only fielder in the covers when Clive threw the kitchen sink at a David Brown delivery. It flew like a missile in the air to the boundary, smacked up against the concrete sight screen and bounced back an enormous distance.

I trotted over to retrieve it and hand it back to big Dave.

'Jesus…' I said.

Dave said, 'Well he won't look so good if he tries that again and it shoots along the deck…'

Amazingly his next ball did exactly that, hardly bouncing and lodging at the base of the stumps…

The home supporters were getting agitated with their heroes. Rum and beer are a huge part of watching the cricket and there was a lot of frustration and disappointment seeing their team losing. It all flared up when Basil Butcher, promoted to number four in the batting order, feathered an attempted leg glance from Basil D'Oliveira and Jim Parks dived and caught it.

Butcher didn't have the time to look around and see whether he had been caught or not. He heard the appeal and waited for the umpire. The few seconds of Basil standing there – correctly – for the decision just got the better of some of the crowd.

Disbelief and annoyance at the umpire for giving him out, and anger at another wicket going down was all too much. Bottles came flying over the fence and onto the ground. Colin Cowdrey went over to the main body of irate supporters to try and calm them, but more and more bottles were thrown. They were so mad with their players and their team going down so easily that they just exploded. Reason and common sense went out of the window, exacerbated by plenty of alcohol. As the riot police appeared and charged towards the bad boys, we ran to the pavilion. Tear gas was fired at the mob but the breeze wafted it into our dressing room. Now I know what dreadful stuff it is when it gets in your eyes. I put my head in a sink full of cold water to try and keep it away.

Seventy five minutes of playing time had been lost in unusual circumstances, so our manager and captain asked if that time could be made up on a sixth day. We were in a very strong position to win the Test, and we didn't want to find ourselves short of time and denied a victory because of the mob. West Indies administrators and umpires all readily agreed.

The key to beating West Indies is always Garfield Sobers. On a pair, but how would he play second innings? Snow bowls to him and he nicks it towards second slip. Tom Graveney tries to catch it but it bounces just in front of him and Tom has to go off the field with a bleeding, damaged hand.

The skipper motions for Basil D'Oliveira to take Tom's place and the very next ball Garry nicks again, straight to Basil who drops a regulation catch. John Snow could have had the great Sobers out for a pair and we would have been home and dry with a fantastic victory.

Ifs and buts…

If Tom hadn't hurt his hand.

If Basil had caught it.

We all go through life thinking our lives would have/could have been different if only. If only doesn't count!

The pitch was playing more and more tricks as the cracks opened up. Sobers was magnificent. He scored a century but just as vital for West Indies while he was there, his presence helped the late order make significant contributions.

Then, just towards the end of the fifth evening, when we are beginning to feel the win has slipped away from us, Garry declared. None of us saw that coming and it really caught us by surprise. All day, West Indies had been fighting to survive and now we required 159 to win - which on that pitch was out of the question - or survive a short session that evening and 75 minutes on the sixth morning. That night England closed on 19 for 4, with myself, Edrich, Cowdrey and Barrington back in the pavilion. The cracks on the pitch were so wide that I could put my hand down right up to the wrist.

Who asked for the 75 extra minutes to be made up because of the riot? Idiot!

Sobers bowled me a ball that pitched outside leg stump, hit a crack, and like a fast leg break hit leg stump not very high up. I was taking my pads off when I heard the roar as he did for Colin Cowdrey with a fast shooter. Nobody was talking as we made our way back to the hotel that evening.

What a tense hour and a quarter of cricket next morning, with us trying to hang on and West Indies rushing through as many overs as possible. They had so many fielders around the bat that the Jamaican umpire Douglas Sang Hue, in only his third Test, moved to point to get a clearer view for any decisions required.

Lance Gibbs was bowling to Fred Titmus and the ball bounced off his pad through all the close-in fielders and out towards point. Umpire Sang Hue got so caught up in the tension and drama that he picked up the ball and threw it back to the bowler! That caused a few alarms in our dressing room. We felt like saying, whose side are you on? Anyhow, we made it for a draw and knew we'd had a lucky escape.

 **17** and **0**

* * *

*Sun-streaked images of Tests played long ago… Wes Hall, Garry Sobers and you, three knights in waiting, different stations on the journey. Wes nearing the end. You at the start. Garry in his prime. Balls and bats and bottles flying. What a player Sobers is. What a human being. He can do anything: run, play tennis, play golf… On the cricket field he is West Indies' best fielder, bowler and batsman and he is the captain. Sobers says that he plays cricket for two men after the death of his friend Collie Smith in a terrible car accident as they travelled to a game together, and when he does the things he does, it's easy to think that's true.*

*On the field, he believes anything is possible. Maybe some of it rubs off on you…*

*You go to St John's Antigua to play the Leeward Isles on a pitch prepared by inmates from the prison that overlooks the ground. You open with Ollie Milburn, who is desperate for a chance to play. He is a cult hero in the West Indies after the radio coverage of the 1966 series in England, but he cannot get in the Test side. The crowds want to witness this man mountain entertain them. When you get out there, the umpire says, 'We are all very pleased to see you Mr Milburn. We want to watch you bat.'*

*'Ollie will be alright with umpires like this,' you think, but in the first over he edges one onto his pad, a clear deflection, and the same umpire fires him out.*

*'I hit it… I hit it…' Ollie says mournfully, but he is gone and the crowd watch you instead, watch you make 168.*

*Tom Graveney leads the MCC against a strong Barbados side. He calls you together and says, 'Lads, this is the sixth Test match…'*

*He tells you to bat for two days. That's exactly what you do. You make 243. The match finishes in a draw. No-one moans about you getting a double hundred this time. No-one drops you for it.*

*The lads take a boat trip and while they are swimming, Fred Titmus gets one of his legs caught by the boat's propeller and loses four toes.*

\* \* \*

## Third Test, West Indies versus England, Bridgetown, Barbados, 29 February – 5 March, 1968

### *Thirtieth cap*

A good batting pitch with a bit of pace and both batting teams too strong for the bowlers, yet the scoring rate wasn't great. West Indies batted for two days, 143 overs to make 349. Eventually John Edrich and I got a turn. At close of play on day three, we were 169 without losing a wicket. I was in top form, 90 not out, and John on 64. I was going so well and certain to get a century before close of play when a message came out from Cowdrey for me to slow down, make sure I didn't get out so as to be there when West Indies took the new ball after the rest day. I did exactly that and shut up shop.

Monday morning was a different day. Sobers took the new ball and bowled out of his skin, swinging it all over the place. John stuck it out and showed that wonderful phlegmatic character: he had the ability to forget the ball before, as if it never happened. He sailed on to a terrific 146 while I didn't add to my overnight score, pinned leg before by Garry.

I was completely mortified to miss out, as I knew I was batting so well. Whenever I experienced a disappointment, I never threw my equipment around or shouted and screamed. I just took my pads and stuff off and went for a walk around the streets adjoining the cricket ground to settle my frustration.

`90` and `DNB`

\* \* \*

*Fred Titmus flies home minus four of his toes, flies home to an uncertain future. MCC offer him £90 compensation. You are all one accident, one injury, one cracked and dangerous pitch, one sea swim, away from losing your livelihood. Just like your father lost his.*

*The selectors send for Tony Lock, who is 38 years old and the captain of Western Australia. Lock is years past his prime and without a first-class county to play for. He bowls with an action remodelled after he was called for chucking back in the 1950s, when he was starring for Surrey and England. Locky is aggressive and abrasive. The old pros joke that when he appealed at The Oval, the umpire raised his finger at Lord's, so loud was his 'Howzat?'*

*Maybe there's nostalgia behind his selection, maybe it's an urge to replace the 2,000 wickets of Fred Titmus with the 2,000 of Tony Lock. Or maybe it's because Locky seems indestructible, indestructible in a fragile game*

*While you bat in Barbados, Mrs Hilda Watson, who is sitting in the crowd, turns to her husband and asks, 'Why is that young man wearing spectacles?'*

*When she returns to England, Mrs Watson writes to you. The letter will change your life.*

\* \* \*

### Fourth Test, West Indies versus England, Port of Spain, Trinidad, 14-19 March, 1968

*Thirty-first cap*

The most important, most contentious and surprising match of the tour. Aged 38, Tony Lock was selected more than four years since he last played a Test. A tremendous achievement and however he bowled, you had to admire the character of the man coming back after being told his previous wickets had been achieved as a 'chucker.' I was impressed then, and more so as I have got wiser and more knowledgeable about cricket history.

The West Indies batsmen made our bowlers toil into the third day with a huge total.

Then I batted well for 62 until I swept the wrist-spinner Willie Rodriguez and got a top edge to the man on the sweep.

Colin Cowdrey was up for any challenge this tour. When he was in the mood, we watched a master batting. His 148 held our innings together until the occasional leg-spinner Basil Butcher had him caught behind. Basil then bamboozled our tail to finish with an unlikely 5-34. Although we were 122 behind, four days had been played and the match appeared certain to be a draw.

But after lunch on the last day Sobers suddenly and inexplicably declared, leaving England to score 215 runs in 165 minutes. Garry said after the match it was a sporting declaration that misfired. To me it would have been very generous in a county match. It was not the sort of thing you did in Test matches.

It was a fifth-day surface, dry and cracked, taking some spin and with the odd ball keeping low. There was a lot of rough from the bowlers' footmarks. It had become hard to time the ball and so scoring was slow. But thinking this through, the teams had amassed 1,022 runs for the loss of only 19 wickets, so it can't have been that bad to bat on – unless it had miraculously deteriorated...

\* \* \*

*Opening batsmen know when they are going to bat. It's one of the reasons that you like to open. No surprises. But this is a surprise, this declaration from the maverick genius Garry Sobers. You rush from the field to the dressing room. Some of the tour party who are out on the balcony overhear the West Indies discussing their plan.*

*They don't think Cowdrey has the balls to chase the runs. If England lose a few early wickets, West Indies have the spinners to exploit those footmarks, to make the ball jump or shoot from those cracks... Lance Gibbs with his champion off-spin. Willie Rodriguez, who wins games for Trinidad on this ground with his fast wrist-spinners. Sobers the genius with his mixed bag of wrist and finger spin. Basil Butcher, the part-timer who tore the England first innings down from 373-5 to 404 all out.*

*You listen to the senior players. They try to work out how many overs England might face if Sobers bowls the spinners all day.*

*Cowdrey says he wants to play for the draw. Tom Graveney backs his captain. Ken Barrington tells them they're talking rubbish. He tells them Garry has got this wrong. This is our chance to win a Test match, take a lead in the series...*

*John Edrich agrees with Ken. You're trying to get your box in and your pads on, five minutes to go.*

*Voices are raised, things get heated. You can't have that, not before you are about to bat, when you need to clear your mind and slow your heartbeat, so you go out on the balcony to finish padding up. Finally, Colin comes out and tells you to bat normally until tea.*

*As you and John Edrich walk to the wicket, he asks you what you are going to do. You tell him you're playing normally but if the ball is there to hit, you will hit it. You reach tea on 28 not out, England 73-1, Colin in the middle alongside you.*

*At tea, Kenny raises his voice again. Jim Parks speaks out. Then you speak out too...*

\* \* \*

At Yorkshire we would have expected to try for a win. We needed 142 for victory off 26 overs. A fifth-day surface, awkward and slow, but opportunities like this one are rare in Test match cricket. Eventually, Colin told me to play my normal game but seal up one end so we wouldn't lose. He would try to push the score along and play a few shots. Smart and clever to hedge his bets!

I took him at his word, getting singles to give him the strike. His ability to place the off-spinner Lance Gibbs into the gaps was educational and he scored a beautiful 71, while after tea I scored 52 runs off 69 balls to be there at the end.

When Garry Sobers made his declaration, I was told that most of the press lads felt the match would peter out to a draw. That was the norm, as very few teams took a chance. But Brian Close disagreed and said, 'We'll win this if GB stays in. He'll take his time and win it with a few minutes to spare. Not before he has to.' Brian knew me so well. I finished with 80 not out and England won with three minutes left on the clock

**62** and **80 not out**

\* \* \*

*As the team flies to Guyana, your suitcase comes off the carousel with 'Mister Runs' chalked on it. When you walk the streets, the locals come up to you and ask about your batting. Clyde Walcott and Everton Weekes say that you remind them of Leonard Hutton in your style and attitude.*

*You're allocated a room with Ken Barrington, but Ken sleeps with the air conditioner on full blast while wearing two jumpers and a*

*pile of blankets. You wake up freezing cold. Ken tells you this is how he likes it and he won't be changing. You ask Colin Cowdrey if you can use the spare bed in his room.*

*The ICC has ordered that if the last Test of any series can still affect the overall outcome, it should be played over six days to give more chance of a result. With England leading one-nil, Colin asks you whether they should select Colin Milburn as an extra batsman and play for the draw?*

*You think about the Yorkshire dressing room. You think about what Brian Close would do. You tell Colin that England should select a balanced team and set out to win.*

\* \* \*

### Fifth Test, West Indies versus England, Georgetown, Guyana, 28 March – 3 April, 1968

#### *Thirty-second cap*

In the end we had a sensible team with two spinners, because the pitch would almost certainly turn over six days. We bowled well but were held up by the West Indies' two world-class batsmen, Rohan Kanhai and Garfield Sobers, who each made 150.

We got the rest for only 103 runs off the bat, which was a terrific effort.

Our reply was held together with a century from me and a half-century from our skipper. It was hard going after Colin and I were out, and we were in a bit of trouble when Tony Lock walked in and played the innings of his life. He had been flown half-way around the world to help our spin bowling but had gone for 190 runs and only two wickets. Now he changed the course of this match as he attacked their bowling for a priceless 89. What a game-changer. We finished only 43 behind West Indies.

By the fifth morning, the pitch was turning. John Snow bowled magnificently and took six wickets on a now very dry surface that didn't really give assistance to seam or pace. West Indies were all out a second time, more than three hundred ahead and with a full day to take the ten England wickets that would square the series.

So many teams fail to bat out the last day. A worn pitch, the pressure of the occasion and bowlers who somehow find that extra ingredient are all against them. We got off to a bad start with Sobers getting John Edrich early. I got out on 30 to a ball from Lance Gibbs that turned and kept low out of Sobers' footmarks.

Gibbs quickly got two of our very best, Ken Barrington and Tom Graveney, for ducks. Then he caught and bowled Basil D'Oliveira for two. We were in big trouble and there was some panic in our dressing room. 41-5, with the cream of our batting back in the pavilion and an age left in the match. There was so much tension and a stunned silence amongst the team.

Colin Cowdrey was still there, yet to get going, with the young Kent wicket-keeper Alan Knott in only his fourth Test alongside. Slowly and stubbornly, they hung in there, yet it always felt like a matter of time until they copped something unplayable. Colin was finally out lbw to Gibbs for a wonderful 82, and we thought that with an end open, West Indies would polish off our tail.

They did, or almost… Snow, Lock and Pocock were in and out so fast that our number eleven Jeff Jones had to face the last over from Lance Gibbs, who was spinning and flighting the ball so skilfully. Jeff was a terrific lad, but as much as we loved him, he was a terrible batsman. Most of our players couldn't watch, but I sat outside with our manager Les Ames.

Jeff was surrounded. I couldn't see him surviving the pressure of the situation, not with his non-existent skills, the pitch turning and the class of Lance Gibbs. But with the series on the line, he did. Jeff kept out all six balls… England had drawn a memorable Test and pulled off a series win that not many expected.

116 and 30

\* \* \*

*You fly back to England. It is already April, the season almost upon you, but you don't need a rest. You know about hard times now. You understand loss. You lost your dad, lost your form, lost your love for the game and for life, but it all came back under the Caribbean sun. More than eleven hundred runs on the tour, almost five hundred in the Tests in just seven innings… Weekes and Walcott comparing you to Hutton… Colin Cowdrey asking for your opinion. Letting you use his spare bed…*

*Mister Runs.*

*You learn something. You learn that runs are the answer. This is what you believe. When you make runs, people stop you in the street. Runs keep the bad feelings away, those feelings of failure, of loss… Runs keep your place in the team, keep a roof over your head, over your family's head. Runs keep you safe. Runs save you from yourself.*

*Mister Runs.*

*This is what you learn. This is what you know. This is who you must be.*

*The season of 1968 comes and the ball looks like a football. You play Sussex at Bradford and hook John Snow into the seats beyond the midwicket boundary.*

*'This isn't Hove,' you tell him.*

*You make a hundred. You make another at Headingley against Leicestershire and then another, one of your best, at Middlesbrough against Warwickshire. You hit David Brown into the seats. You lift Tom Cartwright into the tents at midwicket.*

*'You're just a poor man's Compton,' he shouts.*

*'And you're a poor man's Shackleton,' you shout back.*

*You take a hundred off Gloucestershire and Mike Procter, who bowls fiery inswingers and then rolls his fingers over the ball to make it jag away at high pace. You decide it's too dangerous to cover drive him and put the shot away until you have 125 next to your name. Then you try to cover drive Mike Procter, and he bowls you through the gate.*

*Mister Runs…*

\* \* \*

### First Test, England versus Australia, Old Trafford, Manchester, 6-11 June, 1968

*Thirty-third cap*

To be frank, we didn't bat well enough to ever have any chance of winning the game. Australia totalled a decent 357 and their bowling made runs hard for us to get. John Edrich scored 49 and myself

81

35, but the rest mustered 66 between them. We only just saved the follow on but giving up a lead of 192 on a pitch with just a bit in it for the bowlers was always going to be insurmountable.

Pat Pocock bowled splendidly and took six wickets in the second innings, but the damage was done. I have believed for a long time that after both teams have batted, you usually have a clear idea who is going to win. We had no chance of chasing 413, and it was just a matter of time if it didn't rain.

After his success, Pat Pocock didn't play again in the series. I have no idea why. Basil D'Oliveira easily outscored any of us batsmen in our second innings with a fine 89 not out and yet he was dropped too. Very odd.

**35** and **11**

\* \* \*

## Second Test, England versus Australia, Lord's, London 20-25 June, 1968

*Thirty-fourth cap*

Endless rain, and after three days of stop-start batting, England were 351-7. Our innings seemed to take forever. Our best batting had come from Colin Milburn, who got an excellent 83, yet he was dropped and didn't play again in the series. Another odd decision by our selectors. I batted well for 49, Ken Barrington was good for 75 and captain Colin Cowdrey did well for his 45. I say good, because stopping and starting your batting can be difficult: sat on your backside bored to death, hanging around in dressing rooms and then starting in poor light without a net is not my idea of preparation, so I thought we did well. After the rest day, we had no choice but to declare and have a go at Australia. We were surprised but thrilled as it turned out. Big Dave Brown got a five-wicket haul, Barry Knight picked up three and Australia were all out for 78. Amazing. I think the batsmen got too defensive. They were one up in the series and as they held the Ashes, all they had to do was draw and England would have to win two of the remaining three Tests.

Maybe they factored in more rain, or maybe they just got lucky, because when they were asked to bat again, it did rain. We had them on the ropes but with 15 hours of play lost, we just couldn't get over the line.

Very frustrating.

**49** and **DNB**

\* \* \*

*You play for Yorkshire against the Australians at Bramall Lane and miss out on a hundred when Ian Chappell, bowling his occasional wrist-spinners, pitches one perfectly and you nick it behind for 86.*

*You try to ignore the ache in your back, an ache that began with the season, began in the damp and the cold after the Caribbean sun. Fred Trueman makes the Aussies follow on. The crowd love it. The players love it. Yorkshire give the tourists a good beating by an innings and 69 runs, the Australian batsmen trooping past Yorkshire Annie, the ever-present fan who sits right outside their dressing room.*

*'Wheel them in and wheel them out, Yorkshire,' she shouts in her booming voice. 'Come on Freddie, you've got them now...'*

*The ache in your back is still there. You watch the throwing competition organised by the Milk Marketing Board. Ken Taylor and Fred Trueman take on Paul Sheahan and Dave Renneberg.*

*Jimmy Binks tells you Ken Taylor will win, and he does, with a throw of 112 yards. First prize is £25. Ken takes his wife Avril for a weekend away at the Seahouses in Northumberland and comes back with a fiver still in his pocket...*

*You rub Fiery Jack into your back. You wear a bit of red flannel like the coal miners used to. It gets worse. You can barely move when you get out of bed in the mornings...*

\* \* \*

## Third Test, England versus Australia, Edgbaston, Birmingham, 11-16 July, 1968

### *Thirty-fifth cap*

The first day was washed out. On day two, I was leg before to mystery spinner Jon Gleeson for 36. Edrich with 88 and Graveney with 96 were excellent, but it was all about Colin Cowdrey, the first man to appear in 100 Test matches.

We could tell immediately he was trying hard and batting well on this special occasion. But when he had scored 58, he pulled a muscle in his left leg and asked for a runner. The runner had to be a batsman who had already been dismissed. I was the only England batsman out, and because my back was aching I was laying down and not watching play.

Tom Graveney came up to me. 'Geoffrey, the captain wants you to come and run for him.'

'You must be joking...'

I had to pad up with full gear on and stand at square-leg. On one leg, Colin made a hundred in his hundredth Test Match. How special was that? Mind you, I had run 46 of his runs and I told him he had no idea how lucky he was to survive that long with me running for him

Ultimately, we left ourselves a day to take ten Aussie wickets, but play was abandoned by 12.30pm, so heavy was the rain. More frustration.

36 and 31

\* \* \*

*You can barely get into the car that takes you back to the hotel. Bernie Thomas, the England physio, sends you to see his friend Paddy Armour at Pinderfields Hospital near Wakefield. Paddy tells you that this is not a physiotherapy problem and sends you to see Yorkshire's orthopaedic specialist Reg Broomhead in Leeds. By now the pain is so severe you begin to wonder if your career might be over. You're doubled over in pain and can hardly move.*

*This fragile game.*

*Mr Broomfield diagnoses a swollen disc that has lost fluid. It is very serious. He tells you that you can be in a plaster cast for three months and then rehab for another three months or you can wear a specially designed corset and not move at all for three weeks.*

*You try the corset. Paddy Armour fits it. It goes from under your shoulders down to your abdomen. Paddy places wooden boards over your mum's settee. You lie on them and move only when you need the toilet. You eat your meals on your chest. Your mum washes you. Paddy calls in unexpectedly to check that you are not cheating. He doesn't need to. If lying on wooden boards for three weeks is what you need to do in order to bat again, that is what you will do.*

*After three weeks, you begin gentle exercise. You start to run. You have a net. On 31 August you play for Leeds Freelance against Goole Town at Headingley and make 126. You play at Ackworth the following day and make 98. You return to first-class cricket at Scarborough on 4 September in a three-day game for an England XI versus the Rest of the World and score 93 and 115 against Garth Mackenzie, Eddie Barlow, Garry Sobers and Peter Pollock. You even go to Scarborough to play against an England Under 25 team, looking to prove to the selectors that you are fit for the tour of South Africa, but the game degenerates into a hit and giggle in which you gift your wicket to Keith Fletcher. Fred Trueman gets you a place on his post-season tour of Devon and Cornwall, where you will guest for the opposing club teams alongside Garry Sobers and Lance Gibbs.*

*Yorkshire win the County Championship and play MCC at Scarborough to close the season. You make 25 and 102 not out. Even missing seven weeks of cricket, you score 1,487 runs at 64.65 and top the first-class averages.*

*You are fragile. But you make runs.*

*You understand that these two things are true. These two things are co-dependent. You must look after yourself. You must score runs. If you look after yourself and you score runs then the failure and the loss stay away.*

*While you are flat on your back on your mum's settee hoping that the swelling in the disc will subside so that you can bat again and tour South Africa with the MCC, Basil D'Oliveira is desperate for his chance to be selected too. Desperate to tour South Africa, the country that classifies him as Cape Coloured and designates him a second-class citizen.*

But Basil is no longer in the England team. Not until Roger Prideaux falls ill. And when Roger Prideaux falls ill,

Basil is recalled to play the final Test of the summer against Australia at the Oval and makes 158 as England win and level the series. Anyone can see that Basil should make the tour now. Anyone except Doug Insole and the England selectors, who do not choose him, who know that South Africa will not accept him, who tell the press: 'As far as the selectors are concerned Basil is regarded from an overseas tour point of view as a batsman rather than an all-rounder as he is in this country. I think we have got players rather better than him in the side.'

This is more of Doug's codswallop, more of the rubbish he talks. Rubbish because Basil is a batsman. Rubbish because Basil toured West Indies as a batsman. But Basil goes back to Worcestershire and loses all form with the bat. Instead of touring South Africa as a player, he signs a contract to cover the tour as a journalist for the News of the World. It is mid-September. You head off to Devon and Cornwall to play on Fred's tour. Basil is there to play for Fred's XI. Bowler Tom Cartwright withdraws from the South Africa tour with an injured shoulder. Basil D'Oliveira is selected to take his place, even though Basil is not a bowler.

Basil doesn't care though. None of you care as you head to the bar to toast his selection, an obvious wrong put right. It's wonderful to see Basil smiling and happy, surrounded by his fellow pros.

The feeling lasts a day. John Vorster, Prime Minister of South Africa, announces that his country will not accept Basil as a member of the touring party. Vorster says that Basil's selection is political and inconsistent. Vorster says that he 'has taken a decision for South Africa'.

John Arlott sums it up best. 'No-one of open mind will believe that Basil was left out for cricketing reasons.' John says that even had Basil not merited selection, MCC should have selected him to demonstrate their opposition to Apartheid.

Twelve days after you celebrate with Basil at a bar in Cornwall, the MCC tour of South Africa is cancelled.

# CHAPTER SIX

# 1969

*You are at Hemsworth Grammar School and 17 years old when you first notice that your vision has got worse. You can't read the numbers on the chalk-board. You go to have your sight tested. The optician tells you that you need glasses and you cry for three days. You hate the glasses, hate what they mean. They stop you playing football for Leeds United Under 18s. They make you fear for the cricket career you want so badly.*

*The glasses make you feel more fragile. They make you self-conscious and aware of how you look. You wear them for more than ten years.*

*MCC organise a short trip to Pakistan in place of the South Africa tour but you turn it down. You need to rest your back. Because you have no spleen you worry about your health during six weeks on the road in Pakistan.*

*You stay at home and so you trial the contact lenses Mrs Watson offers. It feels strange to have a foreign body in your eye. Your fear is that the lenses will make you blink too much. Blink just as that ball is coming at you, and anything might happen… But you persevere because the lenses change not just your cricket, but your life. Without your glasses you feel more confident and relaxed. Not the shy introvert in spectacles.*

*Things are changing at Yorkshire. Fred Trueman has come to the end. Your idol departs with no fuss, no farewell and 2,304 first-class wickets to his name. Raymond Illingworth leaves Yorkshire to take up the captaincy of Leicestershire. Ray is a fantastic cricketer, the power behind Brian Close's throne. You go and visit him at his home to persuade him to stay, but Ray has asked Yorkshire for the security of a contract. Yorkshire do not do contracts.*

*Yorkshire chairman Brian Sellers tells the press: 'He can fucking go, and so can anyone else who wants to…'*

*Raymond Illingworth does fucking go, and he is a huge loss. At the end of May, Colin Cowdrey tears an Achilles tendon and Ray is appointed captain of England for the first Test of the summer. Two days before Cowdrey's injury, Colin Milburn is involved in a car accident and loses the sight in his left eye.*

*This capricious, fragile game.*

*There is one more casualty. Before the 1969 season begins, Doug Insole resigns as Chairman of Selectors. The D'Oliveira affair does for him. He is replaced by Alec Bedser.*

\* \* \*

## First Test, England versus West Indies, Old Trafford, Manchester, 12-17 June, 1969

### *Thirty-sixth cap*

My first Test innings wearing contact lenses went far better than I could have hoped.

I was still finding lenses a bit strange, but I scored a hundred and only a dodgy lbw to John Shepherd ended it. Charlie Elliott gave me out even though the ball was missing leg stump. After play I said to Charlie, 'You took pity on Shep and gave him my wicket because he's a nice lad!'

You could chat and banter with umpires then, because most of them had played county cricket and understood the difference between dissent and having a bit of fun. It was a huge relief that I had got off to a better than good start. Tom Graveney made 75 and with a half-century from Dolly we had over 400.

John Snow and David Brown were all over the West Indian batsmen, making it easy for our new captain to ask them to follow on. It had taken our bowlers just 48 overs, so West Indies had no chance unless it rained. They played with more determination second time, all their batsmen getting starts but none could make that telling score. It was all over very early on the fifth morning with a ten-wicket win. A great start for Raymond and a feather in the cap of the England selectors for choosing him as captain.

`128` and `1 not out`

\* \* \*

*England are different under Ray Illingworth. A working-class Yorkshireman who left school at 14, son of a cabinet maker, replaces Colin Cowdrey, son of Empire, born on his father's tea plantation in India, educated at Tonbridge and Oxford.*

*How can things not be different?*

\* \* \*

## Second Test, England versus West Indies, Lord's, London, 26 June – 1 July, 1969

### *Thirty-seventh cap*

Opening bats Roy Fredericks and Steve Camacho put on a hundred runs, and from such a fantastic start West Indies should have batted us out of the game. Charlie Davis scored a steady hundred to hold the innings together, but he got involved in a mix-up with Garfield Sobers and I ran out the great man for 29 from cover point. Their 380 was good but not great.

We closed the day at 27-4, victim of yet another of Sobers' inspired spells. He did for Peter Parfitt, Basil D'Oliveira, and me. Vanburn Holder had John Edrich, leaving John Hampshire, on debut, not out alongside Philip Sharpe.

John was so uptight he couldn't sleep that night. He was awake early and came to sit in the dressing room, alone with his thoughts. He was about to play the innings of his life. Sharpe was out early and with England's batting in a mess, John scored a century, the first batsman to score a century at Lord's on Test debut. A fantastic achievement. Alan Knott made a half-century and the new captain crowned things off with his own maiden century batting at number eight.

Who says there are no fairy stories?

We knew we had got out of jail and finished only 36 runs behind West Indies. Half centuries from Clive Lloyd and Sobers, who batted on one leg and with a runner, set us 332 runs in 240 minutes plus the now mandatory 20 overs in the last hour of play. We had a go but we were always losing wickets and just couldn't get our noses in front. While Philip Sharpe, who got 86, and myself, with 106, were together we kept on trying to win, but once we were out it was a case of saving the game. Garfield Sobers, who had batted with a runner, came out and bowled 29 overs... odd. Very odd.

23 and 106

* * *

## Third Test, England versus West Indies, Headingley, Leeds, 10-15 July, 1969

*Thirty-eighth cap*

Raymond won the toss and batted, which is the sensible decision when you are playing in England in the era of uncovered pitches. It was a cool, overcast and gloomy morning, not very inviting for batsmen against a new ball for sure, but better the devil you know. If there is cloud cover at Headingley, it moves around. If the sun shines it's great for batting. But, and this is always the big but, what if it rains? Then it's a guessing game as to how the surface will play, and on a wet pitch, Derek Underwood was a match-winner. Nobody ever hit Deadly around on a wet pitch. Nobody, full stop. For most batsmen, simple survival was almost impossible.

I once played for Yorkshire against Kent at Canterbury, and as we watched the rain pour down, I said to Derek, '5-40?'

Derek replied, 'Another hour of this and it could be 8-20...' That's how good he was on wet pitches. Sobers bowling left-arm swing and seam with a new ball was a handful every time, but in favourable bowling conditions he shot me, Phil Sharpe and John Hampshire out for next to nothing. John Edrich got a gutsy 79, Dolly 48, and Knotty 44. In the circumstances, 223 all out could have been a lot worse. The four of us Yorkies in the side knew this was a good score if conditions stayed the same.

Most of the West Indies players hadn't come across surfaces like Headingley in cool, overcast conditions, and our bowlers knew how to keep it full and kiss the surface of the pitch. They were all out for 161, giving us a 62 run lead – massive in a low-scoring match. Sobers did me for nought, caught behind with an away seamer, but most of our batsmen scored a few runs on a pitch playing a bit easier as it got drier. West Indies were set 303 for the victory. We felt good about our chances but as the pitch got drier and slower it didn't seam as much.

It felt like Basil Butcher was winning the match for them, and things became tense on the field. I wasn't close enough to hear his exact words, but Ray was asking Snowy for a big effort, as we were desperate for the breakthrough. John hated slow pitches and had his own ideas about the game. He liked to see the ball around the batsman's ears. Raymond wasn't impressed with what Snowy served up next.

The key moment came at the other end as Derek Underwood had Butcher caught behind and then Barry Knight bowled Sobers for nought. After that we mopped up the tail for not many. It was a terrific effort by West Indies as we got home with only 30 runs to spare.

`12` and `0`

\* \* \*

*Ray Illingworth telephones John Snow to inform him that he has been dropped for the next Test match for disobeying captain's orders. He doesn't hide behind Alec Bedser or the selection panel. He puts John straight himself and keeps it in-house. Alec Bedser protects John Snow. He tells the press that the selectors have rested him and want to take a look at Alan Ward of Derbyshire in the first Test versus New Zealand.*

*John is obstinate, truculent, his own man. Nothing wrong with that*

\* \* \*

### First Test, England versus New Zealand, Lord's, London, 24-28 July, 1969

*Thirty-ninth cap*

Another murky English morning with a poor-looking pitch. The Lord's ridge had speckled grass around it and didn't look inviting to us batsmen.

Raymond came up to me: 'What do you think?'

'Don't ask me. I don't want to bat on that.'

'What would you do if you were me as captain?'

'I would bat. The other end is so dry and patchy, Unders will bowl them out as fast as they come in second innings.'

This is where Raymond was clever. Having won the toss, he called all the players together. 'Look,' he said, 'I know batting will be tough this morning but if we scrap and fight then this pitch will turn later on and we can win.'

He was clear-thinking, gave the team his reasons for batting first and he carried us with him. No flannel, just straightforward cricket sense. None of the batsmen were happy with his decision but we understood the logic, so there was no moaning or unrest.

Sure enough, I was out second ball to one that flew off the ridge from Dick Motz, caught at gully. Batting was hard work and Raymond top-scored with 53. We were all out for 190, and I don't think any of us would say it was fun. On another day we could have been bowled out for half of that, but boy, did the players scrap.

New Zealand found it just as tough. Derek Underwood took 4-38 in 30 overs and this was only the second day. Just think what he would do when the pitch turned a lot more.

By the third day the grass had changed colour and the ridge wasn't as menacing. Spin was the problem as wear and footmarks at the other end started to make the ball turn more. Our 340, led by a finely crafted century from John Edrich, plus the lead of 21 on first innings, meant New Zealand had no chance. Only Glenn Turner had played much in England and he battled through the innings for only 43 not out.

Derek dismissed New Zealand for 131 with the astonishing figures of 31-18-32-7. Dick Motz slogged 23 at the death and Dayle Hadlee 19 to make the total look better than it was. It was no contest. Nobody could get Unders off the square. He had great skill, a great mind and hated his fielders allowing singles because he knew pressure would build on batsmen. We'd joke that if he hadn't been a bowler he would have been a rat catcher.

Raymond Illingworth came and thanked me for the advice I had given him before the toss, acknowledging that it didn't help my batting but was right for the team.

 0 and 47

## Second Test, England versus New Zealand, Trent Bridge, Nottingham, 7-12 August, 1969

### *Fortieth cap*

Twelve hours of play lost to rain effectively made a three-day Test, and the pitch was so good there wasn't much chance of a result.

Alan Ward bowled very fast in partnership with John Snow, who'd done his penance, and had us thinking England may have a pair of speedsters to win Test matches. Anyone who has faced genuine pace knows they are like the aces in a pack of cards that make all the difference.

I hooked and missed at Dick Motz. The ball hit me on the arm, cannoned onto my chest and dropped on top of the stumps, dislodging a single bail. It was my third nought in the last four Test innings and was getting ridiculous. There was much talk in the media that it was my change from glasses to contact lenses that was affecting my form. I didn't believe in making excuses and I still don't.

When things go wrong, luck goes against you. Hooking Motz, the ball could have gone anywhere, but if you are on a downward spiral then good fortune is impossible to come by.

0 and DNB

* * *

*Illy understands cricketers, knows what makes you all tick. When he wants John Snow fired up, he puts you at mid-off and gets you to ginger him up a bit.*

*'What's wrong, Snowy?' you'll say, in that voice you have. 'You're only fast-medium. Is something the matter with you?'*

*John Snow tells you what he will do to you when he gets you on a quick pitch at Hove.*

*John Snow goes to Illy and asks him to move bloody Boycott somewhere else.*

*'Keep going,' Raymond tells you... 'It's working...'*

*And then John Snow stirred up and angry, will race in, bowling quickly, not quite realising how much you, Ray and all of the other players admire him.*

\* \* \*

### Third Test, England versus New Zealand, The Oval, London, 21-26 August, 1969

*Forty-first cap*

Not the usual bouncy Oval surface, but a pitch that turned from the start. Underwood took six wickets and Illingworth three to put New Zealand all out for 150.

We had to graft and work hard for a lead of 92. New Zealand's chances of saving the game were slim, and with Underwood in the opposition they were getting slimmer with every run we scored.

Derek liked to sit quietly in the dressing room with a fag in one hand and a cup of tea in the other contemplating... well, who the hell knows what he was thinking! He was the least likely assassin you will ever see. Some bowlers buckle under the weight of expectation. Not Derek, Ask him to bowl a side out to win a game, and he thrived on the chance.

He reeled off 39 overs for 60 runs and another six wickets, giving him 12 for the match. If he'd been allowed to bowl at both ends, we could have all gone home in three days. He was a machine, finely tuned, and I'm glad he was on my side.

46 and 8

\* \* \*

*You do not know it yet, but you will not play an official Test match for more than a year. You pack up your case at The Oval and a week later you are at Hove, where Yorkshire play Sussex. John Snow comes flying down the hill towards the sea, a new red ball in his hand. You hook at a short one and miss. The next ball is short too, but you see it early and play it easily down to third man. As you turn for your second run at the bowler's end, you give Snowy a playful tap on the leg with your bat.*

*Snowy doesn't like it. He's riled by your teasing in the Test match, riled about being dropped by England and about who knows what else… He is a fast bowler and this is how fast bowlers work, by getting angry at the world and everyone in it.*

*John Snow tells umpire Charlie Elliott that he will come around the wicket. There is only one reason why he is doing that, only one reason any fast bowler does that. He turns at the top of his mark and comes flying down the hill at Hove, full of fire and anger and with that new red ball in his hand.*

*He bowls a lethal short ball, chest high, that you are good enough to get behind and play down onto the ground, but the ball strikes the outside of your left glove, and that's that. A few hours later you leave A&E with a plaster cast on your broken hand and miss the Gillette Cup final three days later when Yorkshire beat Derbyshire.*

*You are strong and you are fragile, strong and fragile in this capricious game.*

# CHAPTER SEVEN

# 1970

*Winter comes. Your bones heal. Other things break.*

*The Rugby Football Union hosts the Springboks on a three-month tour that begins in October 1969. They play 26 matches. Almost all of them are disrupted by a loose collective of students, politicians and activists called the Anti-Apartheid Movement. They invade the fields, handcuff themselves to the goalposts, hijack the team bus. The Springboks are rattled. They lose to Oxford University. They lose two of four internationals. They go home. The MCC are rattled. The South African cricket team is due to tour in the summer of 1970.*

*On the evening of 19 January, ten county cricket grounds are broken into during a co-ordinated attack. At Southampton, the scoreboard is defaced. At Cardiff, the pitch is dug up and Wilf Wooller's car is covered in paint. At Lord's a small fire is set. There is damage at The Oval, Taunton, Headingley, Old Trafford, and Grace Road, Leicester. MCC insist that the tour must go ahead, even more so in the face of an unelected mob. Public opinion agrees. MCC ring the Lord's outfield with barbed wire. Test and county grounds are fortified with searchlights and guard dogs. At a meeting in February, the tour is cut from 28 fixtures to 12, the games to be played at the Test venues and city grounds where security is easiest to implement.*

*The Professional Cricketers' Association listens to a speech from its president John Arlott, who advocates the cancellation of the tour. The players, though, vote for the tour to go ahead. Many of them make a much-needed living coaching in South Africa during the winter.*

*The Stop The Seventy Tour protest group, fronted by a 19-year-old student called Peter Hain and a 20-year-old student named Gordon Brown, use the threat of direct action to draw attention to their cause. They make skilful use of television coverage to highlight their protests. The Prime Minister, Harold Wilson, already detests the South African regime and its leader John Vorster, and with a general election looming, says that he will look favourably at peaceful protest. Thirteen African countries announce that they will boycott the Commonwealth Games, due to take place in Edinburgh in July, if the cricket tour goes ahead.*

*Things break.*

*A general election is called for 18 June. The Home Secretary James Callaghan summons the TCCB and tells them to cancel the tour. It is made official on 22 May.*

*Other things heal.*

*In place of the South Africa series, England announce five matches against a Rest of the World team captained by Garry Sobers and including the South African Test players Barry Richards, Mike Procter, Eddie Barlow and Graeme Pollock.*

*Sobers accepts the captaincy on the understanding that the series will be awarded full Test match status. Guinness sponsors the series on the same understanding. The BBC and ITV share broadcasting rights. The TCCB advertise the series and sell tickets as Test matches.*

*The first match is due to start on 17 June, the day before the general election.*

*This season of two halves begins for you in the cold and rain of April at Harrogate for a Gillette Cup first round tie. Three days are set aside to complete the game. The teams of Yorkshire and Surrey spend the first watching the rain come down. On the second, play is halted by hailstones, sleet and rain. Surrey score 134 and bowl Yorkshire out for 76. You make 10. You think, whoever scheduled this match needs their brain examined.*

*You go to Fenners and make fifty against the students of Cambridge, but in the Championship, during the damp and cold of spring and on spring's capricious pitches, some wet, some drying, some juicy, some dead or dying, you cannot score any runs. Every day you are on edge. Every day brings its own kind of heartbreak. Your mood reaches a low ebb. Thirteen innings, 285 runs at 21.92.*

*Thirteen innings. Unlucky for some. Unlucky for you.*

*You have had enough. You pick up the telephone. You call Alec Bedser, the chairman of selectors, and tell him that you would like to be left out of the England team to play the Rest of the World, left out until you can find some form. Alec Bedser agrees. A few days later, the postman brings a letter. It's a personal note from Alec. He tells you to keep going – things that are broken will eventually heal.*

*In July, they do... at last. You go to Sheffield and make 44 and 82 not out against Leicestershire. Then you go to Chesterfield and reach 99 against Derbyshire, who bring South African Chris Wilkins on to bowl.*

*'Be careful of him, Boycs, he's got a golden arm,' Derby's Mike Page tells you.*

*You laugh and smack Chris Wilkins hard off the back foot to cover point, where Edwin Smith dives full-length and catches you in his left hand.*

*No ton at Chesterfield, then, and only – only! – 62 against Sussex, but then it really begins. You make 148 against Kent. Next you travel to the Garrison ground Colchester where you hit 230 in a single day against Essex. In the Sunday League game that occupies the rest day you make 98, and then you resume in the Championship on Monday and take your score to 260 not out.*

*You don't have to ring Alec Bedser or any of the other selectors, they just pick you. Pick you for the fourth Test match at Headingley against the Rest of the World.*

\* \* \*

## Fourth Match, England versus Rest of the World, Headingley, Leeds, 30 July – 4 August, 1970

Sobers won the toss and put us in. He didn't get it wrong, either, although I don't think he was expecting Eddie Barlow to be his main wicket-taker. Eddie was a bustling, brisk medium-pacer and he usually made something happen, basically because batsmen didn't feel threatened by his bowling. He swung the ball out and nipped it back at a pace where batsmen often fancied they could score off him, but then made mistakes.

He had so much confidence and self-belief that he would sometimes say to his captain that he had this feeling or premonition that he would get wickets. His team-mates used to laugh at him, but when he kept breaking partnerships and snaring the big wicket, the smart captains let him bowl.

He strangled me down the leg side for 15 when I was playing well. He got Keith Fletcher for a fine 89, then later he polished off Alan Knott, Chris Old and Don Wilson for a hat trick. What a game-changer. England 222 all out, Eddie Barlow 7-64. And psychic Eddie was the only one who saw it coming!

Yet when we had the ROW at 152-4 and with Barry Richards and Rohan Kanhai injured and out of the game, we felt we were in with a chance. Then came Garfield St. Aubrun Sobers. He usually gets most people's vote as the best all-rounder in the history of our game. I have seen plenty of him, and for me when he was really trying, he was the best batsman I have ever seen, never mind all-rounder. His competitive juices were flowing and he just took the match away from us with another splendid hundred. When you have done your best and someone plays that well at a critical moment, I believe you just have to put your hand up and acknowledge greatness.

We knew it was a tall order, but we set about batting with determination. At the back of every players mind was the trip to Australia that winter. Don't let anyone tell you we weren't aware of selection. It's human nature. Brian Luckhurst played the best, a tough battle-hardened county cricketer. He got 92 and with me batting well, we got a great start. Eddie Barlow, that man again, got me caught at slip for 64 with one that just left me a bit. Soon, Eddie had another five wickets, which added up to match figures of 12-142.

ROW needed 222 with two batsmen injured, and if we could just get Sobers out cheaply we could win. We bowled and fielded like demons and by close of play on the fourth evening they were 75-5, with Barlow, Murray, Pollock, Lloyd and Mushtaq all gone to some inspired and intense bowling. Next morning early, Tony Greig dropped Intikhab Alam at slip off John Snow. Tony was an excellent slipper with huge hands so it was a big surprise and huge disappointment, but it does happen even to the best.

The difficulty with playing against a galaxy of world-class players is you are never through them. Normally when you get a team eight wickets down, you are into the bowlers. This World Xl had Barry Richards coming in at number nine, and even with an injured back he was miles better than any tail-ender. They needed 40 runs to win and got them because who should join Barry but Mike Procter at number 10. Can you believe it – Procter at number 10! Mike was that good a batsman he went back to play for Rhodesia and batted himself into the record books with six consecutive first-class centuries in the Currie Cup. The only others to do that were Don Bradman and CB Fry.

It was a great game of cricket and we were a bit disappointed at the end. So nearly there. But this England team had put up a fight against some of the world's finest cricketers and if we were being honest, man for man, they were better than us.

**15** and **64**

*After tea on the Saturday of this rollercoaster game, Ray Illingworth takes you aside and tells you that tomorrow he will be announced as captain of England for the Ashes tour. Colin Cowdrey is fit and playing again after his Achilles tear, but Alec Bedser and his panel have watched Illy's England scrap and fight all summer against one of the greatest teams ever to take the field.*

*Illy's appointment is a battle between the old and the new, between the Establishment and the North. Jim Swanton, the most powerful cricket writer in the land, has been lobbying the selectors on Colin Cowdrey's behalf. Jim Swanton whispers in the selectors' ears, whispers that Colin has been on four Ashes tours and never skippered the side there...*

*The MCC send a message of their own. They appoint gentleman farmer, former amateur captain of Kent and close friend of Colin Cowdrey, David Clark, as tour manager.*

*But for once, the Establishment does not get its way. MCC's power has waned after the Brian Close affair. The selectors do not listen to Jim Swanton. They do not take the MCC's hint. Raymond Illingworth will be captain of England Down Under...*

*Raymond tells you that the new ball in Australia will be crucial. He will negate it by using three opening batsmen at the top of the order. He wants you to open the batting with either Brian Luckhurst or John Edrich. He asks if you have a preference. You tell him that you don't, so Illy speaks to Brian and to John. Brian wants to open, John isn't bothered, so Brian will be your opening partner and John will bat three.*

*Illy asks which other fast bowlers he should take alongside John Snow. You both agree on Alan Ward. Illy is surprised when you tell him that Peter Lever of Lancashire is your choice. He bowls outswing at a lively pace and can really slip himself when he needs to. He bowls well in big games, in Roses matches... Illy has Peter Lever selected for the final game against the Rest of the World so that you can both take a closer look.*

*What Ray Illingworth doesn't tell you is that he wants you as his vice-captain. He tells the selectors, but the selectors are not ready for two Yorkshiremen to lead the Ashes tour. The selectors ask Colin Cowdrey instead. But Colin Cowdrey still feels hard done by over the captaincy. He takes weeks and weeks to accept.*

\* \* \*

## Fifth Match, England versus Rest of the World, The Oval, London, 13-18 August, 1970

We batted pretty well on a good pitch, but against such a talented attack it was hard.

Cowdrey batted beautifully and top-scored with 73 of our 294. When the World XI went in, it was all about two left-handers, Graeme Pollock and Garfield Sobers. Together they put on 165 in a breathtaking display, the ball disappearing to all parts of the ground.

Pollock never played county cricket and it had been five years since his Test hundred at Nottingham. He sparkled, and may have outshone the great Sobers himself. Once he got on that front foot the ball whistled away, and as he got into his stride he would change his stance, making it wider and wider and hitting the ball on the up through or over the covers. He stood there threatening the bowler, almost intimidating him like a baseball slugger. Sobers and Pollock gave the World Xl a 61-run lead: decent, but not insurmountable, especially having to bat last on a wearing pitch.

The best thing for England was a magnificent bowling performance from new boy Peter Lever, who took 7-83 in 33 overs. We had our third fast bowler for the Ashes tour.

When we batted again, I played what I regard as one of my finest innings. By now the pitch was dry and taking turn, but by the third evening we were doing okay at 118-2. Come Monday, the pitch started playing the odd trick. It wasn't dangerous but the occasional ball went through the top and jumped.

Just when I had seen off all of their best bowlers and we were getting into a winning position, Sobers tried Clive Lloyd bowling medium-pace seamers and off-cutters. One of his off-cutters pitched just outside my off stump, spat from a length and made me lob up an easy catch. I was out for 157, and I had the feeling that even in setting them 284, we were 50 or more runs short, such was the brilliance of their batting.

We got rid of Eddie Barlow and Barry Richards quickly, but Rohan Kanhai chose this moment to show his great ability with a century, Clive Lloyd made 68 and Garry Sobers – who else? – saw the World Xl home. I was awarded a cheque for £250 and the Lawrence Trophy for 'the most valuable innings by an England batsman in the 1970 series.'

**24** and **157**

\* \* \*

*Rest of the World win the series 4-1 but everyone knows it was closer than the scoreline says. Illy's team they fight like hell, every session of every day, all summer long.*

*In the second game at Trent Bridge, Colin Cowdrey becomes Test cricket's highest run-scorer, surpassing the 7,249 of Walter Hammond. England win. The third and fourth games are terrific contests. Crowds grow throughout the series. While only 16,000 people come to Trent Bridge, 53,000 go through the Oval turnstiles. CAN WE RETAIN THIS? Clive Lloyd takes some of the things he learns on the tour into his captaincy of West Indies. He says, 'It was interesting for me to see how great some of these players were. It made me realise how far West Indies still had to go.'*

*Two years after the series the ICC strip its Test status. The players' records are amended. Alan Jones of Glamorgan loses the only Test cap he is ever awarded. Wisden Almanack does not agree. It lists the games as Test matches until 1979, when the ICC reaffirms its decision. In 1971–72 Australia cancels its series against South Africa and plays a Rest of the World XI. The same thing happens again.*

*In 2005, the ICC selects a World XI for a one-off 'super Test' against Australia, and awards it Test status.*

\* \* \*

*The arrow flies. England arrive in Australia at the end of October, 1970. You practise at Adelaide in the immaculate nets, and then you start like the player you now are, batting straight through the first day of the opening State game against South Australia for a dream-like and chanceless 173 not out. You go to bed thinking about batting right through the second day, too, bringing up your first triple century, but as you prepare to take the field, David Clark and Ray Illingworth pull you to one side and ask you to get yourself out once you have passed 200. Let the others have a knock.*

*'Bugger off,' you tell them, tell the captain and tell the manager. 'There is a second innings plus three more four-day matches for the others to have a knock...'*

*You get upset, not about the triple hundred like they think, not about being selfish, but about being asked to give your wicket away when you have spent your life doing the opposite. Built your life around doing the opposite. Getting out means failure and you have always hated failure, loathed it, brooded over it for days, weeks sometimes...*

*You know you can't disobey your captain and you never would, but the row spins around in your head as you walk out to bat and you're out in the first over of the day, out to a daft leg-side strangle. The argument continues in the dressing room, because what they don't understand – what no-one understands – is what getting out means to you.*

*You simmer for the next few days, your mood not improving as Barry Richards smashes 224 for South Australia and John Snow is reduced to bowling medium-pace, and keeps over-stepping. Snowy gets irritated with the umpire and you get irritated with Snowy, unable to complete this endless eight-ball over, you stuck at mid-off until he does...*

*'For fuck's sake,' you tell him. 'Stand at the wickets and finish it or we'll be here all day...'*

*Eventually you calm down and explain that you don't like to give your wicket away and you never do it, even in benefit matches or club games. When you make 124 against Queensland a couple of weeks later, you happily retire hurt. You make a second-innings hundred against New South Wales and John Gleeson, who spins the ball both ways off his middle finger and is almost impossible to pick.*

*In sunshine and in shade, on the hard-baked pitches of this golden land, against the very best of their bowlers, you can't stop scoring runs. Through famine and feast, sunshine and rain, from the far north of Yorkshire to the far south of Adelaide, you live for this, live to play this way, live to play this well. Ted Dexter, in Australia to cover the tour for the Sunday Mirror, says that you have provided 'some of the finest batting I have ever seen... I would say the last of the great English sideways-on players...' Richie Benaud calls your technique, 'as close to perfection as you can get.' Australian writers compare you to the Master, Jack Hobbs.*

*This is your life, the life you have made.*

*Fred Perry is right: it can be lonely here.*

\* \* \*

## First Test, Australia versus England, The Gabba, Brisbane, 27 November – 2 December, 1970

### *Forty-second cap*

Ashes series traditionally start at the Gabba, and usually with England teams getting thrashed. Australia got off to a lucky start with me running Keith Stackpole out with a direct hit when he had scored 18, and the umpire giving him not out. Keith was well short and we were aggrieved. We felt it was a hometown decision. Next morning there was a photo in the paper of the bails coming off with Keith well short of his ground. He went on to make 207, and with Doug Walters striking 112, Australia had a pretty good total of 433 on the board.

If we had been given the correct decision on the run-out, Australia would not have sniffed a score that good. As the away team you tend to think the home umpires are biased. They may have made a genuinely bad decision, but the thought of them unfairly favouring the home side lingers.

John Snow took 6-114 in 33 eight-ball overs. Looking at the stats, you would think John did alright. Factually true, but he wouldn't have frightened my mum batting! There was no penetration and to be honest he bowled powder puff stuff. He got two more wickets in the second innings, but he was a shadow of the great fast bowler he could be. Unless he bucked up maybe we were going to struggle to bowl the Aussies out...

Our batting held up well with Brian Luckhurst, John Edrich and Alan Knott all getting into the 70s. The good thing was countering the two wrist-spinners, who bowled 71 eight-ball overs for just four wickets. I had been caught behind off John Gleeson for 37 in the first innings and I was the only wicket to fall in the second innings, caught and bowled by Terry Jenner as the game petered into a draw. What is the point of scoring all those hundreds in the State matches to get into form and then giving it away in the matches that matter?

37 and 16

\* \* \*

*Before the first Test begins, you go to Ray Illingworth and tell him that you are concerned about John Snow's lack of overs and lack of pace when he is bowling. Illy knows that you and Snowy have history. Illy tells you that he has to look after Snowy, and Snowy must look after himself. It's a long tour, six Test matches…*

*But Alan Ward has gone home injured. The only replacement anyone can find is a quick bowler from Surrey recommended by John Edrich, who has faced him in the nets and played a couple of County matches alongside him. A lanky young colt named Bob Willis…*

*You tell Illy that you understand the need for fast bowlers to rest, but before that they need to find rhythm in competitive matches. Once everything clicks into place, they can rest all they want. Snowy has bowled 67 eight-ball overs in six bloody weeks! He's only taken six wickets…*

*You say your piece. You feel better for it. Illy listens. He understands your need to speak your mind. He understands Snowy's rebellious nature, too. You and John Snow are his twins, polarising forces at either end of his team. For England to win here, you both need to succeed…*

*You go to Perth to play the inaugural Test at the Western Australia Cricket Association ground, the quickest, most brutal pitch in the Big Brown Land… First you play the State team on the same WACA ground. Bob Willis bowls fast and takes two wickets. You bat, and first ball get a sharp bouncer that has you jerking your head back and losing your cap. The bowler comes down and glowers at you. His*

*name is Dennis Lillee. The boys come out onto the balcony to watch*
*the kid who has knocked Fiery's cap off. You make 126.*

*Snowy sits the game out after bowling 50 eight-ball overs in*
*Brisbane. Team manager David Clark has a go at him and tells him*
*to go and bowl in the nets. Snowy tells David Clark where to go. Illy*
*bites his tongue, says nothing to David Clark and smooths it out with*
*John Snow...*

*This team... This tour...*

\* \* \*

## Second Test, Australia versus England, WACA, Perth, 11-16 December, 1970

### *Forty-third cap*

First ever Test in Perth, and Australia put us in to bat. No idea why. Maybe they thought the pitch would be at its fastest on the first day, and we would have trouble with the notorious pace and bounce.

Whatever, Brian Luckhurst damaged his thumb fairly early on, but he was a tough so-and-so and stuck it out to make a tremendous 131. I admired his guts and determination. He was my sort of cricketer. I made 70 and John Edrich 47, so we had a very good platform before Australia could get at our middle order.

We had Australia down at 17-3 and 107-5 in reply to our 397, but then Greg Chappell, making his Test debut at number seven, and Ian Redpath both made hundreds. Chappell in particular took advantage of the conditions, especially when the very strong afternoon wind that the locals call the Fremantle Doctor began to blow in. Chappell was tall and upright, with a slight preference for hitting to wide mid-on. When Ken Shuttleworth had to do a stint running into the Doctor, Chappell kept taking him from outside of off stump through the on-side.

Ken wasn't used to that sort of treatment and couldn't get his head around how he was being dismissed from outside the off. I tried telling him the wind was negating his pace so just bowl wider of off stump and don't fight it. I love Ken, but it was like knocking on wood.

Second innings I was stumped for 50 off John Gleeson as I stretched forward and just over-balanced a touch, which made my back foot slide out of my crease. I could make runs against Gleeson by staying in and so could some of our team, but he could block up an end as none of us could pick him. Because we didn't know which way the ball was turning we were uncertain, and had to stay in the crease and play for our stumps. We scored so slowly against him and were very frustrated at his ability to pin us down.

It didn't help when our manager announced publicly that, 'positive and challenging tactics were needed from both sides.' That didn't go down well with us batsmen and Raymond wasn't thrilled with him interfering in the cricket.

Raymond declared and left Australia two-and-a-half hours batting. It allowed a short session for our bowlers to get match overs. Particularly our main fast bowler who hadn't exactly shown himself a speedster.

Well it did the trick because the real John Snow found his rhythm, and boy was he sharp. At his best he could get the ball to lift awkwardly off a length very fast into the ribs. Raymond placed a bat and pad man and a leg gully and he did for Keith Stackpole and Ian Chappell caught at leg gully. We left the field a lot more upbeat about our ace fast bowler.

Next morning we were able to read in the newspapers our manager criticising both teams for slow play and saying he would prefer to see Australia win the series 3-1 than watch four more draws.

Oh for William Shakespeare: 'Who will rid me of this meddlesome manager?'

70 and 50

* * *

*The team spend Christmas in Tasmania. You sit out the game in Hobart but have a knock in Launceston against a Combined Tasmania XI in a rain-ruined game. David Clark says nothing to Raymond Illingworth and nothing in the weekly team meetings, but now he briefs the Australian newspapers. He tells them that both teams are scoring too slowly. He says that if England's players keep on like this, they 'will be out of a job in five years'.*

*You keep a close eye on David Clark. A close eye and close ear. You understand that he is a Cowdrey man, out to undermine Raymond Illingworth. He's another Doug Insole, trying to taint you for the way that you play. Another Establishment man trying to retain the Establishment hold on a changing game. A game about to enter a brand new year in this new, uncertain decade.*

# CHAPTER EIGHT

# 1971

## Third Test, Australia versus England,
## MCG, Melbourne, 31 December 1970 – 5 January, 1971

Both England and Australia named their teams and Raymond put Australia in to bat.

The MCG outfield was sodden and it was murky, cloudy... As soon as we marched out to field, the rain came. From then on it was rain, rain and more rain that waterlogged the outfield. All we could do was practise in the indoor nets or go for a run to keep fit.

Colin Cowdrey taught me how to play Real Tennis on one of the few courts in Australia, at the Royal Melbourne Tennis Club. Not an easy game to pick up, but Colin was pretty good and I had great fun with him. The Test match was abandoned on the third day without a ball bowled.

\* \* \*

*While the rain falls and you play Real Tennis, David Clark meets with Sir Cyril Hawker and Gubby Allen, President and Treasurer of MCC. Without speaking to Raymond Illingworth or any of the players, they make a deal with the Australian Board of Control, who have watched aghast as spectators continue to arrive at the MCG because the radio announces each morning that play will begin as soon as the rain stops.*

*David Clark, Sir Cyril Hawker and Gubby Allen agree to a one-day match on what would have been the last day of the Melbourne Test. They agree to cancel the tour game between Victoria and MCC and schedule a seventh Test match in its place.*

*You find out about the deal when Don Bradman comes into the MCG dressing room to thank you all for your co-operation. When you study the itinerary, you realise that you will have only five rest days in the last six weeks of the tour, and you will play four Test matches consecutively. What a shambles! Winning the Ashes in Australia is hard enough over five Tests, let alone six or seven. As for the one-day game...*

*You don't want to play it. No-one wants to play it. The ground is soaked, the pitch has been covered for days on end and has not been cut. You will be expected to bowl, bat and throw yourselves around in dangerous conditions and with another Test match beginning four days later.*

\* \* \*

*5 January 1970. Forty-six thousand people come to the MCG and pay $33,840 to see England play Australia in a one-day game of 40 eight-ball overs per side. You take first ball, which comes from Graham McKenzie. You don't know it yet, but you are making history, facing the inaugural delivery in One-Day International cricket. You and John Edrich add 21 before you fall for eight. John makes 82 of England's 190 all out. Alan 'Froggy' Thomson delivers 22 bouncers in eight overs in an attempt to limit the scoring.*

*Australia bat and knock the runs off easily. They win the first one-day international on the same ground where they won the first Test match almost a century before. The crowd love it, roaring as Ian Chappell whacks Basil D'Oliveira for 14 in a single over.*

*The match sponsor, Rothmans Cigarettes, awards Australia $2,400 and England $400. John Edrich gets $200 as player of the match. Jim Swanton, the great traditionalist, writes, 'there is clearly a future in this kind of thing.'*

*You don't care about that, don't care about some knockabout game. You care about the journey to Sydney and the fourth Test match. You care about John Gleeson, the mystery spinner who no-one can pick and no-one can score off... Care about facing him on the SCG's famous turning track...*

*You receive a letter from Uncle Algy. He has been watching the television footage of the second Test. He writes: 'You look hesitant and cramped and a long way below your best... Remember you are the batsman they fear most. Get in and then go for your shots. You can do it.'*

*John Gleeson is the bowler on your mind, the bowler stopping you from following Uncle Algy's advice. Gleeson bowls more quickly than most spinners. He has very little wrist action, instead imparting the spin from a flick of his finger and thumb, making him even harder to pick. You sit with Ray Illingworth and watch film of Gleeson, trying to unravel the mystery. You spend hours with Alan Knott, sitting in a hotel room while Knotty grips a ball and tries to work out how Gleeson produces the spin.*

*'Watch the fingers!' He shouts at you, as he brings his arm over, flipping the ball towards you. He 'bowls' in slow motion: 'Watch the fingers... watch the fingers...'*

*Eventually... finally... you figure something out. You think he bowls the off-spinner from his index finger and the leg-spinner from his middle finger. He's like a magician producing a coin from behind your ear, the trick over before you see it happening.*

*You have the theory, but no chance to practise, no way of finding out if you are right or wrong. Not until Sydney... Not until the fourth Ashes Test. Australia drop Froggy Thomson and pick John Gleeson. Raymond drops Ken Shuttleworth and gives Bob Willis his first Test cap. He drops Colin Cowdrey, and plays Derek Underwood.*

*Australia's captain Bill Lawry takes one look at the green, green SCG pitch and says, 'this time there will be a result for sure...'*

\* \* \*

### Fourth Test, Australia versus England, SCG, Sydney, 9-14 January, 1971

*Forty-fourth cap*

Raymond won the toss and decided to bat. There has always been a bit in it at Sydney early on with the new ball. It's easy to be fooled when looking at the green grass and thinking, 'seam movement, put the opposition in'. But the captain is making a decision for five days of the match, not just the first few hours. As opening batsmen we accept that.

Didn't matter anyhow, as we got off to a flyer with Brian and myself reaching lunch at 100-0. Right from the beginning the runs flowed, and this was the best I had played on the whole tour. As soon as the spinners came on I was down the pitch and driving Ashley Mallett. Could I do the same to John Gleeson? Could I read him? I had Knotty's voice in my head...

Watch the fingers. Watch the fingers...

I did and I could read him. Fantastic. Different game now.

I was out straight after lunch pulling Alan Connolly to a deep, wide fine leg for 77 wonderful runs – ironically it was Gleeson that held the catch. John Edrich made a half-century and John Snow and Peter Lever scored priceless runs. 332 all out wasn't a bad total, but after our start it was a bit short of what we should have scored.

We got stuck into them and the key for us was the variety of our six bowlers. Growing up at Yorkshire, I had seen how even on low-scoring result pitches where some teams played an extra batsman, Brian Close and the senior players would always prefer a full quota of bowlers. Raymond had played Underwood ahead of an extra batsman and it paid off.

On the third morning, Australia must have thought they were doing okay at 189-4, but Derek bundled out four of them pretty sharpish and Basil D'Oliveira, with his off-spin and off-cutters, finished with the other two. A lead of 96 on a result pitch was huge. As long as we didn't cock it up and collapse in the second innings, we were sitting pretty.

In no time at all we were 48 for three with Luckhurst, Edrich and Fletcher gone. When Basil joined me, he was on a pair with the ball doing a bit. He was our last recognised batsman, so another quick wicket and we could have a collapse on. What a marvellously calm character he was, inwardly very strong and with a superb temperament.

Between overs, I went down to him: 'You know what may happen if we get out,' I said. 'This is the Test match, here and now. We have to play well.'

So much depended on us, and he was excellent under such pressure. To me it has never been just how many runs a batsman makes, it is about how many runs you score in vital moments that swing a game. I felt relaxed, confident that I could read Gleeson and in control of myself and my batting. The longer we were out there, the drier the pitch got. The sun was baking it, making it deteriorate, and it was beginning to turn more and more, but because we were set, we could handle it. Raymond came in late on and played a few shots for a quick fifty, and he was able to declare in the afternoon on 319-5 with a lead of 415. By the time he did, the ball was going through the top. I knew that this innings of 142 not out was one of the best I'd ever played, and it put us in a brilliant position to win.

By the end of the day's play they had lost four major batsmen. Snowy had done for Ian Chappell, Ian Redpath and Greg Chappell, and Peter Lever got Doug Walters.

Game over. Only rain could save them.

Next morning, Snowy got Keith Stackpole out very smartly, then Rod Marsh, and now he was bowling really fast on a dodgy pitch. The odd ball was lifting alarmingly. Garth McKenzie was expecting a bouncer but misread the length and ducked into a fuller ball. Sadly, he had to retire hurt. Some Australians wanted to make out our fast bowler was intimidating their tail-end batsmen with short stuff. Not true, but never let the truth get in the way of a good story or an even better headline!

After seeing Garth go off injured, Gleeson and Connolly were not hanging about to get hurt, and Snowy finished them off without either scoring. Bill Lawry had batted through the innings for 60 not out but it was of no use. Our mercurial fast bowler had figures of 7 wickets for 40 runs in 18 eight-ball overs – that will win any Test match. We were home by a whopping 299 runs and we were ecstatic about it.

Up yours, manager!

**77** and **142 not out**

\* \* \*

*Geoffrey Boycott and John Snow… Ray Illingworth's polarising forces… Together you put England 1-0 up in the Ashes battle… One-nil up and miles from home…*

*Ollie Milburn drags you all off to a nightclub to celebrate, where you watch the great blind Puerto Rican guitarist José Feliciano. You sit out the up-country match against Northern New South Wales, still feeling on top of the world, but you know this battle is not over, not over now, not over yet. There are three more Test matches on this foreign soil.*

*The Aussie press lays into its own. 'Sack The Lot!' the headlines say, but the Australian selectors keep faith with their failing batsmen. It's the bowlers that go… Garth McKenzie, Ashley Mallett and Alan Connolly out, Alan Thomson, Ross Duncan and Kerry O'Keeffe in.*

*You return to Victoria, to Melbourne, to the MCG, last week's runs counting for nothing now…*

* * *

## Fifth Test, Australia versus England, MCG, Melbourne, 21-26 January, 1971

### *Forty-fifth cap*

Australia won the toss and batted us out of any chance of victory. We made it impossible for our bowlers by dropping six catches on the first day. Lord Hawke, the great man of Yorkshire cricket in the early 1900s, got it right when he wrote that if you only have to take ten wickets, you have a better chance of winning. We were giving top batsmen two innings each.

Dropping Ian Chappell hurt us most. He wasn't in great form, with four failures and only two fifties in the Tests, but he got out of jail and went on to score 111. Ian Redpath, Doug Walters and Bill Lawry got half centuries, Bill coming back onto the field after an x-ray on a damaged hand. He was a tough so-and-so was Bill...

Even Rod Marsh enjoyed himself with his highest score of 92 not out and could/should have got a century, but his captain declared on him. We didn't think Rod was much of a batsman, or much of a keeper either. This was his first series and he kept dropping the ball. Simple deliveries that went straight through to him were shelled. We started to call him Iron Gloves. Just shows how you can never be sure how a cricketer will develop. He improved way beyond what we saw that first series and became a very fine Test cricketer for Australia. On top of that, when you got to know him, Rod was a fantastic person.

Brian Luckhurst had a fractured little finger and damage to a couple of others, so John Edrich opened with me in our second innings. We put on 161 runs in 58 overs and never looked like getting out, but it had got so hot and humid that we were too tired to summon up any energy to try for a century. I had never been as exhausted in my life and was just relieved to get off the field. Even after a shower and a change of clothes it was impossible to stop sweating. This was the most uncomfortable I had ever felt and we had an evening plane to catch to get to Adelaide ready for the next Test.

Another draw.

**12** and **76 not out**

***

## Sixth Test, Australia versus England,
## Adelaide Oval, Adelaide, 29 Jan – 3 February, 1971

### *Forty-sixth cap*

It was a big blow for us when Brian Luckhurst could not overcome the problems with his broken hand. John Hampshire came in, and Keith Fletcher returned for Colin Cowdrey. Colin was a shadow of the great batsman he could be. You could tell his heart wasn't in it. It was as if he'd received a body blow to his ambition of being captain of an MCC tour of Australia, and try as he might he just couldn't get up for it. I didn't know at the time that he hadn't accepted the invitation to tour immediately and had struggled with being overlooked. Batting is in the mind, because that dictates how you bat. You have to be up for the challenge.

Colin tried. I would never say he didn't try, as that would be insulting to any professional, but his heart wasn't in it. When your heart isn't in it you bat in a dream or in a fog, and it is like a lead weight pulling you down. In retrospect, he should have declined to tour because he wasn't himself and therefore wasn't able to give our team his best. Harsh maybe, but although I didn't know it then, I was to experience something similar three years later. The problem is that well-meaning friends encourage you to go and play because they believe you will feel better if you are playing. At the back of your mind, you worry that the media will crucify you for opting out. I would come to understand exactly what Colin was going through.

The Adelaide pitch was a beauty. I loved playing here, and the form I was in got me thinking that if I got in, I was going to make a big one. Dennis Lillee made his debut, but this time my cap stayed on... And I was right about the pitch. John Edrich and I had put on 107 when I pushed to midwicket, took a sharp single and was given out to a direct hit from Ian Chappell. It was a tight run but I thought I had made it.

Max O'Connell from South Australia, standing in only his second Test, gave me out at the bowler's end. I was furious. I dropped my

115

bat and stood there, hands on hips in disgust. Greg Chappell picked my bat up and handed it back with a few well-chosen words to help me on my way. I didn't say a word to the opposition players or the umpire, but when I had cooled down, our manager said I should apologise. He helped me put out a statement saying sorry for my behaviour after the umpire's decision.

I will always believe I wasn't out. Television wasn't so good then as to capture every wicket and every incident, and even with all those Australian photographers present, no pictures were ever published showing whether Max had made a good decision or not. I told Max that if I ever saw a photo showing me out of my ground, I would personally and publicly offer him the best and most handsome apology you have ever had or are ever likely to get. Two very experienced English umpires, Charlie Elliott and Arthur Fagg, were watching from the pavilion, which is sideways on at Adelaide, and both said they thought I was in. If it was that tight, where was that benefit of the doubt that usually goes to a batsman?

John carried on to a fine 130, and Keith Fletcher did well again with 80. Another half century from Basil and one from John Hampshire gave us a very good total of 470. Yes, we were thinking maybe Australia will make runs on this pitch too, but it will take them a lot of time to get up to our total.

We were a bit surprised then, when our seamers knocked over four of the Australian top order for only 27 runs. Snowy got rid of the limpet Bill Lawry. Peter Lever had a beautiful spell of sharp fast bowling around off stump, making the new ball leave the right-handers a touch. Early in any batsmen's innings if you can just get the ball on the perfect length and line at pace, it doesn't need to do much. Peter did for Doug Walters and the Chappell brothers to put the skids under them.

There was some resistance from Keith Stackpole and the tail, but the damage was done. We couldn't believe they were all out for only half our total, and hadn't even avoided the follow-on. It was hot in Adelaide, and the bowlers were facing back-to-back Tests so Raymond decided we would bat again.

There was a lot of sympathy for Max O'Connell, fuelled by the Australian newspapers. When John Edrich and I walked out to bat for our second innings there was booing and cat-calling and abuse aimed at me. So much anger and hostility was directed my way, but I wasn't going to let the bastards get me down. I was so determined not to let them get to me... By the close, John and I had put on 47, and I was 27 not out. Next morning, I got the same treatment from plenty of Aussie supporters, but I was in great nick, angry with their reaction and still mad as hell at that first innings run-out decision. Throughout my career whenever I was batting and got angry, I only once lost my cool, and I wasn't going to do that here. In my heart I would be cross, but I was cold and calculating in my head and I usually batted well.

Talk with your bat is always the best way to shut people up. I was also looking for that Froggy Thomson and his histrionics, particularly when he bounced me. I had had enough of him and I hooked and cut him all around the ground. When I came off the field I got a marvellous reception from the home crowd. I was thrilled that I had changed their opinion of me with my positive strokeplay. I was delighted to hear Barry Richards saying, 'while he is stacking up runs for himself he is at the same time helping the team,' and even more thrilled when he went on to say, 'he is the most dedicated player in the world and one of the greatest.'

I watched the TV highlights that night and heard effusive praise from Richie Benaud. With those sort of remarks my 119 not out was so satisfying, and allowed Raymond to declare and try to bowl them out again. The pitch was good, though, and Stackpole and Ian Chappell both made hundreds. Our bowlers used up a lot of energy bowling 115 eight-ball overs and never looked like getting through the Aussies.

I didn't field on the last day as something lodged under one of my contact lenses. Under an anaesthetic I had a very small piece of metal removed and wore a patch until it healed.

**58** and **119 not out**

\* \* \*

*The Australian selectors react to another draw by sacking Bill Lawry, the first time that it's happened to an Australian captain during a series. Don Bradman tries to find Bill to tell him, but he has already left the ground. Bill hears the news on the radio. Hears that Ian Chappell has been appointed in his place. Hears that he has been dropped not just as captain but from the team despite averaging 40 in the series and 47 across his career. He is 33 years old and will never play for Australia again.*

*While Bill Lawry pays the price, the run-out row rumbles on... The papers find your apology not fulsome enough. Keith Miller says that the incident will cost you any chance of the England captaincy.*

*What they don't understand is why you are like this. Cricket is a capricious game. Success is a fleeting thing. When it is taken away like that... taken away not by your mistake but by someone else's... Taken away while you are in the form of your life, trying to win the Ashes for your country...*

*That is what they don't understand.*

*You fly to Sydney for the final Test, and before that, on the same ground, a meaningless one-day game against the Western Australia team that has won their domestic knock-out trophy, the Vehicle and General Knockout Cup. Western Australia fly more than 2,000 miles to play. Sydney is wet and cool. It has rained every day for a fortnight. The ground is saturated and when he can get on the square, the SCG curator is concentrating on his Test match pitch, not the pitch for this knockabout. When the tarpaulin comes off, it has an uneven covering of grass and has been sweating for days.*

*Garth McKenzie opens the bowling for WA and his loosener takes off past your chin from just short of a length. His second ball hits you in the chest. His third flies at your face and you throw up an arm to protect it. The ball strikes you just above the left wrist. They tell you later that the sound of your bone cracking could be heard in the dressing room.*

*You go to hospital to have the break pinned and set. Richie Benaud comes to commiserate. You will miss the final Test. You will finish the tour with 1,553 runs in Test and first-class matches, 18 short of Walter Hammond's record for an MCC tour. In the Tests you have made 657 runs in five matches at an average of 93.86.*

*And now you must watch...*

*Watch as Ian Chappell takes one look at the Sydney pitch and puts England into bat. John Edrich, Keith Fletcher and Alan Knott eke out 30s. Ray Illingworth makes a priceless 42. England 184 all out and up against it, up against it until John Snow tears in and knocks over the top three for 15, tears in despite having been in traction a few days before the game.*

*Snow bowls faster than any Englishman since Tyson. On the second afternoon, Terry Jenner ducks into a short ball and is struck on the head. Umpire Lou Rowan, a former policeman, warns Snow for persistently bowling short. You know Lou Rowan is wrong. Snowy's length is deceptive, his pace is such that the ball bounces from much fuller for him, bounces into the ribs and shoulder...*

*When John Snow takes up his fielding position on the boundary at the end of the over, he is manhandled by some of the crowd. They throw bottles and cups at him and onto the outfield. Raymond asks Lou Rowan to protect John Snow. When Lou Rowan refuses, Illy leads his team from the field.*

*You sit in the dressing room with your arm in a sling as Illy and the players come in, shocked and angry at what is happening. David Clark orders them back out. Raymond tells him where to go. Voices are raised and tempers are lost. Colin Cowdrey tut-tuts as Raymond stands his ground, unwilling to listen to a manager who's been stabbing him in the back all tour long...*

*Lou Rowan and the other umpire, Tom Brooks, come in. Rowan insists England must go back out. Brooks is more conciliatory. Raymond asks that the rubbish be cleared from the field and for John Snow to be protected from the crowd. England take the field and concede an 80 run first-innings lead.*

*John Edrich and Brian Luckhurst clear the deficit before a wicket falls. The team fights for Illy, fights for one another. Everyone chips in to set Australia 223 to level the series. The bowlers fight for Illy, fight for one another. They take four Australian wickets that evening. They take the rest the following day. Australia are bowled out for 160. England win the match by 62 runs. Win the series 2-0. Win the Ashes on Australian soil.*

*Win despite David Clark. Win despite Alan Ward going home, and you breaking an arm. Win despite playing four Test matches back to back. The team chair Ray Illingworth from the field. You watch from the balcony, your arm in a sling.*

\* \* \*

*August 1970. At Old Trafford, Manchester, Lancashire beat Yorkshire in a John Player League game to retain the trophy. The Honourable Lionel Lister, chairman of Lancashire, invites himself into the Yorkshire dressing room. Brian Close does not recognise Lionel Lister. He sends him on his way with a few choice words. Lionel Lister runs off to find Yorkshire chairman Brian Sellers and report Close's rudeness.*

*Brian writes a letter of apology to Lionel Lister, which he copies and gives to a member of the Yorkshire committee. The letter goes astray. Three months later, Brian is summoned to meet Brian Sellers. He is told that he can resign the captaincy of Yorkshire or be sacked. At first he chooses to resign but later that day, after time to reflect, he calls Brian Sellers and tells him he chooses to be sacked. Brian Close leaves Yorkshire to join Somerset. The Committee vote for a new captain. Don Wilson receives six votes. You receive six votes. Brian Sellers has the casting vote.*

\* \* \*

*The invitation to captain Yorkshire CCC for the 1971 season arrives while you are in Australia. When you get home, you meet with the Committee and undertake media interviews. You tell the press: 'It is the greatest thing ever to happen to me. It has left me just speechless, shivering like a leaf'. You say that you believe Yorkshire 'should be at the top in all competitions'.*

*When the plaster cast is removed from your arm you're shocked to see how emaciated it has become. You begin some hard physio and strengthening to regain fitness. You keep a squash ball in your pocket and squeeze it constantly to build up the muscles and maintain blood flow. Somehow, by May, you are playing again.*

*The runs don't stop. You make 93 in your first Sunday League game against Warwickshire, then a second innings hundred in the Championship game. Your wrist hurts so you sit out the University match, and then you make 112 against Middlesex and 169 against Nottinghamshire, a game you cap by asking John Hampshire to bowl his occasional leg-spin at Garry Sobers, and when Garry lashes a short one to midwicket, you dive and hold the catch in one hand.*

*But there is a price, there is a cost. Your runs are scored at a certain emotional and physical pitch. They demand everything from you. They give you meaning and drain your reserves.*

*The runs, the captaincy, the injury, the Ashes.*

*These things drain you. You miss the first Test against Pakistan. You return to Fitzwilliam after the Roses match, finally exhausted, emptied of cricket, taking tablets to help you to sleep.*

\* \* \*

### Second Test, England versus Pakistan, Lord's, London, 17-22 June, 1971

*Forty-seventh cap*

The First Test at Edgbaston had been drawn and there was little chance of a result in this one, either, as 17 hours were lost to rain. A Lord's Test is the highlight of an English summer yet there was no play at all on the Saturday. By the fourth morning, because of rain, I was 72 not out in our first innings. When we did start again, soon after lunch, I completed my century and Raymond decided he would declare and have a little bowl at Pakistan. The two openers batted well and we didn't get a wicket. Next morning was very different. Once our seamers started to get amongst them it was a procession. John Price, Peter Lever and Richard Hutton were far too good and bowled them out for 99 more.

With only three hours left in the match, I suggested to Raymond he give our debutant all-rounder Richard Hutton a knock. I felt time in the middle and a few runs would get rid of any nerves he had and stand him in good stead for the next Test match. Richard and Brian Luckhurst made half centuries and batted out time.

**121 not out** and **DNB**

\* \* \*

*You return to the Garrison Ground at Colchester and make 233. You play Surrey at The Oval and make 58 and then Middlesex at Lord's and make 182. Your wrist still hurts.*

\* \* \*

121

# Third Test, England versus Pakistan, Headingley, Leeds, 8-13 July, 1971

*Forty-eighth cap*

A wonderful cricket pitch that encouraged all types of bowlers, and yet if you batted well you could make runs. Usually the most exciting matches are when bowlers are more in control than the batsmen. I have played in a number of high-scoring games and I have scored many runs at times, but the lower scoring matches create more tension and pressure and bring out the best in the best.

Raymond and I had played a lot of cricket at Headingley, and read it correctly. If it is overcast the pitch can be juicy and rightly has a reputation for seam movement. If it is sunny and the pitch is dry then it gets slower and negates pace. The surface was dry and would spin later, albeit slow spin. We played one out-and-out seam bowler in Peter Lever and the new ball would be shared with our all-rounder Richard Hutton.

We batted first. Brian Luckhurst was quickly gone for nought and John Edrich soon followed. I came together with Basil D'Oliveira for a partnership of 135. I liked batting with Dolly as he was always so calm and collected, and quietly spoken when you had a chat at the end of an over. I wasn't one for talking a lot and Basil suited me. He was in control of his emotions and nothing bothered him.

On top of that, he could bat under pressure. And that is the key for me. We played really well, without any mistakes, and probably made the pitch and the opposition bowling look easier than it was. Basil scored 74 and myself 112 before Intikhab got us both with his wrist-spin. It was my third century for England in consecutive innings.

This was a strong Pakistan, though. What a batting line-up they had, with everyone scoring runs. The best innings came from Zaheer, who never seemed hurried. He had such ease of movement with feet gliding forward and back, and that long flowing bat swing made him a delight to watch. Except we needed him out. Mushtaq Mohammed made a fifty with his wristy manoeuvring of the ball into gaps you didn't think existed. Wicket-keeper Wasim Bari has never been much of a batsman, but he chose to play one of his very few good innings for Pakistan and hurt us with 63 runs. Instead of

England having a small lead, Wasim edged Pakistan ahead by 36 runs. It was now a one-innings match, Pakistan just in front but with the pressure of having to bat last.

Pakistan's opening bowler Asif Masood immediately put us in big trouble, getting Brian Luckhurst out for a pair on the third evening, and next morning, before I could get going, he had me caught at bat pad to one that jagged back and kept a bit low. Dennis Amiss came good with a half century and Basil, once again when we were in trouble, scored a fine 72. Raymond worked hard for his 47, and no shame in that as the pitch was wearing with batting getting a bit trickier. 264 all out wasn't great and when you took off the slender Pakistan lead, they only required 231 runs to win.

That's not many to play with. But England had been there before in Sydney!

Pakistan knocked up 25 without losing a wicket on the fourth evening, which was a downer for us. They only needed 206 to win with ten wickets intact on the final day. Talk about pressure. This is when your captain needs a cool head and to be seen to be quietly in control. Raymond sometimes asked my opinion, and when he came to me that fifth morning he had a clear idea that the ball was still hard, the pitch was turning and he fancied a bowl straight away before the batsmen could get in. He wanted a little reassurance that his thinking was on the right track. Many times for Yorkshire, I had watched when Raymond had to bowl a side out and he rarely failed. He could handle the pressure and I had seen for myself when he read the pitch correctly and fancied a bowl he usually got wickets. I said go for it.

Raymond immediately did for Aftab Gul without him adding to his overnight score and then grabbed the big wicket of Zaheer, caught at short leg for nought. He wasn't finished either, as he put Mushtaq under pressure before getting him for just five, and with left-arm spinner Norman Gifford at the other end winkling out Saeed Ahmed, the situation had changed dramatically. From nowhere, Pakistan were 65-4.

Asif Iqbal and the left-handed Sadiq Mohammed held us up until Norman Gifford deceived Asif and Knotty stumped him, but while Sadiq was batting we were still in trouble. One big innings could do it for Pakistan. It was Basil with his mixture of little seamers and off-cutters that did the trick, having Sadiq caught and bowled for a superb 91. Raymond wasn't going to chance the tail-enders slogging a few off the spinners. He brought back Peter Lever, and Peter polished off the last three wickets in four balls. We had won a nail biter by 25 runs, through excellent captaincy, knowledge of the game and the ground, and some superb, disciplined bowling.

112 and 13

\* \* \*

*Batting is repetition.*

*Repetition and routine.*

*Routine and ritual.*

*Innings after innings, day after day. Month after month.*

*Success and failure flow through it. Each innings has one of those two outcomes, but they must be met in the same way: with routine. With repetition. With ritual.*

*So you wake up. You go to the ground. You drink tea. You sit quietly and visualise your innings. The shots you will play and the shots that you won't. You pad up. You walk out, quickly, right behind the fielders, let them know that you are there. You mark your guard. You take your stance. You watch the ball. You play your shot. You repeat. Again and again, innings after innings, day after day, month after month. The same voice in your head:*

*'Watch the ball...'*

*The same tap, tap, tap of the bat behind the toe, the same chew of the gum... ball after ball... over after over... session after session... day after day... month after month...*

*You come off the field. You sit down. You put a towel over your head. You take off your kit. You shower and dress. You go to the hotel. You eat. You sleep. You do not dream about cricket.*

*Batting is repetition. And you bat... Bat for the whole summer of 1971... Even though the captaincy of Yorkshire is sapping your time and your energy. Taking your mind away from batting... The whole summer of 1971.*

*You go from Headingley to Scarborough to play for Yorkshire against Derbyshire and score 133. You go from Scarborough to*

*Sheffield to play for Yorkshire against Gloucestershire and score 34 and 0. You succeed and you fail. You bat and you bat, lost in this hinterland.*

* * *

### First Test, England versus India, Lord's, London, 22-27 July, 1971

*Forty-ninth cap*

Everyone was aware of India's great spin bowlers and the quality of their catching close to the bat, but I was out before I had got in to a little-known seamer called Abid Ali. Playing Test match cricket, you get used to fast bowlers on the first morning with a new ball taking early wickets but this was different.

Then Bishan Bedi and the wrist-spinner Chandrasekhar worked their magic, getting two each to have us in a mess at 71-5. Alan Knott chose this moment to play one of his best innings. Sometimes an orthodox stroke and then other times a cut, a pull sweep or just a slog. He could be an infuriating guy to bowl at or to set fields to because you could never be sure what he might do. If you can bat that way it's fantastic, because it puts doubt in the bowlers minds as they are running in to bowl. He got 67 priceless runs and once again Raymond managed a vital 33. The value of these type of innings is that in Test cricket, anything may happen if you keep yourselves alive. And to prove the point, enter John Snow, who chose today to make his highest ever first-class score of 73. We topped 300 and from 70-odd for five, we were right back in the game.

It was a Test that swung this way and that. India lost early wickets but got late-order runs to edge past our first innings score by just nine. Another one-innings game, then, India having to bat last, but us facing one of the great spin attacks to try and set them a score challenging enough to feel that fourth innings pressure.

The Indian attack was like being caught in a vice. They bowled with such control of flight and line, and surrounded the bat with close catchers who would smile disarmingly at you. Starting an innings against them was hugely difficult. I made 33, caught at

125

short-leg from an off-spinner that bounced and turned. John Edrich was our top scorer with 62 and Dolly, Knotty and Illy all fought hard, but in the end 191 all out wasn't a lot.

To us, India were favourites to win and we were in big, big trouble. Then came the incident for which the match would be remembered. We had a couple of early wickets, but not the big one of Sunil Gavaskar, India's best player, who was batting nicely.

Sunil went for a quick single and collided with John Snow. The Laws of cricket are quite clear: a bowler doesn't have to move at the end of his follow through and it is the batsman's job to run around him. But the bowler cannot obstruct the batsman or deliberately move to impede the batsman running to make his ground. Our bosses interpreted the incident as John deliberately shoulder-charging Sunil, and John was left out of the next Test as a disciplinary measure.

From where I was fielding did John 'bump' Sunil? Yes, but it was a bump, not John moving toward Sunil and smashing him to the ground. An apology for something that happened in a flash in the heat of a tight match would have been sufficient, but not for our authorities. They had to make an example of John, which ensured that the incident got more publicity than the fascinating and marvellous cricket being played.

Norman Gifford got the vital scalp of Gavaskar for 53 and had Farokh Engineer stumped for 35. Wickets tumbled as later order batsman struggled to start against spin with men around the bat. Just as we fancied we were ahead, it rained. Can you believe it? India needed 38 runs to win and we required only two wickets for another improbable victory. Sadly, match drawn.

**3** and **33**

\* \* \*

*You go to Sheffield to captain Yorkshire in the Roses match. You score 169, but you cannot force the win and you strain your hamstring and miss the rest of the India series. You return to captain Yorkshire against Leicestershire at Bradford. A couple of the Leicester players hover around the dressing room trying to catch sight of you. They ask your team-mates, 'Is he playing? Is he fit?'*

Graham Stevenson tells them, 'Of course he's playing. He could get a hundred against you lot with one leg…'

You do play on one leg. You get 151. Herbert Sutcliffe approaches you. He tells you that he once finished a season with a batting average of more than 90. Bradman had once achieved the magical 100.

'You could do that,' Herbert tells you. 'You should do it. It would be good for Yorkshire cricket.'

The great Sutcliffe puts the thought in your head. Your leg heals. Your wrist gets stronger. You make 111 against Hampshire. You make 138 against Warwickshire. After speaking to Herbert, you make 453 runs in six innings.

The last game of the season is against Northants at Harrogate. Yorkshire lie 13th in the Championship table. Wisden Almanack calls it 'the worst season in their history.' At one point, the county goes 17 matches without a win. Don Wilson, your vice-captain, has the yips and endures a miserable year. When you don't play, the side are bowled out easily, and they win none of the seven Championship games you miss. You make a century in all four of the games that Yorkshire do win.

There are murmurs. Murmurs from some of the players. Murmurs from some of the committee, (the half that did not vote for you as captain). Murmurs that you are too wrapped up in your own batting to be a good skipper.

This fractious, fractured Yorkshire team go to Harrogate and bowl out Northants for 61. You walk out to bat. You know that Northants just want this over with, just want the season to end so that they can get off the field and get back to their homes and their families, but first they have to face the greatest, hungriest batsman in the land. You do not want the season to end. You bat on and on, bat until Yorkshire's score is 266-2 and you are 124 not out. Only then do you declare, and let the bowlers take you to victory.

You finish the game with an average standing at 100.12 for the season, the first Englishman to achieve the feat. In all you have made 2,503 runs from 30 innings, with 12 centuries and one double-century.

Later, you will wish that you had given up the captaincy of Yorkshire at the end of your first season.

But you don't.

# CHAPTER NINE

# 1972

*January. You leave the cold and dark of England and fly to South Africa, at the invitation of Wilfred Isaacs. You stay in Pretoria with the Murray family and play club cricket at the weekends. Every Wednesday you appear for Wilfred Isaacs' team of Currie Cup pros who play against the best schools teams in Johannesburg. You guest for Northern Transvaal against Mike Procter's Rhodesia in a three-day game, and make 107 and 41. You guest again for Northerns against Natal and Barry Richards in a Gillette Cup match and make 45.*

*April. You leave the sun of South Africa for the cold and damp of England. The miners' strike and the dockers' strike. One million people unemployed. The Bloody Sunday shootings. Leeds United win the FA Cup for the first time. Derby County, managed by Brian Clough, win the first division championship.*

*And a brand new cricket season, the cricket season of 1972…*

*England versus Australia for the Ashes. And the launch of a new domestic competition, the Benson & Hedges Cup, modelled on the football World Cup.*

*For the first time, bookmakers are allowed to operate at cricket grounds.*

*May. Yorkshire play the touring Australians at Bradford. The umpires inspect the ground and declare it unfit, but both teams are desperate for some cricket, so you suggest that you play a couple of 50-overs per side friendly matches. You strike the ball so well through the damp and cold grass that you make 105 of Yorkshire's 176. The bookmakers see the weather and the pitch and offer generous odds against you scoring a century. They lose £8,000.*

*You make hundreds against Somerset at Taunton and Lancashire at Headingley and when the first Test of the summer comes, you are ready. Ready for a summer that will soon fall apart…*

\* \* \*

## First Test, England versus Australia, Old Trafford, Manchester, 8-13 June, 1972

*Fiftieth cap*

Keyed up and ready for the start of the Ashes, we endured the frustration of a 90-minute weather delay. When the covers came off, the pitch looked hard and juicy for bowling. Raymond decided to bat, and we had about half an hour before lunch to get through. Dennis Lillee, bowling fast, hit me hard on the left elbow.

I batted to the break in some discomfort, but I was struggling to grip my bat so I didn't come out after lunch. The physio was using ice to keep the swelling down but it never helped me get my grip back. Raymond took a look at my arm and said that it would likely stiffen up more overnight, so I should get back out and bat today. All very well, but I couldn't grip the bat at all with my left hand, only one-handed in my right, and the injury wasn't responding to treatment.

It was a struggle, and with runs at a premium I believe the team's situation influenced Raymond's decision to send me out again. He had won the toss and batted, and England were in trouble. This was the Ashes. He was showing some stress at our perilous position. It was no good arguing with Raymond when he had made up his mind, and he was the captain. I had to get on with it.

I resumed with England 118-4, but my attempt was futile. It was the first and only time I have batted one-handed and I didn't enjoy trying to score off Test match bowlers. I wasn't able to stay long and added just five more runs. Tony Greig was on debut and from what I saw between treatments, he batted very well for his half century. I think his height helped against the bounce, but it was tough.

At practice the day before the match Raymond suddenly realised he hadn't got a specialist first slip. John Edrich and Raymond were specialist gullies and Tony Greig was an excellent second slip. John Snow volunteered. In Geoff Arnold's first over Snow dropped two and Tony Greig one, all straightforward catches that my mum could have caught in her apron! I know nobody drops catches on purpose but three in one over…

Australia got to 68 before we got our first wicket. It was a relief and after that, it was their turn to fold under pressure, all out for 142.

Arnold and Snowy got four wickets each, but the one I enjoyed the most was Tony Greig bouncing Ian Chappell as soon as he came in. There had never been any love lost between them and it would get worse over the years. Ian hit it very well but Mike Smith took a wonderful catch above his head as the ball was going over the boundary for six. Chappell gone for nought!

Lots of ice and physio had helped with my injured elbow, so I was able to open the batting second innings. I was bandaged up but able to grip the bat much better. I just knew Dennis Lillee couldn't resist a few short balls and bouncers. It's in a fast bowler's DNA to intimidate batsmen, any batsmen, especially one who he has injured in the first innings. Dennis would have to test me out to see if I'd flinch, or if his first innings blow had done any psychological damage. I was thrilled with the way I hooked and ducked for 47 runs. There was still plenty in the pitch for quality seamers but by the third evening we were 136-3, sitting pretty on a lead of 243.

Come Monday, Lillee polished us off with the second new ball. Dennis took six wickets, but another splendid 62 from Tony Greig meant that Australia required 342 to win – way too many unless someone played out of his skin.

It was Greigy's day, as he bagged the wickets of Keith Stackpole and Doug Walters first up. It was easy to underrate Tony's seamers. He wasn't quick, but in English conditions, with his height and skill, he was a dangerous bowler. It was only when we were nearly home that Rod Marsh gave us a fright by throwing his bat. The ball kept disappearing to all parts no matter who bowled. He had us a bit on edge while he was whacking the ball around with John Gleeson holding up the other end. Eventually Greigy got both of them and we were home and dry by 89 runs.

**8** and **47**

\* \* \*

*In the week between Test matches, Yorkshire play Sussex at Bradford in the quarter-finals of the Benson & Hedges Cup. Yorkshire have qualified from the competition's first phase by topping the Northern Group. Sussex have topped the Southern group, with Raymond*

*Illingworth's Leicestershire winning the Midlands' section, and Glamorgan the West. You remind the boys that they are two victories from a Lord's final. You bowl out Sussex for 85 and Yorkshire win easily, a win that lifts spirits, makes the captain think that maybe a trophy is on its way... A trophy to shut up the doubters... A trophy to silence those whispers.*

\* \* \*

## Second Test, England versus Australia, Lord's, London, 22-26 June, 1972

### *Fifty-first cap*

First morning. An absolutely gorgeous, sunny day with blue skies. Perfect for batting. A straw-coloured, grassless pitch that was crying out to be batted on. I was at the ground early for a net at the Nursery End and one of the selectors, Alan Smith, a former wicket-keeper and captain of Warwickshire, said he fancied a bowl at me because it was the sort of morning that made you feel you were glad to be alive!

Wicket-keepers don't usually bowl, but Alan was a rare individual. He was an excellent fast-medium seamer who had once taken off his pads in a match against Essex and bagged a hat trick. He grabbed a ball and started swinging it in and out and all over the place. After a few minutes of that, I came out of the net.

'Alan,' I said, 'If I stayed in much longer I'd be out of form..."

It was amazing how the ball was swinging so much under the sun and blue skies. I had never experienced it at Lord's before. Bob Massie, playing in his first Test and bowling from the Nursery End at a brisk medium-fast pace, should have been no big deal on such a lovely day and nice pitch to bat on. What the hell happened? I have no idea. Why did the ball swing like that? No idea.

We had never heard of Bob, but from over the wicket and around, the ball went like a banana. I got one that shaped to go out but then came back in and bowled me for 11. Massie had eight wickets in his first bowl in Test cricket and we were all out for 272 on a beauty of a pitch. Hard to explain, except I believe that they were freak atmospheric conditions.

The Australian innings became a tussle between John Snow, who bowled superbly for his five wickets, and Greg Chappell, who made a vital and telling 131 to hold the batting together. That man Rod Marsh stuck around with him and Australia edged a lead of 36. Annoying but not insurmountable. Second innings, Dennis Lillee got me in a freakish way bowling from the Pavilion End. The ball bounced a little and came back down the slope to hit my thigh pad, rebound over my left shoulder, drop into the footmarks and spin onto the stumps, just dislodging a bail. Out bowled for six. Lillee got John Edrich, too, then it was the Bob Massie swing show, as he took the next eight wickets. An easy win for Australia made possible by an amazing performance.

Afterwards there were whispers that maybe he used a foreign substance on the ball to get it to behave in a way none of us had seen before. But just because something is odd or unusual, and we can't explain it or understand it, shouldn't mean we denigrate it with innuendo. I don't believe he did anything wrong or illegal, as I had first-hand experience of how much the ball swung in the nets. I prefer to accept it was his moment, a phenomenal and outstanding performance of great skill in unusual conditions. Although I was one of his victims I put my hand up and say well done. You were fantastic.

**11** and **6**

\* \* \*

*You go to Headingley to captain Yorkshire against Gloucestershire in the semi-final of the Benson & Hedges Cup. A Lord's final would be just the thing for Yorkshire, just the thing for your captaincy... Just the thing to stop those whispers... Whispers from some players and some committee men who did not want you, who wanted Don Wilson as captain instead...*

*The Yorkshire bowlers get to work on a damp pitch and skittle Gloucestershire for 131. Knocking off the runs is slow going but you make 75 not out and are declared man of the match. A Lord's final... Just the thing... Just the ticket... And against Raymond Illingworth's Leicestershire, too... You're feeling good, and feeling even better after the Championship game at Worksop when you take the Nottinghamshire attack for 100 and 75.*

*It is 5 July, 1972. You lead Yorkshire into a Gillette Cup second round tie against Warwickshire at Headingley. Bob Willis takes the new ball, bowling fast down the hill from the Kirkstall Lane End. He makes one lift and traps your bottom hand between the hard new ball and the unyielding bat handle. There is blood everywhere. When you get your glove off, the tip of your middle finger has burst open from the impact. The pain is instant and excruciating. The physio takes one look and tells you to get to a hospital, quickly...*

*Young Phil Carrick volunteers to drive you in his new car. You sit in agony as he takes every corner at a snail's pace, trying not to jolt the car, but you just want him to get there, just get there... Come on... you could bloody walk faster than this...*

*When you finally arrive, the surgeon comes to look at your finger and – at last – slides a needle into your hand and kills the pain. He explains that the tip of your finger is packed with nerve endings that provide your sense of touch. Yours have been exposed by the trauma. It takes all of his skill to stitch the flesh back together. He tells you he will have to amputate the top of your finger if you damage it any further.*

*All you feel once the pain is gone is anger, anger that you will miss the Benson & Hedges Cup final against Ray Illingworth's Leicestershire. Miss out on the chance to lift that new gold trophy and stop those whispers...*

*The day before the final, Raymond comes to see you. You show him the injury, and he is shocked to see it. With you absent, the bookies make Leicestershire favourites, and the bookies are rarely wrong. Yorkshire's batting subsides without you. They score just 136 from 55 overs, and Leicestershire win with almost ten overs to spare.*

*You need to get back out on that field, out there for Yorkshire, out there for England, but how can you when the slightest knock could cost you the top of your finger? John Temple, Chairman of the Yorkshire CCC Cricket Committee, suggests a metal stall that you could wear under your glove to cover it. He has one made from aluminium.*

*Exactly one month after you were hit and with the aluminium stall over your finger, you play for Leeds in a club game at Headingley and make 108 not out. The next day, you go to Settle and appear in a Don Wilson benefit match. The Sunday papers report the news. Ray Illingworth and Alec Bedser read with interest. When you get home,* the telephone goes. It's Alec Bedser, asking if you are able to play in the final Test match at The Oval.

You tell Alec Bedser that you haven't batted for a month, and facing club bowlers is a little bit different to facing Dennis Lillee... You tell him that you are nervous and worried about being hit on the hand by better and faster bowling, and that it is much too soon to ask you to play. You tell him that the Yorkshire committee are pushing you to return, too, and they have made you an aluminium stall to fit your finger...

You yield to that Yorkshire pressure and play for Yorkshire against Surrey at Scarborough. You are scared to push forward and hover on the back foot. You make 4 and 19, but Yorkshire win. As the final Test match begins, you continue your comeback for Yorkshire against Leicestershire at Grace Road. You win the toss and bat first. Graham McKenzie hits you on the injured finger, and despite the aluminium stall, it hurts like hell. You hang around, though, hang in there, because the alternative is getting out, and getting out means failure, and you hate failure more than you hate the fear and pain of losing the top of your finger. Garth gets tired and Leicestershire's spinners, Jack Birkenshaw and John Steele, send down 53 overs throughout the afternoon. You make 204 not out.

England are losing the Oval Test. Defeat will end Raymond Illingworth's dream of winning Ashes series at home and away. Raymond hears the news as he walks off the field at The Oval after Saturday's play. You have made a double hundred against his county team-mates. He goes to the press and says that Geoffrey Boycott should be playing for England at The Oval, not scoring runs in a county match. Raymond knows that a Boycott headline will distract from impending defeat at the Oval. Raymond knows that you will read it and get the message.

You do read it. You get Ray Illingworth's message loud and clear. You admire him as a cricketer and as a captain. You'd do anything for him. You have done anything for him. But now you are angry and disappointed in him. When you join up with England to play in the one-day international series that follows the final Test match, you try to talk to him, try to say your piece, explain that your finger is still healing, but Raymond is as stubborn as you are, and will not talk to you. He will not listen to your explanation. He is beside himself with anger, too angry to talk.

*You recall the words of your Yorkshire team-mate Ken Taylor. 'Never argue with Raymond. You cannot win and he will always hold a grudge.'*

*So you bite your tongue. The atmosphere festers. As you and Raymond play for England, Yorkshire meet Leicestershire in the final match of the John Player Sunday League. Victory for Leicester means that they will win the John Player title for the first time. As the England players gather together to watch the game on television, Yorkshire win by three runs.*

*Raymond blames you for the defeat of England at The Oval and the defeat of Leicestershire at Headingley. You try to tell him that you didn't play in either game, but Illy is not listening.*

*It is not the final argument of this fractured season. Relations between you and Don Wilson sink to an all-time low when Don gets drunk at the team hotel in Southampton and blows his top, calling you every name under the sun, blaming you for everything. You finish with centuries against Essex and Hampshire, and top the national batting averages again with 1,230 runs at 72.35. But Yorkshire finish just 10th in the County Championship and fourth in the John Player League. Lose the final of the Benson & Hedges Cup and the first round of the Gillette Cup.*

*You go home to Fitzwilliam.*

# CHAPTER TEN

# **1973**

*Six months earlier.*

*You receive the MCC letter asking for your availability to tour in the middle of July, 1972. You speak to Donald Carr, Assistant Secretary of the TCCB. You outline your misgivings. You tell him that you had your spleen removed in an emergency operation when you were eight years old, and you have been left susceptible to infection. Two Pakistani and one Indian doctor have advised you not to tour because of your increased risk. You hear that Raymond Illingworth, John Snow and John Edrich have decided not to go. You inform Billy Griffith, secretary of MCC, that you will not be touring either. He asks you to reconsider. He tells you that you will be made vice-captain to Tony Lewis of Glamorgan. He tells you that your captaincy ambitions will be looked kindly upon in future. You remind Billy Griffith that he saw for himself how ill you became in Ceylon in 1965. You tell him that you cannot risk becoming that ill again.*

*Billy accepts your decision with reluctance. He asks that you not make any public remarks about your health fears because they may not go down well in the host countries. You agree to his suggestion and issue a statement saying that you are declining the tour 'for personal and domestic reasons.'*

*Winter, 1972. As the season fades from view, the newspapers stop writing about you. It is wonderful. In the new year, you fly to Johannesburg for a holiday. You play a few practice matches and coach the local kids. You lie in the sunshine, let it warm your bones. You forget about being Geoffrey Boycott and all that it means.*

*England win the first Test against India, but lose the next two. The stories start again. Start again and shatter your peace. Stories that say Geoffrey Boycott is sunning himself in South Africa when he should be helping England in India. Stories that say Geoffrey Boycott has lucrative business interests in South Africa (you wish – you are playing club cricket and coaching kids). Stories that say that you wouldn't tour because you were not made captain. Made-up stories that distort the truth and blacken your name.*

*No-one mentions that Raymond Illingworth, John Edrich and John Snow are not on the tour... No-one mentions that Alec Bedser, Chairman of Selectors, once turned down a tour to the sub-continent. So did another selector, Cyril Washbrook. So did former captains Leonard Hutton and Peter May. No-one mentions them while they are writing about you.*

\* \* \*

*The season of 1973 begins with you in the runs, hundreds against Cambridge University and Lancashire, half centuries against Warwickshire and Hampshire. After the Roses game you catch a train to Hove to play in a match between Tony Lewis' XI of players that toured in the winter, and Raymond Illingworth's XI of players that didn't. The papers are calling it a 'Test trial'. You know that it's not. You make 22 in the first innings and then, with the permission of the selectors, retire hurt on 22 not out in the second and catch a train back north to play for Yorkshire.*

*Anyone with eyes can see you are the best player in England. The selectors reappoint Raymond as captain, select you and John Snow, but leave out John Edrich. Still the newspapers write that the non-tourists should not play.*

\* \* \*

### First Test, England versus New Zealand, Trent Bridge, Nottingham, 7-12 June, 1973

*Fifty-second cap*

There was an atmosphere around the team that gathered at Trent Bridge. I felt there was still an air of 'them and us' between the players who had toured and those of us who had not. I was to open with Dennis Amiss, who had made his maiden Test hundred in Lahore and then another in Hyderabad.

It turned into a crazy, topsy-turvy Test. Dennis and I began our partnership well, adding 92 before Dennis went. I followed a bit too quickly and after that we fell in a heap, only Knotty's dogged 49 seeing us up to 250 all out. Then New Zealand fell in an even bigger heap.

137

John Snow, Geoff Arnold and Tony Grieg bowled beautifully, and only three batsmen reached double figures. New Zealand all out 98.

Early on in the second innings, Amiss hit the ball through a vacant mid-off and as he passed me for the first run, called two. I turned and ran, and as I got well down the pitch for the second, Dennis stopped half way, turned his back and made his ground, leaving me stranded and run out for one. This time it wasn't my fault. I can honestly say I have never turned my back on a partner and 'upped the ladder' on him.

I was mad as hell. There was no apology and Dennis went on to score 138 not out. Not a word was spoken and the atmosphere between us was icy. I was feeling particularly vulnerable as I sensed that undertone with the players that had toured, and I was anxious to re-establish my place in the England team.

Tony Greig got 139 to go with Dennis' ton, and the rest of us didn't get out of single figures – a lopsided scorecard! It got even crazier, New Zealand chasing a massive 479 and getting within 38 runs of winning thanks to Bev Congdon's 176 and Vic Pollard's maiden hundred. Bev was uncomplicated and stayed back to our seamers. He played for his stumps and made our bowlers bowl him out. He had a method that worked and it was tough to get him out of his comfort zone. Vic's technique was very simple and very orthodox, too. Watching him make his hundred I was puzzled why it had taken him so long – more than 50 innings. It was too close for comfort and that second new ball was a godsend. It did the trick, but what a magnificent effort by New Zealand.

**51** and **1**

\* \* \*

**Second Test, England versus New Zealand,
Lord's London, 21-26 June, 1973**

*Fifty-third cap*

Raymond sensed the mood between Dennis Amiss and me and called us together on the pavilion steps to clear the air. It developed into heated words and accusations. There was so much mistrust, because if I was not the best judge of a run around the county circuit then Dennis was known to be a close second...

England batted and I was in top gear as I pulled Bruce Taylor into the Mound Stand twice during my 61 runs. A cricket lover from Barbados called Ron Griffiths had come to the game, and he christened me 'Sir Geoffrey'. Ron would shout out, 'Sir Geoffrey...' when I was batting or fielding the ball and it attracted a lot of pleasant support and publicity. He started coming to all the London Tests and singing my praises. It was very flattering and very welcome, and 'Sir Geoffrey' began to catch on!

Graham Roope made 56 from number three, and Tony Greig 63, but there were too many failures. A total of 253 on a good batting pitch wasn't good, especially as we'd blown a terrific start.

Then that man Bev Congdon did it again for New Zealand. He batted the same way as he had done at Nottingham and it was as if he just carried on from where he left off. No frills but not giving us a sniff at getting him out. Another 175 for him, and this time his mates joined in: Brian Hastings drove the ball well for 86 runs and Mark Burgess scored an easy-on-the-eye century. Vic Pollard had evidently got a taste for hundreds and batted as if he was still at Nottingham too. Another century from him allowed Bev to declare with a lead of 298. With a lot of time left in the match, defeat was staring us in the face, so we had to pull our finger out. Big time.

When you are so far behind, good starts are crucial. Fortunately Dennis Amiss and I played really well: an opening partnership of 112, and no problems with the running. I was batting beautifully and felt in total control with a hundred-plus on the cards, when, because of the hot weather, drinks were taken. Drinks breaks in England were not the norm then. So often, a break of any sort works for the bowling team and sure enough, I was down the pitch to the left-arm spinner driving the ball straight, and I hit it too well and a tiny fraction too early. Caught and bowled low down for 92. It made me want to scream! The big, big innings that sealed a draw for England was a splendid, controlled 178 from Keith Fletcher.

61 and 92

\* \* \*

*You are sat in the dressing room after your first innings at Lord's when someone comes to the door and asks to see you. It is Neville Cardus, the most famous cricket writer on earth. He tells you that your batting is on a par with all of the greats he has witnessed, including Len Hutton and Herbert Sutcliffe. 'The world is your oyster,' he says. 'With your skill, you can do whatever you like. I came to watch you bat and now I am going home.'*

* * *

## Third Test, England versus New Zealand, Headingley, Leeds, 5-10 July, 1973

### *Fifty-fourth cap*

A topsy-turvy series continued as New Zealand went in first on a good pitch to face some high-quality new ball bowling from Geoff Arnold and Chris Old. They gave nothing away and extracted what early movement there was, nipping the ball around off the seam with great skill and accuracy from a full length. Soon New Zealand were 24-3 and then 78-4. Batting at Headingley usually gets easier after lunch as the pitch settles down and the ball loses its shine, and so it proved. They ended day one at 262-9. You never know whether a score like that at Headingley is good or bad. It all depends on the weather next day. If it's overcast then the bowlers will love it, but sunshine on a second day and I am queuing up for a bat!

When day two dawned, it was the latter, lovely light sunshine, and I was in heaven as I made my way to a hundred. Keith Fletcher was in good touch for 81 runs and Raymond batted really well for 65. Knotty and most of our late order made a few runs to swell the total to 419. A lead of 143. Geoff Arnold, John Snow and Chris Old made a huge mess of all the New Zealand batsmen except for Glenn Turner. Although Glenn had achieved something special in scoring a thousand runs in May for Worcestershire and should have been in top form against England, he had only made 35 runs in five innings. But now he showed his class and was the one batsman to handle our bowlers, last man out for 81 from a total of 142. The seam bowling by our guys was superb, and only 58 runs were scored off the bat by the other ten players.

**115** and **DNB**

\* \* \*

*You get a taste of what the New Zealanders faced when Geoff Arnold does you for four and nine at The Oval in the Championship game against Surrey, Yorkshire broken and beaten, all out for 60 and 43. The team is going backwards again, humiliated in the Gillette Cup by Durham, a minor county, finishing third in the Northern Group of the Benson & Hedges Cup, languishing in the bottom half of the Championship table, and you called away again to play three more Test matches against the touring West Indies...*

\* \* \*

### First Test, England versus West Indies, The Oval, London, 26-31 July, 1973

*Fifty-fifth cap*

Garfield Sobers had relinquished the captaincy of West Indies to Rohan Kanhai, who won the toss. On such a good pitch, someone was bound to bat well. Clive Lloyd was that man, with a powerful 132, and then Alvin Kallicharran a neat 80. Clive bristled with intent to smash the ball. As bowlers were running in at him some felt intimidated and rightly so... If he got going, the ball was very likely to come back at them faster than they could bowl it! Alvin was a tiny, slim guy, so power was not his forte, but he placed the ball in the gaps as if using a rapier instead of a bat. Both were left-handers but one tall and one very small made it awkward for bowlers to have to keep changing their lengths. Keith Boyce hurt us, thrashing 72 from number nine. He was a chancy shot-maker and if it came off, as it did here, it is so demoralising. A total of over 400 batting first usually puts a team in a decent position whatever the state of the pitch.

141

Amiss and I added fifty but as soon as Dennis was out, none of our batsmen stayed long enough to play a substantial innings. I felt good and batted well enough to hit Keith Boyce into the stand at backward square-leg for six. Just when I had a hundred beckoning, I edged a good ball to the wicket-keeper off a lively debutant left-arm seamer called Bernard Julien. Out for 97. Keith Boyce was the enforcer and took five wickets while Sobers and Julien pitched the ball up with great skill, using the advantage of the left-arm over the wicket angle. A West Indies lead of 153 runs was substantial.

We did well in our second bowl at West Indies, stopping any of the batsmen making a big score. Although we had them all out for 255, it's that first innings lead that hurts you. We needed 414 runs to win. That seemed to me an awful lot. With our batting line-up I wasn't confident, and by now a dry Oval pitch had started to take spin. So often The Oval is a wonderful cricket pitch that gets every type of player in the game at some stage. And so it proved. It didn't take long for off-spinner Lance Gibbs to be on at one end. Lance prised me out, and then Graham Roope, both caught and bowled for 30 and 31.

Lance was a tremendous bowler with a fantastic personality. He would bound in using a high action, tossing the ball in the air with a big loop that got overspin to make the ball bounce awkwardly as well as plenty of turn. He was never afraid to tease batsmen with a variety of flight and loop. Never worried about giving you a run or two. All he was interested in was wickets. The tail was blown away by the pace of Keith Boyce.

The one bright spot was a not out century by debutant Frank Hayes.

97 and 30

\* \* \*

### Second Test, England versus West Indies, Edgbaston, Birmingham, 9-14 August, 1973

*Fifty-sixth cap*

West Indies won another toss and batted, but not especially well. Roy Fredericks put his natural stroke-playing game away and grafted.

He just kept on going, all Thursday and well into Friday, to score 150 out of their 327. A terrific individual performance. Late on, we got our first glimpse of this young kid Bernard Julien with the bat, scoring a half century. He looked too good to be at number eight.

By close of play on the second day, we appeared in great shape at 96 without loss. I was 52 not out and Dennis unbeaten on 42. But the real story came early in my innings. West Indies had appealed for a caught behind against me off the bowling of Keith Boyce. Umpire Arthur Fagg said not out, and Rohan Kanhai, standing at slip, took off his cap, threw it to the ground and jumped on it in disgust.

From then on it was a stream of abuse, invective and swear words at me and Arthur Fagg. Captain Rohan was the ringleader, encouraging some players to follow suit. At the end of every over, as they changed positions, they took the opportunity to directly and indirectly make nasty remarks. The hostility and anger was far worse than the day-to-day sledging you got from the odd bowler. The atmosphere was a disgrace. That evening, Arthur Fagg sat in the umpires' room taking stock of it all before he decided to venture home. Two well-known journalists had waited around for Arthur to leave and engaged him in conversation as if they were members of the public. They chatted to him, being sympathetic about Kanhai jumping on his cap at slip. They buttered him up and gained his trust when he was in a raw emotional state. Umpires never experience abuse like he had to put up with, and they asked him what he was going to do about it. Arthur had no idea that they were journalists and opened his heart to them.

'I haven't decided,' he said. 'But I might not stand tomorrow.'

The journalists had their scoop and a big headline for next morning's paper. On the Saturday morning, Arthur stayed in the dressing room when the players went on the field. Alan Oakman, a retired former England player on the coaching staff at Warwickshire, had to go stand at square-leg. Arthur had to be talked into continuing and he came out after one over.

Early in my innings, Dennis had sent me back when attempting a run, and as I turned to run my bat in, I collided with Deryck Murray, the Windies' keeper. No problem at the time, but next morning my ribs were badly bruised, stiff and painful. I needed lots of tape and pain-killers, and even then I was in so much difficulty I had to retire after a couple of runs. I returned with the score on 249-6. West Indies were still feeling aggrieved at me being given not out early in my innings the day before, so Vanburn Holder put everything into his first ball at me, a very fast short one that hit me on the left arm. I had to go off again and returned only to hang around with our tail for a bit.

West Indies batted so long in their second innings that a draw was inevitable, so the England lads got some batting practice as a rancorous game petered out into nothing.

**56\*** and **DNB**

\* \* \*

### Third Test, England versus West Indies, Lord's, London, 23-27 August, 1973

*Fifty-seventh cap*

A no-contest. West Indies absolutely slaughtered us. We were only in the game for the blink of an eye on the first morning, when their stand-in opener Deryck Murray was dismissed by Bob Willis. After that we seemed to toil forever as their batsmen brutalised us. Roy Fredericks stroked his way to a half century and when he was out, Clive Lloyd smashed a half century too, while at the other end we were treated to a Rohan Kanhai special. He put on a show that thrilled the many West Indian supporters in the crowd.

It got even better for them when Garry Sobers joined him, and the two greatest West Indian batsmen of the day went shot for shot, each trying to outdo the other with the excellence of their stroke play. If I hadn't had to field, I would have stood back and applauded. When finally Rohan was out for a superb 157, in came this precocious youngster Bernard Julien, and struck the ball to all parts. He didn't slog or chance his arm, just sliced us up with a marvellous exhibition, scoring a run-a-ball 121. He was supposed to be a front-line bowler yet here was a maiden hundred in only his third Test. Sobers carried his bat for 150 not out, and West Indies decided they had punished us enough, declaring at 652 for 8.

England were three down that night. I hooked at a Vanburn Holder short ball and must have got into the stroke too early because it hit the back of the bat and finished up caught at slip. There are some unbelievable ways to get out. Only Keith Fletcher made fifty, with Tony Greig a gutsy 44. We were 419 runs behind, so I bet there wasn't much of a discussion in the West Indies dressing room about whether to make us follow on or not!

At 2.40pm on the Saturday, a bomb scare took us off the field for almost an hour and half. The ground was evacuated, and the photographers got a famous picture of Dickie Bird sat all alone on one of the covers. We were left with just a short session that evening. Keith Boyce, bowling very fast, got Dennis Amiss and nightwatchman Alan Knott out quickly. In the last over of the day, I was out hooking when the field had been clearly positioned for that shot. I liked to hook against certain bowlers I fancied. I could play it down or try to hit it out of the ground, and I had two double hundreds for Yorkshire against Essex when Boyce had bowled, so I felt comfortable hooking him.

I hooked him down, with the ball bouncing well in front of Alvin Kallicharran on the backward square-leg boundary. I set off for an easy, ambled single and got halfway down the pitch before I realised Brian Luckhurst wasn't running. I even had time to ask him what the hell was going on as I scuttled back to make my ground. Brian just flatly refused to run. I was so angry with him that I stopped thinking, and when Boyce delivered a bouncer, I hit at it out of frustration and it sailed straight down the throat of Kallicharran!

It was the only time I have lost my wicket through hot-headedness. I was so angry. In my mind Brian had done as much to get me out as the bowler or the field placing. Hundreds of West Indian supporters couldn't control their delight and ran on to the field to manhandle me. Some of them jumped on me, others danced around taunting me, unable to conceal their joy at my demise.

When Brian and I got back to the dressing room, I was absolutely livid and launched into him. I told him he was chicken and looking after number one, refusing an easy run so he could stay at the non striker's end for the final over of the day. Brian made excuses that I was in and he felt I was best placed to finish the over. I said I was only 15 not out, and it wasn't as if I had been in a long time and could or should protect him.

Raymond stepped in and told us to cool it. I found it very difficult to calm down, and although I admired and liked Brian Luckhurst, I couldn't at that moment forgive his lack of professionalism. I don't like excuses and never have. My recollection of what happened and a factual account of why it happened should not be taken as me making excuses. It is not.

I accept that I played the shot, and I hit the catch, and I should never have allowed anything to interfere with my decision-making or concentration. In the end I take full responsibility for the stroke. It was my fault and I should not have lost my cool. West Indies had beaten us by an innings and 226 runs in three-and-a-half days. It was a monumental and embarrassing defeat.

**4** and **15**

\* \* \*

*This capricious game.*

*This summer of 1973.*

*The stress builds.*

*Fred Trueman, your idol, tells the Sunday People that the captaincy of Yorkshire 'is the only failure in a brilliant career. The time has now come to find another man capable of doing the job.' Len Hutton and Herbert Sutcliffe, players that you once worshipped, question your captaincy.*

*14th*

*You can be moody and self-absorbed, insecure despite your talent and your record. The hatred of failure eats at you every game, every innings, every day of every season. You don't understand yourself sometimes. Raymond smooths out the row with Dennis Amiss. He tries with Brian Luckhurst but you are not speaking to Brian. Not yet. Not for years. You return to the hotel and awake at 3am with a nosebleed so severe that you have to go to hospital to have it cauterised. Word gets out and totally untrue rumours that Ray Illingworth punched you during a dressing room argument begin to spread.*

*The whispers and the rumours.*

*The rumours and the lies.*

*The stress. The relentless stress.*

*You lose the final Test ignominiously and Raymond calls you to his hotel room. He will not be re-appointed as captain of England for the winter tour of West Indies. The selectors have decided that he is too old at 41, and have appointed Mike Denness of Kent instead.*

*Mike Denness of Kent, and not Geoffrey Boycott of Yorkshire.*

*Mike Denness, who couldn't get in the England side all summer. Mike Denness, who captains a Kent side with seven internationals, including Asif Iqbal and Bernard Julien. Mike Denness, who accepted the tour of India and Pakistan as vice-captain to Tony Lewis.*

*You do not respect Mike Denness. You worry about playing for England under his captaincy.*

*Ted Dexter tells the newspapers that you should have been made England captain.*

*You speak to the Yorkshire Committee. You try to explain that the team has been weakened by the departures of Fred Trueman, Brian Close and Raymond Illingworth. That the younger players are not of that standard. That the other 16 counties each employ two star overseas players, while Yorkshire do not field any cricketer born outside of the county lines. You are a skipper with one hand tied behind his back, looking on while Lancashire, Kent and Leicestershire win cups and lift trophies.*

*The Yorkshire Committee retains you as captain and awards you a benefit season in 1974. You appreciate the gesture. A benefit year is vital for any cricketer, offering the chance to raise a tax-free sum to supplement the working wage that you are paid. It is a nest egg and peace of mind for a future after cricket, this capricious game.*

*You agonise about the West Indies tour. It goes around and around in your head. If you go, then you lose three months of organisation for the benefit – all of those events and committees that you need to set up and run. If you don't, then the newspapers will be at you again, calling you selfish, disloyal, blaming defeats on your absence…*

*Round and round… Back and forth… The stress…*

*Friends get in your ear. Friends urge you to play, to go on tour. You know that they mean well. They want the best for you. You know that you shouldn't go, that you don't want to, not deep down, not under Mike Denness.*

*But you do.*

# CHAPTER ELEVEN

# 1974

*You receive a letter from Mike Denness. In it, he asks if you will take charge of net practice in West Indies. You wonder why Mike Denness has not picked up the telephone or come to see you.*

*If he had, you would have told him that asking you to arrange net practice is asking for trouble. Your personal standards are so high that it would cause frustration and arguments between you and the team. You don't need that, not when there is a captain and a vice-captain who will have an authority over the players that you won't. Anyhow, your relationship with practice is complex, too complex for an exchange of letters with Mike Denness. You write back to decline his offer. Instead they ask you to be a part of the Selection Committee on tour, alongside Mike, tour manager Donald Carr and vice-captain Tony Greig. You accept this offer because you have experience of conditions in West Indies and know your team and theirs inside out.*

*And then Mike Denness begins making speeches. Speeches about batting and how to do it in Test cricket. Speeches about the importance of not hooking. Speeches made by a man who has batted 15 times in Test match cricket with a highest score of 76 and an average of 34, who has never batted in West Indies, never really batted any bloody where in Test match cricket except the sub-continent, where the ball barely gets above knee height.*

*But you know why Mike Denness is doing this... Why he is speaking about hooking... Because it is a way of getting at you, putting you under pressure. Because it is an admonishment of your dismissal to Keith Boyce at Lord's and of your altercation with Mike Denness's friend Brian Luckhurst. Because he knows that the West Indies bowlers are about to pepper you and you are now obliged not to play the shot. You can see the headlines already if you do... You've not even left England yet and Mike Denness is telling you how to open the batting.*

*'What a pillock...' You think. 'Having a go at me... Wouldn't even be in the team if he wasn't captain...'*

*...And you should be captain. You land in Barbados and play the President's XI at Bridgetown. You get plenty of short stuff but you*

*do not hook, not one single time. You do not give Mike Denness the fucking satisfaction.*

*You make 261 not out, your highest first-class score.*

\* \* \*

### First Test, West Indies versus England, Port of Spain, Trinidad, 2-7 February, 1974

*Fifty-eighth cap*

The pitch was wet and not surprisingly, West Indies put us in. Our new captain came into the dressing room and said that he was happy because if he had won the toss he would have batted, too. There were some raised eyebrows and questioning glances over that. Did he take us for fools and think making a stupid comment would somehow give us false confidence? Some of us knew from experience that in West Indies, pitches that started wet are to be avoided at all costs. The soil is not like in England because here, the ball flies.

And so it proved, as England were all out for 131. Batting was a nightmare, and one ball from Keith Boyce leapt up at my throat off a length. I just managed to jerk my head out of the way before it hit me. There is a picture of me jumping up with my feet off the ground and head back, the ball whistling past my chin. It nearly decapitated me and was too close for comfort. I got tired of signing that photo for autograph collectors!

The sun dried out the pitch and West Indies could have the heavy roller before they went in near the end of the day. At sunrise on day two, the covers came off and the pitch had more time to dry, and then West Indies got another roller before the start of play. We nipped out Roy Fredericks and Lawrence Rowe while the ball was new, but Alvin Kallicharran batted so well and stayed in all day. None of our bowlers could control his strokeplay, and, as Tony Grieg prepared to bowl the last delivery of the day, Alvin was leaning on his bat at the non-striker's end, no doubt thinking about the reception he was going to get from his team-mates and the West Indies fans.

Bernard Julien pushed the ball back down the pitch, and Tony, in his follow through, picked it up and in one fluid movement threw down the stumps at the bowler's end. Alvin was already walking happily towards the Pavilion and was way out of his ground. Umpire Douglas Sang Hue gave him out, which was, by the letter of the Law, the correct decision. Whatever the player or players may think or believe, play for the day is never over until the umpire at the bowler's end calls 'time.'

Alvin was furious and he smashed his bat on the pavilion steps, putting a huge gash in it. There was mayhem, the West Indies' players upset with Greigy, believing it was sharp practice to run Kalli out when he wasn't attempting a run. There was a discussion and debate over the fact that Alan Knott had pulled up the stumps as soon as Bernard Julien had played the last ball, too. Surely that signalled the end of play? Not so, only the umpire can do that. The ball is live until the umpire calls time.

The players shared a balcony, and the home fans gathered around the dressing rooms, followed by the media. I was glad I wasn't part of that press conference... Overnight, the management agreed that for the good of cricket, England would ask Sang Hue if they could take their appeal back so that Alvin Kallicharran could resume the next day. Douglas agreed, and honour was satisfied. Alvin came out next morning to huge applause and Tony Greig met him in the middle with a handshake that went down well with West Indians everywhere. Alvin was soon out, but that young kid Bernard Julien again batted splendidly for 86 not out. He ran out of partners just as he looked like scoring a second consecutive century against us. More than 250 runs behind and eight sessions left in the match was about as bad as it gets. Fortunately, Dennis Amiss and I batted so well that at close of play we had put on 201, with Dennis 92 not out and me 91. I don't think either of us was getting carried away and thinking that we could save this game. We had salvaged some pride and we would do our best, but every cricketer knows that when the bowlers have had a night's rest, the next day can be very different.

The pitch was turning a bit and Lance Gibbs opened up at one end. He got me out before I could get in, caught very well and very low down at bat pad by Roy Fredericks. Dennis played an outstanding innings, though, sealing up one end and scoring 174 excellent runs. He got a bit of support from the captain, who made 44 before Dennis ran him out, but the rest didn't make many. Our second innings score of 392 exactly matched West Indies' first, so they were left with 132 to win. They closed on 77-1, so only rain could save us. There wasn't much of that around, and we went down by seven wickets.

6 and 93

\* \* \*

*You fly to Jamaica. At Sabina Park you play against the island team and score 83. You watch Lawrence Rowe bat for Jamaica, watch him make 41 and 118, the most impressive batsman on either side. You sit on the Selection Panel for the second Test. You are still in turmoil, about the captaincy, about not hooking, about the unfairness and stupidity of it, the calculated bloody stupidity of it, and when Mike Denness turns first to Tony Greig and then to you, you can't stop yourself, can't stop yourself from turning to Tony and saying, 'They always ask you first. Nobody ever thinks about me...' and you sit there, alone, with tears of frustration and pain running down your face. Mike Denness says, 'come on, all we're doing is picking teams here...'*

*And Donald Carr says nothing at all.*

\* \* \*

### Second Test, West Indies versus England, Sabina Park, Jamaica, 16-21 February 1974

*Fifty-ninth cap*

We won the toss and batted. The correct decision, but we didn't make it count. I played well for 68 and the captain had his best innings of 67, but no-one who got a start went on to that crucial big hundred. Tony Greig 45. Alan Knott 39. Dennis Amiss and John Jameson out in the twenties. Those sort of scores on a good pitch don't hurt the opposition, and so it proved. Lawrence Rowe, fresh from the island game, carved us up with ease, a sparkling 120 in an opening stand of 206 with Roy Fredericks. From such a powerful base, Kallicharran carried on where he left off in the first Test and by the time Kanhai declared, they had a lead of 230 runs. I watched the whole thing from the dressing room, having freakishly injured myself when my bat got stuck in the ground as I ran it into the crease, jamming the handle into my groin. Painful. The captain wanted me to bat in my normal position as an opener, but Rohan Kanhai objected, and there were heated words. When Rohan got angry there was no discussion or debate: the red mist descended in front of his eyes.

The umpires decided that I had been injured during the course of the match, and our captain could have me bat wherever he wished. It didn't really matter as I was out quickly, caught behind off Keith Boyce for five. By close of play, West Indies had John Jameson, Frank Hayes, Mike Denness and Tony Greig all back in the hutch with me, and we were still 12 runs in arrears.

Dennis Amiss was the only shining light, not out on 123. What an innings to just keep us in the game by a whisker. Dennis was a tough nut with tremendous determination and a fierce desire not to give his wicket away. Once he got in, he had the patience and concentration required to make centuries. Very strong forearms gave him lots of power when driving, and he was as good as anyone off his legs. He was even better on the last day as he sealed up an end and gave our tail the confidence to stay with him. Dennis knew that every run he made was worth two, as it ate into the time West Indies would need to knock off whatever lead he could get us. By the end of play our number eleven Bob Willis was still hanging on, England 202 runs ahead and Dennis unbeaten on a magnificent 260. This was one of the great rearguard innings and ensured an unlikely draw. We felt we had got ourselves right out of jail!

**68** and **5**

\* \* \*

*You miss the game with the Leeward Islands because of the groin, and then fail twice on a wet pitch in the game with Barbados. You lose by ten wickets to an island team, and the whispers get louder, whispers from the England bowlers, who tell you that they are fed up with Mike Denness and the way that he won't let them set their own fields...*

*The selection meeting turns into a big row when you let Mike Denness and Tony Greig have it in plain, unvarnished English. You tell Mike Denness that he needs to start listening to his bowlers, get them onside, because at the moment they are having no impact on the West Indian batsmen. You tell Tony Greig that he is making no effort to get involved as vice-captain, he's just keeping his nose clean while the captain hangs himself. You tell Mike Denness he needs to listen and Tony Grieg that he needs to get involved or else the team are going to capitulate.*

*And then Donald Carr and Mike Denness tell you that they have been thinking about the batting order, which is top heavy with openers. They ask you to drop down the order, to come in at number four...*

*That is a shock to hear, but you've made a rod for your own back telling Mike and Tony that they need to listen, and now you can't really refuse to do so yourself. You hear yourself agree to what they're saying, hear yourself agree to bat in a position you haven't batted in for ten years...*

*Ten years.*

* * *

*You go and talk to Ray Illingworth, who is covering the tour for a newspaper. He tells you that it would be good for you to be seen to be helping the team's needs by batting at number four. You see the sense in it, reluctantly.*

*Things are still uneasy between you and Tony. You sit down together. 'You are obviously unhappy,' Tony says. 'And you are upsetting other people...' You know deep down that he is right. You are unhappy. You want to be England captain. You should be England captain. You do not respect Mike Denness, do not respect him as a cricketer or as a captain. Maybe it's a measure of how unhappy you have become that you have allowed yourself to be talked into batting at number four. Batting at number four while Mike Denness opens...*

* * *

## Third Test, West Indies versus England, Bridgetown, Barbados, 6-11 March, 1974

*Sixtieth cap*

With me at number four, captain Denness and Dennis Amiss reached 28 before Dennis fell. John Jameson went out to bat and I had to sit padded up ready to be next man in. John hooked at every short ball bowled at him and hardly ever connected. There were top edges, leg byes off his arms, balls which he gloved that looped just short of the outstretched hands of fielders. There were two men out for the hook, and when he did connect, the ball looked as if it was going straight down the throat of a fielder and then would fall just short.

Every time, I would jump up, start putting my gloves on and picking up my bat. Then he would somehow escape and I would sit down until the next false alarm. I was up and down like a yo-yo. I was a nervous wreck for half an hour, and after all that, John had only scored three runs. It was the worst scenario for any opener who for years has not had to wait to bat.

When I finally got to the middle, we were two down for 34 and under a lot of pressure. I found it tough and eventually nicked Bernard Julien to the wicket-keeper for 10. Tony Greig stood up and got us out of trouble with a splendid 148, and just when we needed him, Alan Knott came to our rescue with 87 vital runs. A total of 395 all out wasn't bad, but a lot depended on whether our bowling could finally impact on the West Indies batting.

Sadly, the answer to that was no. Someone came up with the idea to bounce Lawrence Rowe early in his innings. Most West Indian batsmen hooked. It was almost a badge of honour for them. The supporters expected it, and a successful hook created vocal support and admiration. The first bouncer Lawrence received from Bob Willis he hit out of the park, way out over the longest boundary.

After that, our seamers were scared to bowl any more short stuff. What a player Lawrence was. He appeared so calm and relaxed, and he whistled to himself as he waited for each delivery. He was so still and very much at ease at the crease, and if you chatted to him between overs or off the field he had such a warm smile and friendly nature. He appeared comfortable with himself and his batting was so simple and effective.

He and Alvin Kallicharran put on 249 before Alvin was out for 119, but Lawrence went on and on. He was so much in control that I felt Garfield Sobers' world record score of 365 was in serious danger. I was surprised when he was out for a gorgeous 302 runs. Tony Greig had six wickets – heartening, even though he laboured through 46 overs at a cost of 164. Not very penetrating but it was a good batting pitch. West Indies declared with a lead of 201. It seemed no matter how many runs we scored, they could always do better.

Andy Roberts, on debut, got the early wickets of Dennis Amiss and John Jameson, and we were in trouble right away. I was in with the scoreboard reading at 8-2, and so I might as well have opened. Sobers got me out cheaply with the new ball, and at 40-4 we were in danger of getting beaten again. Keith Fletcher saved us with 129 not out in tandem with another fine contribution of 67 from Alan Knott. We were outplayed but somehow managed to escape defeat again. Surely we couldn't keep doing it?

10 and 13

\* \* \*

*You hear whispers... Whispers that you are batting down the order because you are afraid of the short ball, afraid and no longer hooking... You fly to the South American mainland, to Georgetown, Guyana, where the cricket field sits below sea level and the monsoons fall. The rain stays away for the tour match. You go in first and score 133. In the selection meeting for the Guyana Test you tell Mike, Tony and Donald, 'I'm opening. Now let's sort out the rest of the batting order.'*

*You still do not hook.*

\* \* \*

### Fourth Test, West Indies versus England, Georgetown, Guyana, 22-27 March, 1974

*Sixty-first cap*

There wasn't much chance of getting a result, as rain and a soggy outfield meant more than two days' play was lost. We batted first, with

155

me back at the top of the order. I hated the fact that I daren't hook, and it allowed Keith Boyce to bowl short at me without any retaliation. He hit me in the ribs and it was bloody painful. The bruising meant it hurt like hell if I laughed. Not that I was doing much laughing...

It was a bad decision, and one that I have regretted. Yes, the hook shot is fraught with danger and occasionally you are bound to get out. But every shot a batsman attempts will get him out at some point. It has to be a balance of weighing up how many runs you get with that stroke against how many times you get out with it. Not hooking allows the bowler to dictate by bowling short at will. If you hook him with success, it can make him pitch it up, so you get more balls to drive, or he may give you lots more short balls. Selective, rather than compulsive, hooking is necessary, but the Mike Denness public directive had cramped my batting and made me too passive.

Dennis Amiss was in fine touch again with 118 and Tony Greig got his second century of the series. But our biggest and best total was only good for batting practice as the rain fell and fell, washing away the chances of a result. Yet going into the last Test, a series in which we had been constantly behind and absolutely second best was somehow still alive.

**15** and **DNB**

\* \* \*

*The series may be alive, but the captaincy of Mike Denness is almost dead, hanging by a thread that another defeat will surely sever... This is how it feels, this is how it seems, as relations between Mike and a number of the players fall apart. As Donald Carr lets it be known that he sees the appointment as a mistake. As the press begin to question Mike Denness's future...*

*On the Saturday of the final Test, you return to the hotel and find a letter waiting for you. It is from Jim Swanton, inviting you to have a private dinner in his room. You show the letter to Bernard Thomas, England's physio and assistant tour manager, who tells you to play along, so you go to eat with Jim Swanton.*

*Inside room number 427, he grills you on your views of the game and its players. When he asks who you could work with as your vice-captain, you feel a mixture of flattery and offence at this pompous establishment man auditioning you, vetting you for the highest honour in the game.*

*'Tony Lewis,' you tell him, your tongue lodged so far in your cheek it might not come out again. 'Nice fellow, Cambridge University...'*

\* \* \*

## Fifth Test, West Indies versus England, Port of Spain, Trinidad, 30 March – 5 April, 1974

### *Sixty-second cap*

I'd broken all my bats, and so I had been trying to borrow one from any team member who would let me use their spare. In the end I had to settle for a heavier bat than I preferred from John Jameson. I practised every morning and late afternoon to try and get used to this new bat, and the pitch we were about to play on. The nets were very similar to how I felt the match surface would play, and it looked a result pitch.

And surprise, surprise, who should be having extra nets in the late afternoon but the great cricketer himself, Garfield Sobers... It was very rare for Garry to have second helpings of net practice! I even bowled a few overs to him, but my bowling didn't trouble him as much as his did me...

Because the pitch was pretty dry to start with, I was sure that as the game progressed there would be more and more spin, with some awkward low balls and shooters. Winning the toss would be a big bonus, and Mike Denness called it right.

We got off to a great start with Dennis Amiss and me putting on 83 before Dennis departed for 44. Then came trouble, as 83-0 became 165-4. The wrist-spin of Inshan Ali did for the captain, while Lance Gibbs got rid of our in-form middle order of Keith Fletcher and Tony Greig. We were wobbling, and our batting had shown it could go either way. The West Indies bowlers had us under enormous pressure. Nobody could trust the bounce, or force the ball away, as it came on so slowly. Every run took a lot of concentration, patience and sheer determination. It was a long day of struggle, but at the close we were just about okay on 198-4, with me not out 97. The crux was how many more I could score, and could our last few wickets make a telling contribution? Next morning, I was out right away, strangled playing a leg glance for 99, and only Alan Knott handled the situation for a tremendous 33 not out. 267 wasn't a great total but on result pitches you can never be sure what is a good score until both sides have batted.

Straight away we were in big trouble as Roy Fredericks and Lawrence Rowe put on 110. Roy was difficult to keep quiet at the best of times, and although he wasn't as flashy as normal, he showed us some fine strokes. Lawrence played it similar to how I had done: stay in, watch the ball, accept it is tricky and score when you can. At the close of play, he was still whistling away and smiling, another day at the office on 76 not out. Nothing ever seemed to bother Lawrence.

Before the Barbados Test, Tony Greig had a long chat with Raymond Illingworth about his bowling. Ray told him that the swing he used in England was never going to work, and advised him to use his height and bowl his off-cutters. Being so much taller than most slower bowlers, Tony could get bounce as well as turn the ball away against the four left-handers in their top order. When Tony dismissed Clive Lloyd for 52, it was his first wicket with the new style, and West Indies were still bossing the game at 224-3. That changed very quickly as Greigy immediately had Sobers out for nought, Kanhai for two and Deryck Murray for four. Wonderful crazy game, this cricket. Only Lawrence Rowe, still batting serenely, held them together with a priceless 123 before he mistimed a drive to me off Tony. West Indies had a lead of 38 runs. In low-scoring matches, every run is so important, but it wasn't as many as it had looked like being early on, and West Indies had to bat last on a pitch that was deteriorating quickly.

They had found Greig's off-cutters to be a handful, and Tony had the most remarkable and wonderful figures of 8-86. Fantastic. As Raymond had thought, he delivered the ball from a height that batsmen aren't used to, and this gave him disconcerting, exaggerated loop, with bounce and turn. The West Indies batsmen wanted to drive the ball, but that wasn't wise against him on this surface.

For the only time in the series England had a chance to win a Test match, and it was all riding on how well we batted this fourth day. Dennis Amiss and Mike Denness didn't make many, but Keith

Fletcher and me put on 99. Keith was always an excellent player of spin, and with runs hard to get, we gritted our teeth, dug deep and just wouldn't give our wickets away. When we did hit the ball, it wouldn't come off the bat and didn't go anywhere, which was very frustrating. Neither of us had the power to whack it, and we had to use our technical skill, along with patience and concentration. It was tiring, almost exhausting, having to stay in for such a long time without being able to push the scoring rate along. When Keith went for 45, Tony Greig and Frank Hayes made one run between them, and we were sliding out of the game at 176-6. Take off the 38 run deficit and we knew we didn't have enough runs to bowl at.

But Alan Knott was there when we needed him again. Small in stature, yet a giant of a player. Averages don't tell you everything. This guy got his runs when the going was tough, in pressure moments, at difficult times in a match. Alan made a huge contribution with his 44. When I was finally out, bowled by Lance Gibbs for 112, I stood there in disbelief. I don't remember missing a ball until that one, and I didn't expect to get out. On difficult pitches, it's all about mind over matter and self-belief. You have to be convinced that you can achieve whatever goal you set yourself. After getting out in the first innings one short of the magic figure, I was so much in the zone and so determined to get one in the second innings, that I was shocked to see one bail on the floor near my foot. I thought the keeper must have caught the stumps with his boot and it took a few seconds before Lance came up and said the ball had just clipped the stump. I believed him. Lance was a good guy, and I knew him well. 263 all out, less that 38 run lead, meant West Indies needed 226 to win.

The Imperial Cricket Conference had decided that this was to be another six-day Test match, as the series was in the balance, and as day five closed, West Indies were 30 without loss. It didn't look too promising, but we had got our bowling selection right. At our meeting, I'd held strong in my belief that spinners would be more important than our seamers, and I got my way. England played only one seamer in Geoff Arnold, which allowed us to accommodate three spinners in Pat Pocock, Derek Underwood and Jack Birkenshaw, plus Tony's cutters. We had variety, and could always call on a fresh spinner to exert some pressure.

We had two slices of luck on that final morning. Roy Fredericks was run out for 36, and then Lawrence Rowe played back to a slow, orthodox Jack Birkenshaw off-break and, inexplicably, missed it. He just missed it completely. For a second or two, there was a stunned silence. Lawrence was in control and had hardly played a false shot all series. It struck him on the back leg, hitting middle stump halfway up. What a huge wicket. Tony Greig was coming around the wicket to the left-handers and there was plenty of rough from the bowlers' boots. This, on top of a surface that was already crumbling, was to prove helpful for us. Tony got Alvin Kallicharran caught at slip, a huge wicket as he had plundered our bowling throughout the series. It soon got even better as Tony caught and bowled Clive Lloyd for 13 and then, even sweeter, Rohan Kanhai, in his last Test match, nicked him to slip to leave his team at 85-5. Two hundred now looked a long way off and we were buzzing.

Garry Sobers walked in. It was a remarkable moment. He was almost 38 years old and on a pair. This was to be his final innings in Test cricket. Garry had first played for West Indies as a 17-year-old, half a lifetime ago, and I knew from talking to him that he was tired and burned out. He was a true great, a legend of the game, probably the best all-round cricketer ever. A few years earlier, he would have relished the chance to get West Indies home for a victory. Now, at the end of his days, it was tougher. He fought hard for 20 before Derek Underwood bowled him out of the rough.

Keith Boyce was a natural striker of a cricket ball, a free spirit with a good eye. He gave us some concern as he put on 31 with Inshan Ali, until Inshan's patience let him down and Tony got him hitting it in the air. When Lance Gibbs walked out to bat, West Indies needed 27 more to win. As much as I love Lance, he was a hopeless batsman and it was obvious Keith Boyce would have to try and hit them to victory. Mike Denness nipped any chance of that in the bud, bringing on Geoff Arnold, who bowled Lance very quickly.

We had won, with Tony taking 5-70 to give him match figures of 13-156. A magnificent performance. I have always believed batsmen put you in a position to win and bowlers then win the match. I was proud of my 211 out of a team total of 520 runs. Forty per cent of England's total was good. The press had criticised my

A bespectacled Boycott in 1965.

Losing his cap to Dennis Lillee at the WACA in 1970.

Read all about it! Local reaction to Boycott's 100th hundred in 1977.

Chatting to Mike Brearley, 1977.

Mobbed at Headingley, 1977.

In action for Yorkshire, 1978.

Captaining England at last, tossing up with Wasim Bari, Karachi, January 1978.

Mid-summer, 1978.

At the WACA with Ian Botham and other team members, December 1978.

Before yet another Test against the West Indies, July 1980.

slow scoring in the first innings, but most of them haven't a clue about pitches and how their quality dictates the type of batting and the run rate.

Mike Denness accepted all the plaudits and congratulations, basking in the glory of an astonishing win and a drawn series. He quite rightly praised Tony, but made not one reference to my batting. Tony laughed. A few players came to me afterwards and said how embarrassed they were by his deliberate avoidance of any praise. Victory was bittersweet for me, because had England lost, there is no way Mike Denness would have clung on. I had batted myself out of the captaincy of England.

`99` and `112`

\* \* \*

*You could have finished Mike Denness. You think it. You know it. You could have given your wicket away in that second innings and he would have been gone, done for, and no-one would have known. You would be the new captain of England.*

*But that is not you. That is not your nature. Your nature is to fight, for every run, no matter what it means.*

*As you walk off the field at the Queen's Park Oval, you say to Tony, 'that's the worst day's cricket for England... We've just kept Denness in his job...'*

*The papers are full of the triumph of Mike Denness's England team. Donald Carr sings his praises. He is safe. There are no more invitations to dinner with Jim Swanton. Instead the team fly home via Bermuda, where Mike Denness, whose job you have just saved, accuses you of faking an injury to get out of the three-day game against the island team. He insists that you play, so you strap up your thigh and make 131.*

*Back to England, back home, your mind still not right, your mood low. Back to the English spring and to your benefit year, back to the problems at Yorkshire...*

*You return to find that some of your benefit functions have been cancelled. An organiser has opted out. The Yorkshire CCC Cricket Committee are insisting on a trophy while refusing to sign overseas players. You try to explain, explain why Yorkshire are falling behind, explain it all to those who are for you and those against.*

*You pour even more of yourself into these problems. You get your benefit back on track. You practise and prepare for the new season, you try to improve as a player and as a captain. You are 33 years old now. You have been playing international cricket for a decade. You feel the weight of it, the constant worry, the constant absorption in the game. You wonder how much longer all of this can continue.*

*You pick out some new bats. You play the students of Cambridge University and make 140 not out. You play the touring India team at Bradford. On a juicy pitch, you are lbw to Abid Ali for 15 and then lbw to Eknath Solkar for 14. You are summoned to play for MCC against India at Lord's, a game that Yorkshire try to get you out of so that you can captain them in an important Benson & Hedges Cup group game, the Benson & Hedges Cup that would be just the thing for your precarious captaincy, but the MCC insist, so you go to Lord's and are dismissed cheaply twice by Eknath Solkar, each time caught at second slip by Sunil Gavaskar.*

*The newspapers pick you apart, say that you are struggling against Solkar's medium-pace left-arm seamers. They do not mention all of the left-arm seamers that you have scored hundreds of runs against: Garfield Sobers, Keith Boyce, Trevor Goddard, Dick Collinge, Karsan Ghavri...*

*A journalist approaches Sobers, hoping he'll put the knife in. Garry tells him you have no problem with any type of bowler: 'All shots in cricket must first be played in the head and this is where Boycott is having his problems. The moment he believes in himself again the runs will flow.'*

*A week later you are dragged away from Yorkshire once more. This time, the selectors place you in the Rest of England team to play England at Worcester.*

*The Rest... That's what they think, is it?*

*Being placed in 'The Rest' team makes you angry, pisses you off. You score 160 not out and 116 against the best bowlers in England.*

*On and on it goes, this unending, capricious game, played out endlessly in your head.*

\* \* \*

## First Test, England versus India,
## Old Trafford, Manchester, 6-11 June, 1974

*Sixty-third cap*

The least enjoyable Test match I have ever played in. I had a miserable time, as our captain Mike Denness made it obvious he wanted nothing to do with me. By snubbing me, he made me feel he didn't want me around, and I wasn't in a good enough state of mind or form to shrug it off. I got out lbw to Abid Ali again for 10 and in the second innings caught behind to Solkar for six. The bowling wasn't special, and in a good frame of mind I should have been making runs. Keith Fletcher scored a first innings century to take us to 328 and John Edrich a second innings not out hundred to allow an England declaration. The match was hard-fought, but England were just too strong, and had the more penetrating seam attack. Usually I watch every ball and can remember all the major moments in every Test match I was a part of, but towards the end of the game I just wanted to go home. I didn't enjoy being snubbed. There was no satisfaction and very little pleasure or involvement.

If Mike Denness had a plan to alienate me and get me out of his team, then it had succeeded. There is no fun in being cold-shouldered by your captain. Taking stock of my situation over the next few days, I came to the conclusion that the drive and desire to play for England had gone. I was wasting my time and I couldn't see my relationship with the captain getting better. It was going to be easy for England to beat India and Pakistan that summer and Mike Denness was now unassailable. He wasn't going anywhere so I had to be the one to leave.

I put my thoughts and feelings to Alec Bedser. He called me before the selectors sat down to pick the team for the second Test. I told him that I hadn't changed my mind, and I walked away from playing for England.

`10` and `6`

\* \* \*

# ABSENCE
# 1974-1977

**Co-Author's note:**
Between the Old Trafford Test against India in June 1974 and his
return against Australia at Trent Bridge at the end of July 1977,
Geoffrey Boycott made himself unavailable for selection for England.
During that period, he missed out on a possible 30 Test match caps.
At the point of exile, he had played 63 times, scoring 4,579 runs at
an average of 47.69. That total included 12 centuries, and 26 scores
of fifty or more, in 110 innings. His highest remained the 246 not
out against India that had resulted in him being dropped for slow
scoring by Doug Insole. He was 34, an age at which many cricketers
begin to contemplate retirement, and also by now one of the most
famous sports stars in Britain.

Just like life and society, fame, in 1974, was quite different to its
contemporary equivalent, our atomised and infinite world of social
media and reality television. Fame was more sedate and probably less
intrusive. Nonetheless, Boycott was one of the few sporting greats,
along with perhaps George Best, Brian Clough and Muhammad Ali,
whose exploits would appear on the front page of the newspaper as
well as the back, and who might guest on the biggest television talk
show of the day, *Parkinson*, hosted every Saturday night by Boycott's
friend and former Barnsley CC team-mate Michael Parkinson. Like
his other great friend Brian Clough, Boycott was by now a lightning
rod figure, capable of inspiring tremendous loyalty and passionate
dislike, often in the same person. And in the same way that Boycott
had been overlooked for the captaincy of the England Test team,
Clough was the people's choice for manager of the England football
team, a post he would never fill. He and Boycott were also much
more complex personalities than their portrayal in the media, or, in
fairness, the face that they were willing to show to the public. As
Geoffrey once said: 'I don't understand myself sometimes...'

One thing that does need contextualising is his love for, and
relationship with, Yorkshire County Cricket Club. To Geoffrey
Boycott, the three years he dedicated solely to Yorkshire were in no
way a 'step down' in his mind. He regarded playing for the county

as equal to his role in the national team. Indeed, Yorkshire's fate, so deeply entwined with his own, was a major factor in his withdrawal.

Geoffrey's diary ends after the Test against India in 1974, and picks up again with the events surrounding his recall in the summer of 1977. However, he and I agree that it is important to give an insight into the years of his absence and so the following attempt to describe what happened is a result of reading, research and my conversations with Geoffrey.

\* \* \*

*Alec Bedser is sanguine about your unavailability for the India series or the three Tests against Pakistan that will follow later in the summer. He knows that England should beat India and Pakistan at home with or without you. The tour of Australia in 1974–75 is a different story. For England to have any chance of winning the Ashes down under, you must be there.*

*So Alec Bedser keeps in touch. He keeps that door open... He thinks that maybe a summer at Yorkshire, among your people, might clear your head, free your mind, give you and Mike Denness some distance from one another.*

*And yet Yorkshire is no refuge, no hiding place. Not without trophies in the cabinet. Your form improves as soon as you leave Mike Denness behind, but it is too late for this season, too late for a trophy, as Yorkshire finish tenth in the County Championship, lose in the quarter-final of the Benson & Hedges Cup to Surrey and in the quarter-final of the Gillette Cup to Lancashire, and then finish in joint sixth place in the John Player Sunday League.*

*No titles and no trophies to set before the committee...*

*Senior pros Tony Nicholson, Richard Hutton and Don Wilson circulate a petition among the capped professionals asking that you be replaced as captain, but Phil Sharpe refuses to sign and John Hampshire wrongly tells them that you are considering retirement, so the petition goes in the bin where it belongs. You go before the committee early in September. They examine your record. They ask if you would play under another captain. You are taken aback at the vehemence of their questioning. They re-elect you to captain Yorkshire for the season of 1975 by a solitary vote. It seems clear that it will be your last chance. You worry about that. You worry about what would happen under another captain. You tell your friend Sid Fielden, 'If I don't play for them next year instead of England, then they could finish bottom. I just have to concentrate on Yorkshire.'*

*At the end of August, you receive an invitation to tour Australia under Mike Denness. You do not reply, so MCC send urgent telegrams to your house. On 23 September, you travel to London where you meet with Alec Bedser and Donald Carr. You tell them that Mike Denness is still captain, and you cannot play under him. You need to rest and recover during the winter, try and regain your best form for Yorkshire and the crucial season of 1975. You explain that your mother is in poor health, suffering from rheumatoid arthritis, and as your father is dead and your two brothers married you are the only one at home and you need to look after her. You ask that this final reason is kept between the three of you and not made public.*

*England go to Australia without you, where they are blown away by Dennis Lillee, who after 11 months has made a miraculous recovery from a back injury, and an unknown quick from Queensland called Jeff Thomson, who might just be the fastest bowler on earth. Australia win 4-1. England's batsmen are left shocked and broken by the pace and ferocity of Lillee and Thomson, and the relentless verbal aggression of Ian Chappell and Rodney Marsh. Thomson says in a television interview, 'I like to see blood on the pitch.' Keith Fletcher, John Edrich, Dennis Amiss, David Lloyd and Fred Titmus are struck and injured. England call up the 41-year-old Colin Cowdrey, who is also struck and hurt. Mike Denness is unable to cope with the bowling, dismissed for 6, 4, 2, 3, 8 and 5 in the first three Tests. He drops himself for the fourth, and returns for the fifth, when Australia are without the injured Lillee and Thomson. England win a consolation victory and Denness makes his highest Test score of 188.*

*Even in your absence, the rumours begin... stories that you opted out of the tour because you were scared to face Lillee and Thomson. Rumours that can't possibly be true, because when you turned down your place, Lillee was injured and no-one had heard of Jeff Thomson... But still they begin...*

*But at last there is good news. Your benefit committee announce that it has raised £20,639. It is tax-free, and almost three times more than the previous highest amount for a Yorkshire player. A huge sum when*

166

*you are paid £4,000 per year. You are overwhelmed by emotion. You tell the Yorkshire Post, 'I can't tell you how much this demonstration of people's affection means to me. I have always thought of myself as a people's player... Until last year, I never realised just how many well-wishers I had.'*

*More good news: Phil Sharpe, Richard Hutton and Don Wilson leave Yorkshire, the dressing room clear-out you need. After years of turmoil, the season of 1975 becomes one of your happiest in cricket. You lead the way with the bat, making 1,915 runs at 73.65, with six centuries. You lead the way on the field and in the dressing room. You make sure that you spend your captain's allowance in the bar. You spend time with this new and younger team, talking cricket. The launch of the Prudential World Cup in mid-summer takes many of the star overseas players away from their counties, and with a level playing field, you lead Yorkshire to second place in the Championship, the highest finish since the days of Brian Close.*

*You even play in the Lord's Taverners charity game at Lord's where you entertain the crowds by hitting boundary after boundary and break the habit of a lifetime by giving your wicket away, caught and bowled, to Brian Clough. You love every minute of it. Australia stay on after the World Cup to play a four-Test Ashes series. Mike Denness is sacked after England lose the first Test by an innings. Tony Greig is the new captain, and he leads the team to three successive draws, including the game at Headingley, which ends prematurely after supporters of an armed robber called George Davis dig up the pitch before the final day's play.*

\* \* \*

*The burning summer of 1976. The drought and the cricket. Michael Holding and Brian Close. Viv Richards and Tony Greig. The National Front and the IRA. The Cod War and Direct Rule. The Black Panther and the Yorkshire Ripper. Harold Wilson and Jeremy Thorpe. The Sex Pistols and Bill Grundy. John Stonehouse and John Curry. Eric Clapton and Enoch Powell... A new England, a country of change, a country in shock...*

*Tony Greig tells Alec Bedser he is 'desperate' to have you in his England side. Alec telephones again, just to check on your availability, perhaps you might change your mind? Your answer is the same as last year... Brian Clough tells you that if he was the Chairman of Selectors he would go around to your house and refuse to leave until you were playing for England again. You tell Brian that if he was Chairman of Selectors, you might just agree...*

*Tony Greig tells the TV cameras that he will make the West Indies 'grovel,' a comment that Michael Holding says, 'smacks of racism and apartheid', especially when it comes with a South African accent... England are smashed by the batting of Viv Richards and assaulted by the bowling of Holding, Andy Roberts and Wayne Daniel. West Indies win three games in a row. Without you to face the barrage, England recall 45-year-old Brian Close to open the batting with 39-year-old John Edrich. At Old Trafford in the third Test, on a dangerous pitch, they endure one of the most brutal onslaughts seen on a cricket field. The series assumes great cultural significance for the Windrush generation and the Caribbean people living in England. They fill the stands with light and noise. They rejoice in the electric power of their team. England will not beat West Indies again for a generation.*

*Yorkshire play Sussex at Hove, where Tony Greig pulls you aside and offers you the vice-captaincy of England for the winter tour of India. He tells you that he will arrange for food to be flown in to protect your health. Ted Dexter drives to Canterbury, where Yorkshire are playing Kent. He sits with you for an hour trying to persuade you to play for England again.*

*But you break a finger and have problems with your back and miss matches. Yorkshire slip back into the pack, finishing eighth in the Championship, losing in the second round of the Gillette Cup, losing to a Combined University XI in the Benson & Hedges Cup, finishing third from bottom of the Sunday League. You are third in the national batting averages, with 1,288 runs at 67.78 and five centuries. Selector Charlie Elliott comes to visit. He says that you are a fool not to play for England. But he implies that if you come back against India, it will add to the stories that you do not want to face the fast bowlers of Australia and West Indies.*

*So you turn down the tour of India. Before England leave, Tony Greig travels to Australia for some television work. While he's there, he recommends you to Waverley Cricket Club in Sydney. You leave the English winter and Yorkshire CCC 12,000 miles behind and make*

168

stacks of runs in the sunshine. Tony's friend Ian Macfarlane sorts you out with some media work, commentating on Sheffield Shield cricket and writing for newspapers. You fly all over the country, returning every Saturday to play for Waverley, driving to games in the battered old car they loan to you. You feel better and better, out here by the beach at Bondi, living a more carefree life.

You meet up with the Sussex bowler John Spencer, who introduces you to Kerry Packer. Kerry owns the Channel Nine TV station and loads of newspapers. Kerry asks you to take a look at his son James at the net in his back garden. James is nine years old.

You and Kerry exchange words because Kerry won't stop interfering while you are coaching.

# CHAPTER TWELVE

# 1977

*It is one hundred years since Australia played England at the Melbourne Cricket Ground in the first-ever Test match. To celebrate, the teams play a one-off Centenary Test at the same venue. You are invited to Melbourne as a guest of the Australian Cricket Board. A few days before the game, Kerry Packer asks to see you again. You meet at his office in Sydney. He asks how much money you would want to spend the next winter in Australia coaching outside of the big cities. You pull a figure from the air and tell him £20,000. Kerry says no, too much. Then he says that he is planning some cricket matches between a World XI and an Australian XI made up of recently retired Test players like Ian Chappell, and maybe you could come back and play in those?*

*You do not know that Kerry Packer's Channel Nine are in dispute with the Australian Cricket Board over television rights. You do not know that Kerry Packer is not used to being turned down or not getting his own way. Kerry quizzes you on who should captain his World XI. You tell him Raymond Illingworth. Kerry says no, so you tell him you'll do it if he wants as most of the best players will be playing for their countries.*

*Kerry asks if you're going to the Centenary match. He asks if you'd like to commentate. He makes two phone calls, and you have the job. During the Test, you receive a contract from Kerry for his World XI matches. It is pages and pages long. You realise that he is more serious than you had imagined. You ask to take it to your solicitor in Yorkshire. Austin Robertson, the former Aussie Rules footballer who is working for Kerry and has brought you the contract, says no, it's too secret, but he will be in England soon, scouting players and even grounds where Kerry's teams can play in future summers. You tell Austin Robertson in that case, you are contracted to Yorkshire for the English summer and you will not be signing, even for the almighty Kerry Packer.*

*At the Test you run into Ken Barrington. Ken is now an England selector. He urges you to make yourself available for England again. It gets you thinking.*

*You fly home. You feel great, ready for anything, like you've taken some kind of rest cure. On Sunday 8 May, Yorkshire meet Sussex at Hove in the John Player League. Sussex win. Tony Greig makes an unbeaten fifty. You're getting in your car after the game when Tony comes over and asks you to go to the pub. You tell him that you can't, and he says, 'Well watch out for a story in the papers tomorrow. Me and a lot of other players have signed for Kerry Packer…'*

*You still don't think too much about it. On the way back, you drive past Tony's place, so you call in on his wife Donna to say hello and thank her for being so kind to you with hospitality while you were in Sydney. Richard Lumb and Bill Athey are in the car with you, so they go too. The next day, the Packer story breaks. Tony is all over the papers and the television. He is removed as England captain a week later. Alec Bedser says, 'The English captain acting as a recruiting sergeant left a mixture of numbing sadness and anger.' The British public have never heard of Kerry Packer or Channel Nine. The press dub his idea 'Kerry Packer's Circus'. They call Kerry 'the Man In The Stocking Mask'.*

*Overnight, the game is divided. Among the England players signed to Packer are Dennis Amiss, Derek Underwood, Alan Knott and John Snow. Also signed are Dennis Lillee, Jeff Thomson, Clive Lloyd, Viv Richards, Andy Roberts, Joel Garner, Michael Holding, Lawrence Rowe, Wayne Daniel, Colin Croft, Barry Richards, Mike Procter, Clive Rice, Eddie Barlow, Javed Miandad, Imran Khan, Mushtaq Mohammed, Sarfraz Nawaz and Richard Hadlee.*

*Your name is the glaring omission from that list. The press want to know why, and you tell them the truth: that you met with Kerry at his offices in Sydney and Melbourne, and that you turned him down.*

*As the story grows, they crave any detail: how much the Packer players are being paid, who might sign up next… Kerry flies to England. He appears on David Frost's television programme with Jim Laker and Robin Marlar and makes mincemeat of them.*

*Kerry is direct, charming and the biggest cat in the jungle. He says he is changing cricket for the benefit of the players.*

*But you know what he really wants. The TV rights. His TV rights.*

*As the Packer story grows and grows, Alec Bedser says publicly that the England selectors will consider any player that makes himself available, including you. You ask your friend John Callaghan of the*

*Yorkshire Evening Post to ring Alec and ask if he would be willing to meet you. Alec says yes, so you call him. You decide on a halfway point between your homes: the Blue Boar service station on the M1 at Watford Gap on a Tuesday afternoon. You don't want to be recognised, so you sit in the car park in Alec's new, white Austin Princess. You remember the smell of Alec's new car. You tell Alec that you feel ready to play for England again but you don't want to make yourself available and then have the selectors embarrass you in public. Alec tells you that he feels you will be welcomed back, but that he will discuss your wishes with the other selectors and the TCCB.*

*A week later Alec rings to tell you that you will not be snubbed. Donald Carr, on behalf of the TCCB rings to say the same.*

*You go to Cardiff to play Glamorgan. You sit with Ossie Wheatley, former captain of Glamorgan and a former Test selector and tell him what is going around and around in your head: Would they pick you... What about the pressure from the media... What if you come back and fail... What will happen to Yorkshire without all of your runs...*

*Ossie listens, and he tells you, gently and persuasively, that you should push aside the fear and the doubt, let it all go, and pick up the phone to Alec Bedser...*

*You ask the Yorkshire players. One says, 'Stay with us'. Another says, 'We need you more than England... but I suppose England need you too...' Another says, 'Don't go back unless they make you captain...' Another says, 'We won't do as well without you. But I think you have got to play for England because you are the best player and England need you.'*

*You ask another close friend, who tells you: 'Are any of the current England batsmen better than you? No. Definitely not.'*

*It's now or never. You know it. The soul-searching, this constant questioning of forces that you cannot control, has to end. Yorkshire play Nottinghamshire at Headingley in the second week of June. The first day is rained off. You go home. Early on Saturday morning, you call Alec Bedser. Alec listens politely as you make yourself available for England. He tells you he will inform the selectors right away. He tells you that the team for the first Test against Australia at Lord's has already been chosen.*

*Your long exile is almost over. But not quite... Not yet...*

*The first Test begins in chaos. England are captained by Mike Brearley, and field the Packer-contracted players Tony Greig, Dennis Amiss and Alan Knott. Australia are captained by Packer signing Greg Chappell, and field the Packer-contracted players Doug Walters, David Hookes, Rod Marsh, Max Walker, Jeff Thomson and Len Pascoe. The match is drawn.*

*The Australians come to Scarborough to play a tour match. The Yorkshire public – your Yorkshire public – fill the ground to watch you bat. They get their wish at the end of day one, but it does not last long. You play no shot to a Max Walker inswinger and are lbw without scoring. You sweat it out on a pair but on the final day you bat again and make 103.*

*Mike Brearley tells the selectors that he wants you in the team for the second Test at Old Trafford. They tell him that they don't want to be seen to come running the second you call. Dennis Amiss retains his place. England win, but Dennis makes scores of just 11 and 23 to go with the 4 and 0 that he got at Lord's, and when the game is over, the selectors name you in an England team for the first time in three years.*

*You report to Trent Bridge, Nottingham, the ground where you made your Test match debut 13 years ago. You are nervous and wired, worried about what your team-mates and the crowd will say and do, worried about everything that is about to happen, but when you walk in the dressing room for the first time you are greeted warmly.*

*You go and look at the pitch. You tap it with your bat. It's as hard as concrete.*

*'Bloody hell Ron,' you say to Ron Allsop, the Trent Bridge groundsman, 'it'll be no picnic against their fast bowlers on this...'*

*Ron laughs. Ron looks at you. 'It's a good pitch for them that can bat,' he says. 'You always get runs on my pitches, Geoffrey. You'll get a hundred on it...'*

*Always hundreds... Always the expectation and the pressure...*

*You make your way to the practice nets. Hundreds of spectators have gathered around them. They break into applause at the sight of you. When it's your turn to bat you're still nervous and a little embarrassed by the attention so you nick one behind.*

*'Don't do that tomorrow Geoffrey,' someone shouts. 'We want a hundred from you!'*

*Always hundreds... The expectation and the pressure... The same routine...*

*You go to the hotel. You eat. You got to bed. You think about the Australian bowlers. You go to sleep. You do not dream about cricket. You wake up. You have your breakfast. You go to the ground. You sit in the dressing room while Mike Brearley goes out for the toss. Mike Brearley loses the toss and Greg Chappell decides that Australia will bat first. For once in your life, you're delighted...*

\* \* \*

## Third Test, England versus Australia, Trent Bridge, Nottingham, 28 July – 2 August, 1977

### *Sixty-forth cap*

It was a relief to field first, as it allowed me to get back into the atmosphere of Test match cricket. The crowd were fantastic, and every time I touched the ball, they cheered. Australia were bowled out for 243 just before the close, and a 21-year-old kid making his debut for England took five wickets. His first was a long hop to Greg Chappell, who edged it into his stumps.

Take a bow Ian Botham.

Towards the end of the day, I walked out to bat with Mike Brearley, and I can honestly say I had never felt so nervous in my life. We got through three overs to the close, and I slept that night with a single run to my name.

Next morning, Jeff Thomson and Len Pascoe gave me a real going over with lots of short stuff that tested my technique and courage. They had no doubt seen some of the media articles that said I was supposed to be afraid of fast bowling... And as I hadn't played at the highest level for three years, they would have been crazy not to test me out. Lenny Pascoe bowled so short you could have been forgiven if you thought he was trying to knock his own toe-cap off...

Pascoe did get Mike Brearley and Bob Woolmer early, which brought in Derek Randall, appearing on his home ground to a proper hero's welcome. I was doing okay until I pushed the ball to the on side of the pitch and called for a single. Normally, a right-arm fast bowler would finish his follow through to the off-side and the momentum would make it difficult for him to change direction. Jeff Thomson was the exception. He jumped across the pitch in front of Derek, picked up the ball and flicked it side-arm to Rod Marsh, who demolished the stumps with glee. Derek stopped and then started again, and never, ever got going, out by a street. He told me it was not my fault, and said that if he had run straight and not hesitated, he would have got home. It was nice of him, and I know he was a fast runner, but I accept any blame and criticism.

I was distraught and expected the crowd to give me hell, but instead there was a stunned silence as Derek walked off. I buried my face in my glove, unable to really take in what had happened. The next batsmen, Tony Greig and Geoff Miller, tried to help by talking to me, but they were soon out. I was like a rabbit trapped in the headlights. I couldn't play a shot. I was stunned and mortified by what I had done. I wanted to get out of that pressure cooker, which had become unbearable. The spotlight and embarrassment felt as though they would overwhelm me. It would have been easier to give my wicket away so I could go and hide in the dressing room, yet something in my nature would not allow me to give in. For an age, all I could do was defend and survive. In those moments it was mental strength, a great technique and sheer bloody-mindedness that got me through. The Nottingham crowd's refusal to condemn me was a tremendous help. While I was suffering, England had slumped to 82-5, and we were losing the Test match. Enter Alan Knott to play probably the most important innings of his life against two fine, rampant fast bowlers on a helpful, bouncy pitch. Alan started to talk to me, and as he played his shots it helped get me going at the other end. He encouraged me back from a state of suspended animation so that my brain started functioning again and my hands and feet began to move in sync. We took the score from 82 to 242 before I was out for 107. Our partnership of 215 changed the course of the match and steered us to a winning position. Alan was finally out for a magnificent 135. What an innings! And what a time to deliver. It's never as simple as how many runs you make. It's the context in which you make them, and against what quality of bowling. That innings was one of the greatest I ever saw.

Mine was not close to the longest I've played, nor the best, but physically, mentally, and emotionally, it was the hardest. I was returning to the international stage at 36 years of age, which is when most players are retiring. At 36, every batsman is past his best. And having been out for three years, I had to return to huge publicity and enormous pressure. Some people were so angry about my self-imposed exile that they wanted me to fail.

When I ran Derek Randall out, someone in the press box said, 'Geoff is his own worst enemy...'

Lyn Wellings of the *Evening Standard* replied, 'Not while I'm around he ain't...'

Failure was always a possibility and I was conscious if that happened there would have been more embarrassment and publicity as some in the media would have said, 'What was all the fuss about, he's past it...'

The Randall run-out was an extra unbelievable pressure, so to come through it with a century and to help Alan Knott win the Test match was beyond my expectation. Australia set us 198 to win, and I shared an opening partnership of 154 with Mike Brearley that helped us home by seven wickets. That 80 not out showed my first innings wasn't a fluke, and I became the second player in history to bat on every day of a Test match. At the end of the game, we stood on the balcony with lots of people chanting and cheering. I was thrilled to bits, but honestly, there was a lot of relief, too.

**107** and **80 not out**

\* \* \*

*The high is so high it should last forever, but it doesn't... It doesn't even last a day, because you go straight from the Test match to a meeting of the Yorkshire committee who want to know why the team has lost at home to Middlesex and Hampshire, lost heavily enough to have the members asking questions of the committee.*

*You ask them how you're supposed to know. You were playing in the Test match.*

*'It's your team and your responsibility,' committee member Mel Ryan tells you. 'I don't care if you never score another hundred for England. It's Yorkshire that concerns me...'*

*'I can't be in two places at once,' you tell Mel Ryan. 'Not unless I cut myself in half...'*

*You leave the meeting wondering what the fuck is going on, and when you get home, your mum says to you that she's having problems with a lump under her arm. When you ask her how long it's been there for, she says nearly a year.*

*'Oh no,' you think. 'Oh Jesus…'*

*'Why didn't you say anything?'*

*'You've got enough problems of your own,' she says.*

*Well you have now. You organise a doctor and set off for the match with Warwickshire at Edgbaston, and you're so bloody worried about your mum and the madness at Yorkshire that you get stopped for speeding on the way.*

*In Birmingham it rains and rains, but you get out there long enough to make another hundred. Maybe that will shut Mel Ryan up for a bit. You're so consumed with everything that you are barely aware that it is your 99th first-class century…*

*Barely aware of it until you ring your girlfriend Rachael after the match…*

*'You've done it now,' she says.*

*'Done what,' you ask her.*

*'All the TV and radio is about you getting your one hundredth hundred at Headingley in the Test match…' she says.*

*'Do you know how fucking difficult it is to get a fucking hundred…'*

*You don't usually swear, but now you do.*

*'…Never mind in a fucking Test match and against fucking Australia, and on my fucking home ground…'*

*'Well,' she says, 'nobody else thinks that…'*

*In the whole history of cricket, only 17 players have made a hundred centuries. None of those made their 100th in a Test match. You think of all of the players that were better than you who couldn't do it. The odds are astronomically against it ever happening, let alone it happening to you. But Rachael is right.*

*Nobody else thinks so.*

*They think it is written in the stars. They think that fairy tales come true. They think that you can just pluck a hundred from the sky when you want one. Letters and cards arrive to the Headingley dressing room by the sackful. You don't have time to read them. You practise well enough but then you go to the pre-Test dinner and the stress starts to get to you. Mike Brearley notices and allows you to go to your room early. You go through the bowlers in your head, and then you try to sleep, try to sleep so that you will not dream of cricket, but you can't. Instead your mind churns over and over until it gets so late you call Rachael and ask her to come. She does, but you still can't sleep. It's too bloody hot, for one thing. At 4am you call the night porter to fix the air conditioning.*

*You get so desperate you take a sleeping tablet and wake up late, and now it's all a bloody rush, the soothing routine shot out of the water. You grab a taxi to the ground because it's quicker, but then the driver says, 'I had two of your mates in here yesterday... Thomson and Pascoe... I told them you were going to get a hundred, but they said, no he's not, we're going to knock his fucking head off...'*

*You're so late that the groundsman is taking down the practice nets, and you beg him to put them back up, just so that you can have a hit, feel the ball on the bat, and all the time you're thinking, 'please... just let Brearley lose the toss again...'*

*And then Mike wins the toss and says he'll bat. You rush into your gear, and all you can think about is how bloody tired you are...*

\* \* \*

## Fourth Test, England versus Australia, Headingley, Leeds, 11-15 August, 1977

### *Sixty-fifth cap*

As we walked out, Mike asked if he could take first ball. The way I felt, that was okay by me. As I stood at the other end, he nicked the third delivery of Jeff Thomson's first over and was out for nought. That woke me up pretty quick.

It was a warm, beautiful day and a lovely pitch for batting. After 20 to 30 minutes the ball was hitting the middle of my bat and the tiredness seemed to have disappeared. I wasn't thinking a hundred at that stage, although everyone in the ground was. Michael Fearnley, the older brother of the bat maker Duncan Fearnley and a very good Bradford League seam bowler, helped out as an assistant coach at Yorkshire and used to bowl to me a lot at early season net practices. As Michael sat down in front of our dressing room, he said to some people nearby, 'I'll tell you if he's going to get a hundred. I watch his footwork, right forward or right back, in rhythm. He has a big stride for a man who is not that tall.'

After a short time, he got up and said, 'He'll get a hundred today.'

I had just two awkward moments. Len Pascoe bowled me a corker of a short ball that brushed my left wrist-band and the Aussies did a war dance. I held my breath.

Not out, said umpire Lloyd Budd.

Later, with my score on 75, left-arm spinner Ray Bright bowled me an arm ball that brushed my thigh pad as I went to glance, and the Aussies went up for a caught behind.

Not out, said umpire Bill Alley.

Ray Bright was apoplectic. Greg Chappell had to cool him down and Bill Alley wagged his finger. Bill was a tough Aussie himself and had played Grade cricket and also for New South Wales before coming over for a successful spell with Somerset. Bill knew all the dodges, and Ray Bright's tantrum didn't cut any ice with him.

I am told I spent a long time in the eighties without scoring, and that gave my friends and supporters a great deal of concern. The scoreboard inactivity didn't worry me. I knew that when a batsman was getting near a century, bowlers and fielders deliberately made a special effort to stop the flow of runs in the hope that nerves will come into play and they'll get themselves out. It was an old tactic that sometimes worked. I just held my concentration together and waited for the right ball. As the clock approached 6pm, I went through the nineties. When I'd reached 96, Greg Chappell came on to bowl his medium-pace to try and sucker me into a false stroke.

'Don't hook if he slips you a bouncer,' I told myself. 'Look for the gap at extra cover or the on side.'

As soon as the ball left his hand, I knew I was going to hit it and I knew exactly where it was going. It was an amazing feeling. The ball was around off stump but the length was perfect for me to get over it and work it from outside to in, past the stumps on the on-side. As soon as I middled it, I raised my bat in the air and Graham Roope at the other end had to jump out of the way to make sure it didn't hit him.

On 11 August 1977, at 5.49pm, I scored my hundredth first-class hundred, playing for England versus Australia in an Ashes Test on my beloved home ground, and it was the greatest moment in my cricketing career. The crowd ran on from all sides, and for a while I was mobbed and manhandled, but I wasn't really thinking about that. I was trying to take in that something impossible had happened to me. When the police and the stewards got the crowds back, someone had stolen my England cap. An announcement was made over the tannoy asking for it back. By now the Aussies were sitting down on the outfield, waiting for the game to start again. Someone on the Western Terrace handed my cap back to a policeman, who gave it to David Hookes, who passed it back to me and shook my hand. All the while, the cheering just went on and on, and I was trying to make sense of it all.

At the close, the crowd thronged around the players' balcony. Someone handed me a glass of champagne, and I was interviewed on television by Peter West. I still had my bat under my arm.

'It's a miracle really,' I told him. 'I didn't believe it could happen, but it has. I would like to have done it here more than anywhere.'

That evening, I wanted to share my magical moment with friends. I telephoned Michael Parkinson, and then Brian Clough. Brian's wife Barbara said he was at a board meeting and he had arrived late. He'd rung the Nottingham Forest chairman and told him, 'Start without me, I'm watching my mate make history on TV...'

Next day, the idea was to get as big a total as we could and keep the Australian players in the field as long as possible. Tired legs often become tired minds, and by tea time you could see the fielding side were flagging. Mike's instructions at the interval were, 'Get what you can for 20 minutes or so and then we'll have a good go at their batsmen tonight.'

I was last out, caught at slip for 191. By close of play, Australia had lost five top batsmen for only 67 and the match was effectively won. There was no coming back from that position and it was just a matter of playing out the game for a huge England win by an innings and 85 runs. After everything that had happened, these were some of the happiest and most satisfying moments of my life.

**191** and **DNB**

\* \* \*

*While you are batting for England, Yorkshire lose County Championship games against Sussex and Worcestershire, but this time there is no meeting to be summoned to, no complaints from Mel Ryan or anyone else. No committee on your back like a sack of coal... They're too busy drinking champagne at Headingley, happy to fawn over you, let some of that lovely success rub off on them, bathing in all that reflected glory.*

* * *

## Fifth Test, England versus Australia, The Oval, London, 25-30 August, 1977

*Sixty-sixth cap*

England had won the series convincingly 3-0, the Ashes were regained, and after the emotions of Headingley it was inevitable that some of the sense of occasion had gone. This was compounded by the endless coverage of Packer cricket, which would be starting in the winter. There had been relentless media stories as to how it would work and which players had signed up. It was such a huge story, with our media chasing new developments and information every day, so that this game became less important than a normal Ashes Test. Almost half of the players were contracted to Packer and no-one knew what would happen once the summer was over.

The first day was a wash-out, and as the teams sat in the dressing rooms watching the rain come down, I got the feeling that some of the players on both sides wanted to get it over with, get off home and take stock before the next chapter of their lives unfolded.

England won the toss and the covers had done their job. The pitch was dry. Mike Brearley and I put on 86 before we were dismissed for 39 apiece. I played forward to swing bowler Mick Malone, the ball nipped back a touch onto my pad and lobbed over the stumps behind me, where Rod Marsh ran forward and caught it. He and his mates as usual went up with a strong appeal. I didn't think I'd hit it, in fact I am sure I didn't, but the umpire disagreed. I was Mick Malone's first Test wicket.

Graham Roope scored 38 but the rest of our batting capitulated, and we were saved from embarrassment by our last three wickets surprising us – and themselves – by adding 84 priceless runs. Derek Underwood, Mike Hendrick and Bob Willis were amongst the weakest tail-end batsmen you could see, and their statistics don't lie. They were terrific, but 214 all out was poor.

David Hookes, who got 85, and Rod Marsh, with 57, played really well, and what hurt us most was their tail-enders doing to us what ours had done to them, but doing it bigger and better. That got Australia's total up to 385, and a very useful lead of 171 put them in a strong position to win the match. Unfortunately for them, more rain came and took three sessions out of the game.

As we got showered and changed, it was a bit strange looking around knowing that Tony Greig, Alan Knott, Dennis Amiss and Derek Underwood would not be touring with England. The thought did cross my mind, would we ever play together again?

**39** and **25 not out**

\* \* \*

*There should be time to think, to take it all in, to understand what has happened, but there isn't because the Packer thing is coming to a head. Kerry is running rings around everyone. He recruits Richie Benaud as his consultant. He makes it clear that the organisation he has named World Series Cricket is very far from a circus.*

*All summer long, he engages in a war of claim and counter-claim, the drip… drip… drip… of information and rumour. The Australian team divides into Packer and non-Packer camps. Allegiances form and reform. Kerry and Richie meet the ICC at Lord's. Kerry walks out when he realises that the ICC cannot hand him the Australian TV rights that he wants.*

*It is war, the Packer War. The Cricket War. Kerry spins it as a revolution for the players. Cut adrift from the England captaincy, feeling which way the wind is blowing, Tony Greig begins to lash out.*

*Tony tells Private Eye magazine that you went to his house back in May, when Sussex played Yorkshire. He says that you waited for him to get home and then begged him to call Kerry on your behalf, but Kerry didn't want to know.*

*You wonder what the hell is going on with Tony, why is he telling lies.*

182

*The ICC acts, stripping Kerry Packer's matches of first-class status and banning its players from Test cricket after 1 October 1977. Some of the players wobble. Jeff Thomson and Alvin Kallicharran hold binding contracts with a Queensland radio station that require them to play for the State side. Thomson's manager David Lord extracts the pair from their Packer deals.*

*But contracts and deals are Kerry's thing. He obtains an injunction banning third parties from inducing his players to break their contracts. He uses his money and power to take the TCCB and the ICC to the high court. He backs Tony Greig, John Snow and Mike Procter in a legal challenge.*

*The TCCB ask you to give evidence on their behalf. You almost fall over. You tell them that you are not used to being one of the good guys. When Tony Greig hears the news, he telephones you and says, 'How the hell have you got involved in this... We'll have to find some mud to sling at you...'*

*The day before you testify, you go to the Sports Fair in Birmingham to appear for Slazenger. Tony is there for Saint Peter. He tells you again he'll have to find something to have a go at you with in court. He does not mention the Private Eye story. You both know why, too... because Tony made it up...*

*Doug Insole accompanies you to the High Court. Before you take the stand, Mr Justice Slade is apprised of Tony's remarks to you. He rules them jocular and satisfies legal dignity with a warning. You are examined by Michael Kempster QC for the ICC and TCCB, and cross-examined by Robert Alexander QC for Kerry Packer.*

*You're on the stand for four hours. The press loves you. Henry Blofeld writes that you are 'impressive and entertaining'. You are fluent and funny and sure of your arguments. You prove the best witness that the TCCB can produce. Even Deadly Doug can see the irony in that...*

*Mr Justice Slade rules in favour of Kerry. The ICC and TCCB incur costs of £200,000. And the whole thing seems pointless anyway because Mr Justice Slade decides that the selectors retain the right to choose whomsoever they wish on the basis of 'form and team spirit', qualities that are so subjective as to be impossible to define.*

*There is no time to think about it, though. No time because the decision is handed down on the day that England fly to Pakistan for the winter tour, with you as vice-captain...*

*No time to think about anything else, either. No time to think about the Yorkshire Committee member Don Brennan, who, at the end of the season, calls for you to be sacked as captain...*

*No time to think about the Reform Group that the Yorkshire CCC members form to defend you. No time to think about a year that began with you unavailable for England and ended with you as a national hero and spokesman for the Establishment.*

*There is no time to think, because in the middle of all of this, the doctors tell your mum that she has cancer.*

*The England party flies to Pakistan. You are vice-captain to Mike Brearley, but get no say in selection. You score a couple of hundreds in the warm-up games and take a trip through the Khyber Pass, where you are scared half to death as the driver takes you on narrow roads chiselled from the mountain, with no guardrails between you and the precipitous drops.*

\* \* \*

## First Test, Pakistan versus England, Gaddafi Stadium, Lahore, 14-19 December, 1977

### *Sixty-seventh cap*

At this time of year, the further north you go in Pakistan, the more dew there is in the mornings. There is no chance of net practice, because after only a few deliveries the ball gets so wet it's like trying to grip a bar of soap. A knock up on the outfield is often impossible, and if you try, you finish up with your bat covered in red dye from the ball. Play rarely starts on time because of the dew, and darkness comes early, so you may get as little a five hours' playing time. It can be hard to get results.

The pitch was dry, rolled mud with not a blade of grass anywhere. The new ball went through okay, but as soon as it lost its shine and hardness, it was very slow and low. Hard to score, but not hard to stay in. We couldn't get them out and they couldn't hit us around. An uninteresting stalemate.

At the end of the first day, Pakistan were 164 for two, and by the end of the second, they had crawled to 360 for five. Mudassar Nazar took nine-and-a-half hours for his 114, the slowest hundred in Test history – Doug Insole would have had a field day with that one!

There was a bit of drama at the end of the Pakistan innings when off-spinner Geoff Cope, in his debut Test, could, and probably should, have had a hat trick. He trapped Abdul Qadir leg before, then bowled Sarfraz first ball. Iqbal Qasim, a left-hander, edged the hat-trick delivery, and Mike Brearley, diving forward from first slip, scooped it up. Mike said immediately that he wasn't sure if it had bounced. I thought he caught it fairly but I was 30 yards away, and if the catcher isn't sure then how can the umpire give him out?

I batted a long time for 63 and Geoff Miller made his highest score ever in Test cricket, 98. All our players struggled. Guys daren't play back because of the low bounce, and that took away 40 per cent of the chances to score. Cracks like crazy paving appeared in the pitch and we had a couple of crowd demonstrations. I was told they had nothing to do with the cricket, but I couldn't understand the writing on their banners. The match was an inevitable and tedious draw – even Derek Randall had a bowl in the Pakistan second innings...

**63** and **DNB**

\* \* \*

*1977 has one last twist for you Mike Brearley decides he will sit out the second ODI at Sialkot, and so a year that began with you in exile ends with you captaining England for the first time. On the way the bus breaks down and you are asked to get out and push it but when it finally restarts your tour manager Kenny Barrington gets covered in soot from the exhaust. You arrive very late at the official reception to find all the food gone, and then get to the hotel, which is freezing cold. There are no locks on the door but you all have an armed soldier guarding your room. It is so cold that you wear your two cricket sweaters and put your thick wool cricket socks over your hands and feet. Tired, hungry and desperate for sleep, the light above your head won't go off. Your room attendant wraps some cloth around the lightbulb and when you finally get to sleep, the burning rag lands on you and almost sets the bed on fire. You shout for help and the attendant runs in and throws a pitcher full of water over the flames. You lie fitfully on your wet bed only to be woken up at 5.30am by the Mullah calling all to prayer with his megaphone.*

*This is how England's latest captain begins his first game in charge... But you win the toss and on a substandard pitch, England bowl Pakistan out for 151 and edge home by six wickets.*

*You do not bat.*

# CHAPTER THIRTEEN

# 1978

### Second Test, Pakistan versus England, Niaz Stadium, Hyderabad, 2-7 January, 1978

*Sixty-eighth cap*

The pitch was more dried, rolled mud. There was some nice grass on the square, but the majority of the outfield had only a sprinkling of grass, and any kind of breeze blew soil and dirt around like a sand storm. I had a problem fielding on the boundary with grit getting under my contact lenses, and I got sick as well, a general malaise of tiredness and lack of energy. When play finished each day and a bus took us back to our hotel, I just flopped on the bed. Our physio Bernard Thomas helped me undress, and after a shower, I got into bed and stayed there. I couldn't eat anything except for some chocolate I had brought with me from England, with cups of tea and as much sleep as I could get.

Pakistan took a day and a half over 275 all out. When we replied, I was batting really well when Derek Randall came in at number four. I'd pushed a ball towards square midwicket when he gave me a 'Yes... No... Bad luck Fiery!' We did a quickstep in the middle of the pitch, and I was left stranded. I'd made 79 and was fancying a hundred, but I couldn't complain after Nottingham.

The much bigger problem for England was the wrist-spinner Abdul Qadir. I played him with some ease, but as soon as I was out he cleaned up our batting, taking 6-46 and shooting us out for 191. Our guys didn't read him and after I had gone, we only scraped another 50-odd runs. Pakistan had an 84-run lead and the opportunity to get quick runs and see if Abdul could spin them to victory. But they batted with no urgency and meandered to a declaration, leaving England with just over a day to score 344, or realistically to bat all day for the draw.

On the evidence of the first innings, the key contest would be my battle with Qadir. He was new to Test match cricket, but I felt the kid was good, and so I got my bit of gamesmanship in early. No swearing or abuse, but I wanted him to know that I had confidence in my ability to read his variations and play him properly. I told him that he wouldn't get me out, and what's more, I wouldn't be using my pad to kick the ball away either.

Abdul smiled and nodded as if he didn't believe me. He was a tremendous sight, playing in his plimsolls and coming in with a great rush of energy, bouncing around and bowling with a good, strong action that put plenty of spin and dip on the ball. Mike Brearley and I dug in and played well, adding 185 for the first wicket, a lot of them against Qadir and the slow left-armer Iqbal Qasim.

Growing frustrated, Abdul went around the wicket to try and spin the ball across me from the bowler's footmarks. As he was going to pitch outside my leg stump, I wanted to shoulder arms and stand in front of the stumps playing no shot, but it was vital the umpire knew the Law. If the ball pitches outside leg stump and is going on to hit the stumps, a batsman shouldn't be given out lbw. I made sure that the umpire confirmed to me that he knew absolutely what the Law was, and then I frustrated Abdul some more by padding him away.

The same umpire let Mike claim the extra half hour to allow me to complete an unbeaten century before we called the match off for another draw.

**79** and **100 not out**

\* \* \*

*You fly to Lahore for the final ODI, another terrible pitch and this time you open the batting, but Pakistan win.*

*Then it happens...*

*You fly to Karachi for the third Test. There's a warm-up game against Sind at the Gymkhana. You and Mike open, and Sikander Bakht gets one to jump at Mike. The ball breaks his left forearm. Your head is in that much of a spin you lose all track of the game, can't even remember being out stumped for five runs, can't remember anything about it at all, because all you can think is that you are now captain of England...*

*You have four days to prepare. As you do, head still spinning, Kerry Packer allows Imran Khan, Mushtaq Mohammad and Zaheer*

*Abbas, three of Pakistan's greatest players, to fly back from World Series Cricket in Australia to be available for selection for Pakistan. It is a political move, designed to gain favour with the Pakistan Cricket Board, and it seems to be working...*

*As he prepares to fly home and with his arm in plaster, Mike Brearley chairs a meeting of the England team, who make it clear that they will refuse to play if the Packer trio are selected for Pakistan. When Mike arrives in England he informs the TCCB of the players' feelings. Soon there are telegrams arriving from the TCCB, telling you and Ken Barrington to be available on the telephone. Doug Insole, the new Chairman of the TCCB, the same Doug Insole that humiliated you and left a stigma attached to your name, is on the other end of the line when it rings.*

*Doug Insole is worried. Doug Insole is afraid. Doug Insole is scared that the Pakistan Cricket Board will sue the TCCB for damages if the England players strike and the Test match does not go ahead.*

*'I implore you,' Doug Insole says, 'as a personal favour, persuade the players to play...'*

*You listen to Doug Insole. You think, 'How ironic that the man who dropped me for slow scoring is now asking for my help.' Instead you find Chris Old, John Lever, Bob Taylor and Ian Botham and bring them to the phone. You get Doug Insole to talk to them. You let Doug Insole hear how strongly they feel about the Packer players.*

*Doug Insole tries and fails to change their minds. He speaks to you again.*

*'You are their captain,' he says. 'Show some leadership. You can carry the team with you.'*

*You do show some leadership. You tell Doug Insole that the TCCB should send a telegram to the players instructing them to play, and another to the Pakistan Cricket Board telling them that the players have been instructed to go ahead with the Test match, but they will not play if the Packer players are selected. This will cover the TCCB legally. Doug Insole listens to what you say and sends the telegrams.*

*From Sydney, Tony Greig writes a newspaper article that says, 'the threatened strike is the work of Geoff Boycott and his cronies.' He writes that, 'Boycott has the uncanny knack of being where the fast bowlers aren't.'*

*Within a week, Tony Greig has been stripped of the captaincy of Sussex.*

*Just days before the third Test is due to begin, Mr Mohammad Hussain, President of the PCB, announces that Imran, Zaheer and Mushtaq will not play.*

*You go to the hotel. You eat. You go to bed. You think about the Pakistan bowlers. You go to sleep. You do not dream of cricket. You wake up as the captain of England...*

\* \* \*

### Third Test, Pakistan versus England, National Stadium, Karachi, 18-23 January, 1978

*Sixty-ninth cap*

I won the toss and batted on another bone-dry pitch, a pitch I knew was bound to crack as the match progressed. I was bowled by Iqbal Qasim with an absolute beauty that I swear pitched leg stump and clipped the top of off. Years later, I would commentate for TV with one of Pakistan's best batsmen, Ramiz Raja. We became good friends and he loved to tease me about this magic ball that left me speechless at the crease.

It was another war of attrition. By the time both sides had batted once, three-and-a-half days of the game were gone. During our 266, the Pakistan spinners Qasim and Qadir bowled 80 overs, and during their 281, Geoff Cope, Geoff Miller and Phil Edmonds sent down 75.

Phil took seven wickets and bowled as well as I'd ever seen him bowl. He was a strong individual with his own mind. He rubbed Mike Brearley up the wrong way – they played together at Middlesex, as well as with England and were often butting heads – and although Phil could be an arrogant bugger, he respected me and he played for me.

The human limpet Mudassar sealed up one end, and the cricket can't have been great entertainment for the spectators. Even in my first match as captain, it wasn't much fun to play in. As I'd guessed, huge cracks appeared by the time we batted again, and the match fizzled out to another draw. I scored 56, but to be honest, we were all glad the series was over. Three matches, three bore draws.

While we were in Karachi, the team were introduced to the British Prime Minister Jim Callaghan. When he asked me if there was anything we wanted, like some beer, I said a couple of cases of wine would go down well. He promised to look into it, and shortly afterwards two cases of wine arrived. Kenny Barrington got his knickers in a twist, saying the British Ambassador was miffed because he was supposed to look after us and I'd made it look like his staff were falling down on the job! Ken was the sort of guy who could get nervous and jumpy over his own shadow.

I said, 'Ken, the PM asked me. I didn't proposition him…'

**31** and **56**

\* \* \*

*General Zia Ul-Haq, the head of Pakistan's military junta, comes to watch the game in Karachi. He invites you and Wasim Bari for tea after play. You put on your England blazer and get into the limo that Zia sends. It takes you to his official residence, where the General asks you about Kerry Packer.*

*He listens, then tells you about his meeting with Mushtaq Mohammad.*

*He says, 'I asked Mushtaq: 'Why did you not make yourself available to play for Pakistan and instead play for Kerry Packer?'*

*'And Mushtaq does not reply…*

*'So I say to him, why should I allow you to play now?'*

*You smile at this. You understand now who had the final word on whether the Packer players would appear for Pakistan.*

*Maybe General Zia could come and run Yorkshire cricket…*

*You fly from Pakistan to New Zealand for a three Test series. New Zealand have not beaten England for 46 years. You get six innings before the Tests begin and make only 124 runs. You retreat a little deeper into yourself, that place that fears failure, hates and fears it, keeps it at bay by eliminating risk…*

\* \* \*

## First Test, New Zealand versus England, Basin Reserve, Wellington, 10-15 February, 1978

### *Seventieth cap*

Our bowling was strong and our batting weak. We had Bob Willis, Mike Hendrick, Chris Old and a talented all-rounder in the 22-year-old Ian Botham, so as skipper I had some proper firepower. I won the toss and put them into bat on a juicy, green pitch and a gale force wind. First ball from Bob Willis leapt up at new boy John Wright, gloved him and flew through for a straightforward catch to Bob Taylor. John stood his ground and the New Zealand umpire gave him not out. Unbelievable decision, as the gloves were up and away from the body so it had to be out. On a stop-start day full of rain and bad light, he shored up one end and was 55 not out at the close of play. That decision stopped us getting at their middle order with a new ball when the conditions and the pitch were most in our favour. In my view, it cost us the match.

Later, when John came to England to play for Derbyshire, he would sometimes ask my advice about his batting. We became good friends, so one day I asked him why he didn't walk in Wellington. He admitted he was out but said, 'I couldn't. It was my first Test match and getting nought first ball would have been terrible...'

The wind was so strong and blew straight down the pitch, making bowlers with the wind a yard faster and causing those against it to have to toil hard. Our seamers were magnificent and gave up very little to hit, but the wickets wouldn't fall. Graham Roope dropped a straightforward slip catch and up till then, I had never seen him miss one for Surrey or England. The batsmen played and missed so often that we began to believe they weren't good enough to nick the many, many good balls bowled.

After a day and a half of hard labour, Chris Old had the tremendous figures of 6-54, having bowled almost 30 overs into that wind. At times, Chris could be a hypochondriac. He'd come up with all sorts of niggles, strains, soreness, an upset tummy or whatever else may be bothering him, but if you could get him on the park, he was a fine bowler.

When we went in, I was doing a John Wright, shoring up one end with 77 until I nicked big left-arm fast bowler Dick Collinge to slip.

Richard Hadlee and Collinge, alternating with the wind, were very fast and very nasty to face. Graham Roope stuck it out for 37, but the pace and hostility were too much for many of our guys and we slipped away to 215 all out. A deficit of just 13 made it essentially a one innings match, but this time, we had to bat last and the conditions were awful.

We got the first part done, ripping through New Zealand's second innings, Bob Willis bowling very fast indeed and taking 5-32. That left us 137 to win, and if every time you put a side into bat you only required 137 to win a Test, you would take it wouldn't you? Yes, the conditions were tough and it was still blowing a gale, but we fancied our chances!

Well it didn't go to plan. The wind was getting even stronger and batting was a test of determination, mental resolve, guts, fight, character and technique. I can say with all honesty it was as testing as anything I have ever faced. Dick Collinge bowled me off my pads with a quick, full one, and then Brian Rose, my opening partner, got hit on the arm and had to retire hurt. Collinge did for Geoff Miller and Derek Randall, and then Richard Hadlee polished off the rest. It was a procession, all done in 28 overs.

England all out 64, and New Zealand had won a historic victory by the comfortable margin of 72 runs.

I was by now deeply concerned about our batting. I had inherited Mike Brearley's selection of players, and they wouldn't have been mine. Mike Gatting was only 20 years old and not yet ready for the big time. Brian Rose, Graham Roope and Geoff Miller were not my type. They were okay in good conditions, but if a team was in a tight situation I wanted batsmen like David Steele, Barry Wood, Peter Willey, Roger Tolchard or David Bairstow. Men who were not pretty or eye-catching, but who had fighting qualities, who would tough it out. An attitude of 'over my dead body.' Many people believe it is paramount to have wicket-taking bowlers because bowlers win matches. I don't totally agree with that. My belief is batsmen put you in a position to win so that bowlers can take the wickets. Without enough runs, your bowlers will fall short no matter how good they are.

I had wanted to have a go at captaining England, but I was beginning to think having someone else's team was a poisoned chalice.

 77 and 1

*You let the batsmen know what you think. You tell them they played like schoolkids. You give them the truth in plain language. Some of them like it and some of them don't. But that is you. You are harder on yourself than you are on any of them. You have waited a long time to captain England, but these are not your players. The players you really need are not here. The players you really need are not here because they are with Kerry Packer... Tony Greig. Alan Knott. Derek Underwood. Dennis Amiss...*

*You fly to the South Island, to Dunedin to play Otago. You order the batsmen to early nets, but they are sub-standard and it rocks their confidence even more as they play and miss, get bowled and caught and hit on the pads... They grumble and they groan... You battle as hard as you can to find your own form, the doubts and the fears gathering force, the divisions between you and your players beginning to open...*

*The team whisper you are obsessed with nets and practice.*

* * *

## Second Test, New Zealand versus England, Lancaster Park, Christchurch, 24 February – 1 March, 1978

*Seventy-first cap*

The pitch looked green and hard, ripe for bowling first. I won the toss. I was conscious our batting was flaky and had buckled under pressure in the fourth innings in Wellington. I had put NZ in to bat and we had lost. Dare I do it again? I was well versed in cricket history, and a fellow Yorkshireman, Len Hutton, had put Australia in to bat in the first Test at Brisbane in the 1954/55 series. Australia made 601 for eight declared and England lost by an innings and 154 runs. After that defeat Len said: 'If you think of putting a side in... think again and bat yourself...'

That swayed me. I decided to bat, knowing that early on New Zealand had two top-class fast bowlers in Hadlee and Collinge who could damage us. I told myself that the green grass and the new ball would be a handful, but it was a match over two innings not just that first morning.

It was the right decision, although it didn't look that way at 28-3, with me, Brian Rose and Derek Randall all back in the pavilion. If you'd told me right then that we'd still be batting at the end of day two I probably wouldn't have believed it, but Graham Roope steadied us with a fine fifty, and Geoff Miller, sent in up the order at number five, made 89. He took a blow to the face from Richard Hadlee, came off for treatment and went back out again – exactly the sort of fight I was looking for from our batsmen.

Then came Botham. Ian had contracted dysentery in Pakistan and hadn't played a Test on that leg of the tour, but now he showed for the first time what he could do with the bat. He was not out 20-odd overnight, and next day went on to a splendid maiden century in just his fifth Test knock. He dragged Bob Taylor and Phil Edmonds along with him, Bob making 45 and Phil, who thought he could bat but whose record showed he couldn't, a fast and entertaining 50. Not before time, 418 was a first innings score we could work with.

Having starred with the bat, Botham and Edmonds got stuck in with the ball. Only the opening bat Robert Anderson, who got 62, looked at ease. Then there was that strokeless limpet John Parker. He'd put his front foot inches forward, hide his bat behind his pad and kick everything until an easy ball appeared. The modern day DRS would have had a party with him! He got away with frustrating our bowlers to the point where we just had to shake our heads and laugh. It was ridiculous how he was never given out lbw. He was 53 not out by the time we bowled them out for 235. We just missed making them follow on, but a lead of 183 was substantial. Botham finished with five, Phil Edmonds with four.

There were just over four sessions remaining in the game, time enough to set New Zealand a target and bowl them out. But that fourth evening saw two very different run-outs, and both would go down in cricket folklore...

First, Derek Randall was dismissed while backing up at the non-striker's end by the bowler Ewen Chatfield. It was only the third instance in Test match cricket of a batsman out in this manner (a Mankading as they call it, after Vinoo Mankad, who ran Bill Brown out while backing up during India's tour of Australia in 1947–48).

Most cricketers back then saw it as against the spirit of the game. In a tight run chase, emotions can get high if the non-striker batsman is backing up a bit too early for the bowler's liking, and words could be exchanged.

Even so, if a bowler felt that the batsman was taking an unfair advantage, the custom was to offer a warning, or have a few words with the umpire. Derek said that Chatfield did no such thing, he just broke the wickets with Randall out of his ground. Now Derek was an extrovert. He would talk to himself, fidget, pull at his kit and jump around like Pinocchio on those strings, and I suppose his mannerisms could get under bowlers' skin. But he was also the most loveable guy you could ever meet. There was no malice in him, no gamesmanship, just someone having fun playing the game. To run him out was not good for cricket, not great on Chatfield's record, and I hope Ewen came to regret doing it.

The second dismissal was mine, and it's a story that has grown taller and taller as the years pass. I was on 26 and not finding batting easy when Ian Botham came in and after a few overs, ran me out. He tried to hit through the covers, but the ball slipped off the face of the bat towards a fielder at backward point. I was backing up and it was my call. I was trying to tell him 'NO!' yet Ian came thundering down the pitch towards me.

I was stood a few yards out of my crease, perplexed by the stupidity of the run, when the fielder threw the ball to the keeper who broke the stumps at the far end. Ian was past me in a flash. Some of the fielders reckoned we hadn't crossed when the wickets were broken and went to the umpire to say Ian should be the one given out, but before it got messy, I walked off to the pavilion.

Ian would claim later that he had run me out deliberately, egged on by Bob Willis and some of the others, as I hadn't been scoring quickly enough.

All I can say is if he did run me out on purpose, shame on him.

Next morning, I declared and set New Zealand 280 to win. More realistically, we had a full day to bowl them out and level the series. Bob Willis bowled very fast and got rid of John Wright for nought. Chris Old got Geoff Howarth for one, and we had a perfect start at 14-2.

Then Big Bob and I had trouble with the home umpire, Fred Goodall. He started no-balling Bob, so I went to stand at mid-off to see for myself how far over the line he was. If a fast bowler starts to worry about where he is putting his front foot instead of concentrating on his pace and where he is aiming, it often affects his confidence and his bowling suffers.

Sure enough Fred no-balled him again, but I couldn't see anything illegal. Bob was mystified too, so I asked Fred what Bob was doing wrong. He wouldn't answer and turned his back on me.

I said, 'As captain, surely I am allowed to ask you in a reasonable manner?'

It was a stand-off between an intractable, unresponsive, officious umpire and a bowler and captain with no idea of what was wrong or how we might put it right. He wouldn't speak to us and we wouldn't bowl until we knew what was wrong. Fred Goodall was the worst umpire I have ever seen. His decision-making was poor and his attitude appalling. Big Bob was in the zone and bowling fast, and this tight-lipped stubbornness by the umpire just made him madder.

Bob said to him, 'Right, I'll bowl around the wicket.'

I said to Bob, 'You just bowl fast. We can live with the odd no ball – let's just hope it's not a wicket ball.'

Bob stormed off to take his anger out on the opposition batsmen. He hit their captain Mark Burgess on the left elbow, and he had to retire hurt, then he bowled Robert Anderson for 15. Nobody needed to talk or say anything now, as Bob was in the zone and menacing as hell.

He had Bev Congdon caught at slip for nought and bowled the keeper Warren Lees for nought, too. When fast bowlers are roaring in, it's a fantastic sight – if you are not the one receiving the thunderbolts… In six overs Bob destroyed New Zealand, taking four wickets for five runs and putting Burgess out of action.

The scoreboard read 25-5 and game over. What a sensational passage of play. Richard Hadlee played a few shots to make the New Zealand total look a bit better. Ian Botham and Phil Edmonds took two wickets each, and in the end we were thrilled to have bowled them out for 105 to win by a whopping 174 runs.

**8** and **26**

* * *

*The story that Ian Botham tells, the story that grows and grows, the story that follows you around for years to come, goes like this:*

*You are batting, and when Derek Randall is out, Ian comes in at number four, promoted up the order by your vice-captain, Bob Willis. Bob tells Ian, 'Go and run that bugger out...'*

*You bat together for 20 minutes. You tell Ian that you are struggling. He tells you not to worry and then he runs you out.*

*'What have you done, what have you done?' you say to him.*

*'I've run you out, you cunt,' he replies...*

*Phil Edmonds says that you sat with a towel over your head and didn't speak. He says that when he asks you, 'What are we doing now,' you snap back, 'you and Willis are in charge of this tour... You work it out.'*

*Bob Willis says that you delay the declaration and don't give him time to warm up. Bob thinks you are too scared of being beaten. Kenny Barrington is flustered by your plain speaking. You have dreamed of the captaincy. You have fought for it, worked for it, cherished the thought of it, but now that you have it, it is not like you thought it would be... It is not like that at all...*

\* \* \*

## Third Test, New Zealand versus England, Eden Park, Auckland, 4-10 March, 1978

*Seventy-second cap*

Maybe it was a bad omen, but we, the England cricket team, were having net practice at the stadium a few days before the game when we were turfed out by the Auckland CC club side, who said that they needed them and we had to go! That summed up the practice facilities supposedly organised by the New Zealand cricket authorities.

Because there wasn't an outright series winner, we had to endure another six-day Test match. The pitch was so slow we could easily have played a timeless Test, let alone six days. We thought the pitch might have been specially prepared to nullify our quality seamers, but we had no way of proving that.

New Zealand won the toss and batted for almost two days. We found it impossible to get Geoff Howarth off his front foot. A tall man with a good stride forward, he was always comfortable. We wanted to rough him up with short stuff, disrupt his rhythm, but the slow pace and lack of bounce made it impossible. He controlled their innings with 122, and a half-century from the skipper saw them past 300.

By the time Clive Radley had made 158 in nine hours of patience and concentration, and we'd got a lead of 114, we were halfway through the fifth day! Geoff Howarth got on his front foot again, comfortable that the umpires were never going to give him out. He completed another century to achieve that special distinction of scoring a hundred in each innings of a Test match. Whatever the pitch, it was the same for all us batsmen, and Geoff was the one to do something very special. A remarkable achievement he should be proud of.

I couldn't field in the second innings as one of my contact lenses got some grit underneath it and scratched my cornea. I had to sit in the stand and watch with a patch over one eye like a pirate. Not able to see properly and take my place on the field just about summed up my four matches as captain of England...

At the end of the tour, the Chairman of New Zealand Cricket, Walter Hadlee, father of Richard, asked to sit with me. We spoke about New Zealand cricket and some of its challenges. I told him umpiring was a problem. The impression we had was that decisions favoured the home team. I wasn't sure whether that was because the umpires were nervous about giving well-known home players out, or because they couldn't handle the pressure. I felt that asking some leading international umpires to come and hold seminars and even stand in matches would be a step forward.

Two years later, when West Indies toured New Zealand, Michael Holding kicked over the batsman's stumps at Dunedin and Colin Croft deliberately knocked over the umpire at Christchurch as he was about to bowl. The situation got so bad that the West Indies team failed to take the field after tea on the third day of the game at Christchurch. All to do with unfair and biased umpiring, particularly by Fred Goodall. It could have been avoided, but presumably the New Zealand Cricket Board listened to my views yet didn't want to hear them. What was the point in asking?

54 and DNB

*You fly home from the wind and rain of New Zealand to the wind and rain of England. Fly home to find your mum getting worse. You go to see her doctors and tell them that you will do anything in your power, spend any amount of money, to get her well, but the doctor tells you, 'Geoff, all the money in the world cannot cure this…'*

*She is always on your mind, always in your thoughts as the season of 1978 unwinds.*

*The worst months of your life start now…*

*The Yorkshire committee re-elect you as captain, and then a month later appoint Raymond Illingworth as Manager, effective 1 April 1979 once Ray has played his final summer for Leicestershire. The club announce that they look forward to Raymond and you working together in due course.*

*As the new season begins, the papers are full of your name. The papers are stirring it up, making out that you may be retained as captain of England even though Mike Brearley has recovered from his broken arm.*

*You tell them that England have a captain and you get on with your batting. Yorkshire play Warwickshire at Edgbaston in the first Championship match of the season and lose, but you score 115. Alec Bedser comes to see you during the game to tell you that Mike has been reappointed for the first three Tests of the summer against Pakistan. He is not quite ready for the two-match ODI series that precedes the Tests, so you will be captain for those.*

*You play Oxford University in the Parks and a student named Steve Wookey gets you caught and bowled for a duck, and next morning the newspapers are full of your name again, even though Jim Love and Richard Lumb make centuries. You lead England in the ODI at Old Trafford and win easily, but you damage your thumb while batting and can't play again until the third week of June.*

*John Hampshire captains Yorkshire to wins over Worcestershire and Ray Illingworth's Leicestershire, and then a two-day victory in the Roses match. During the Leicester game, Ray Illingworth takes John Hampshire out to dinner. The whispers begin again, whispers that Ray Illingworth would like John Hampshire as his captain next season, whispers that the Yorkshire players would like John Hampshire as their captain next season.*

*When you come back, you make hundreds against Northamptonshire, the New Zealand tourists and Glamorgan, but your thumb is still killing you, and your feel and fluency are missing. You're not batting, you're surviving.*

*At Northampton, your 113 takes 90 overs and once you are out, John Hampshire stages a bizarre go-slow, making 11 runs in the final ten overs of the innings and refusing to chase the final batting bonus point.*

*Yorkshire President Kenneth Parkinson, who was at the match, calls it, 'one of the worst days of my life' and says John Hampshire should be sacked. But he does not have the power to sack John Hampshire...*

*John Hampshire is not disciplined for his go-slow.*

*Your mum gets worse. You worry. Your thumb won't get better. You worry.*

*You worry about the Yorkshire captaincy, about Ray Illingworth and John Hampshire, about your England place.*

*Mike Brearley leads the team to two easy wins over Pakistan and another over New Zealand. But Mike is not scoring any runs. The selectors worry about that. They worry about you, too, worry about your thumb and your form, don't select you until the second Test against New Zealand, when they drop Mike Brearley down the batting order.*

\* \* \*

### Second Test, England versus New Zealand, Trent Bridge, Nottingham, 10-14 August, 1978

*Seventy-third cap*

The selectors wanted to appoint Michael Brearley as captain for the winter tour to Australia but opening the batting that summer, his scores were 38, 2 and 0 against Pakistan and 2 and 11 against New Zealand. To announce him as captain having made 53 runs in five innings would have been embarrassing. Opening at Test match level put his technique under a strong examination, and flaws he could sometimes get away with at Middlesex were exposed by better bowlers with a new ball.

My opinion was that Michael played too far in front of his pad in a firm manner. His hands went at the ball too hard and he was not able to manoeuvre. Once a batsman is exposed that far in front of his pad, he doesn't have full control of the bat. Under your eyes and close to the pad with softer hands is best.

The selectors had a very serious problem because he was a brilliant captain, a clear thinker, tough underneath, but calm and understanding. To solve the dilemma, Graham Roope had to be dropped and Brearley shuffled down the order.

Mike won the toss and batted. A good, firm pitch with pace and carry but a bit of awkward movement early on. Richard Hadlee was a great fast bowler and didn't need much to make him a handful. He was quite sharp, if not express pace, with amazing control. For me, he was the best line bowler I ever batted against, probing off stump with out-swing and in-swing plus movement off the seam. He had this wonderful, easy, fluid action that seemed to take very little out of him as it unfurled. Playing defensively early on I edged an outswinger, but because I played with relaxed hands, it went fast and low. Geoff Howarth got one hand to it, and if it had stuck, the catch would have been a blinder. It didn't!

It was the first time Graham Gooch and I opened together, and it was a good omen as we put on 86 before Graham went for 55. Trent Bridge was kind to me once more, as I made 131. I'd just hooked Richard Hadlee for four when Lance Cairns, fielding at mid-off, said to Richard, 'Give him another, and put everything into it this time.' I fell for it and spliced it up in the air.

That meant Mike was able to come in to bat against the old ball with 300 on the board, and, to the relief of the selectors and himself, score 50 priceless runs. England were all out for 429, but more importantly, were able to announce Michael as captain for the winter tour of Australia.

New Zealand couldn't cope with the hostility of the England bowling and were all out for 120. Geoff Howarth got hit on the head and retired, only to come back later and be not out, a gutsy effort. Bob Willis and Ian Botham bowled with control and aggression and Mike Hendrick gave them nothing. Brearley enforced the follow on and they did a bit better, scoring 190, but they were no match for quality seamers in English conditions. We'd lost three hours to rain but the match was still all over in less than four days.

**131** and **DNB**

*  *  *

*You lead Yorkshire against Nottinghamshire at Scarborough and make 129 and 33, then leave for Lord's to play for England. John Hampshire goes to the Yorkshire committee to tell them that he has been offered the captaincy of Derbyshire, and he will take it if he is not captain of Yorkshire in 1979. He puts the Yorkshire committee under pressure. Ray Illingworth tells the Yorkshire Committee that he wants John Hampshire as his captain. He puts the Yorkshire Committee under pressure...*

*  *  *

### Third Test, England versus New Zealand, Lord's, London, 24-28 August, 1978

*Seventy-fourth cap*

A match that was turned on its head on the third evening showed just how strong our seam attack had become, especially at home, and even more so at Lord's with its slope and how it can change with the weather. And Ian Botham confirmed again what a player England had found.

New Zealand batted first and made 339, led by a Geoff Howarth century. Geoff played well, using everything he'd learned in his time in county cricket with Surrey. Botham grabbed six wickets. In reply, we were bowled out for 289, conceding a lead of 50.

Then came that third evening. Ian Botham and Bob Willis bowled fast and aggressive and New Zealand simply had no answer. The slope on the Lord's pitch gives seam bowlers something to work with, and if there is a bit of rain to liven up the pitch or some cloud overhead then batting can get tricky. All out 67, and another five for Botham, his first return of ten wickets in a match. Ian was so strong, with huge powerful shoulders, a big backside, a bigger heart, massive determination and great skill to make the ball swing. He could be quite sharp and very aggressive. In full flow he was a magnificent sight. He and Bob Willis had led the attack superbly all summer. Five of the six

Tests were won within four days, all down to the strength of our seam bowling.

**24** and **4**

\* \* \*

*The selectors name you in the party to tour Australia, but you will no longer be vice-captain. Mike has chosen Bob Willis instead. He and Bob have become close over the summer. Ian Botham, too. Thick as thieves, those three...*

*Your enemies at Yorkshire get braver. 'England don't want him as captain,' they whisper... 'And neither do we...' Yorkshire finish fourth in the County Championship. They lose in the group stage of the Benson & Hedges Cup. They lose in the quarter-final of the Gillette Cup. They finish seventh in the John Player Sunday League. There is still no trophy, still nothing for those committee men who live in the past and think they have a divine right to silverware.*

*Despite the thumb and the pain, despite the stress and the worry, despite the committee men plotting against you, despite John Hampshire and Raymond Illingworth, despite watching your mum get worse and not being able to do anything about it – especially despite that – you make 1,074 runs with five centuries and average 51. But John Hampshire scores 1,596 runs and averages 53, the first time in 16 years that you do not finish top of the Yorkshire averages.*

*You need a holiday, need to get away. Your mum tells you to go. 'Don't let the buggers get you down!' she says. You book a trip to Bermuda. The family rally around. You fly out and while you are there, your mum dies.*

*27 September, 1978. The worst day of your life.*

*These are the words that you will write in your book, Put To The Test, published a year later:*

*'We were very close, my mother and I, and I relied on her a lot. It is always a hard thing to lose a very special parent. If you are married and live away from home it is bad enough, but it is a dreadful experience to live with someone you love and see them deteriorate from week to week.'*

*You fly home immediately. You walk through the door to the ringing phone. It is Joe Lister, the Yorkshire Secretary, asking if you're coming to the committee meeting tomorrow. Still in shock, not thinking, you tell him, 'Yes'.*

*You walk into the committee room and without looking you in the eye, John Temple, Chairman of the Cricket Committee, sacks you as club captain. Joe Lister issues a statement. Mel Ryan rushes from the meeting to phone John Hampshire and ask for his official acceptance of the Yorkshire captaincy. Then they go to the pub... Don Brennan, Billy Sutcliffe, Harry McIlvenny... Go to the pub and toast your sacking... Drink to John Hampshire and to Yorkshire cricket without you as the captain... Go to the pub and leave you to bury your mum.*

*The funeral service is overrun by the press and the TV cameras. You and your brothers and the family struggle to get through them and into the church. Five days later, you appear as a guest on the Parkinson show. You tell Michael Parkinson: 'In their haste to sack me, they could not even wait for my mum to be buried.' You say of the Yorkshire committee: 'They are small-minded people, people who feel that they always know best, always feel that they are right.'*

*But you are a son of Yorkshire...*

*And the Yorkshire public have not forgotten you. They have not forgotten that they have the greatest batsman in the land, even if they no longer have the greatest team. They have not forgotten the three years of international cricket that you gave up to serve them. They have not forgotten Kerry Packer. They have not forgotten that your dad was a miner, that you live in a pit village, that you graft hard every single day, that you are one of them. They have not forgotten the letters that you write to the supporters who are ill and in hospital, the phone calls that you make to elderly fans, the times you let kids bowl at you in the nets, the thousand small acts of kindness that don't fit with your public image.*

*They have not forgotten.*

*You are them and they are you.*

*The Reform Group marshals their forces once more. The Reform Group wrap their arms around you. They tap into the Yorkshire public's feelings for you. They demand your reinstatement. The movement gathers pace.*

*You are still in a haze, in grief, in shock. The last thing you want to do is get on a plane to Australia. What you want to do is shut the door, shut out the world, come to terms with your losses, but you can't. You can't because you did not tour Australia last time, did not play for three years. Can't do that again, however much you want to, however much your brain screams at you...*

*So you fly to Australia with England captain Mike Brearley, vice-captain Bob Willis and tour manager Doug Insole.*

*When you land, Doug tells the players that this is the most important Ashes tour ever, because Kerry Packer's World Series Cricket will be taking place alongside it. 'Whether you like it or not, comparisons will be drawn,' he says. 'So use your heads, and don't put yourselves in an embarrassing position...'*

*Bob Willis warns you all about the Australian media, who are worse than the English lot...*

*You hear it but you don't hear it. Take it in but you don't take it in because all you can think about is the Yorkshire committee and the Yorkshire captaincy. About Raymond Illingworth and John Hampshire. About the one-year contract that you have been offered and the January deadline to accept it.*

*You think about the impossible. About leaving Yorkshire County Cricket Club.*

*Your home. Your birthright...*

*Round and round it goes in your head while you bat seven times in the warm-up games and score just 165 runs, all the while wanting to be anywhere else, anywhere else but here...*

\* \* \*

## First Test, Australia versus England, The Gabba, Brisbane, 1-6 December, 1978

### *Seventy-fifth cap*

Australia were in difficulties from the off. All their best batsmen had signed to Kerry Packer. Their new captain, Graham Yallop, told the Aussie papers that they would win the series 6-0. He was joking but they took him seriously.

Our fine seam bowlers cleaned them up for 116 in just 38 overs. Even the Brisbane humidity was barely enough to have us breaking sweat. We sailed past their total thanks to 75 from Derek Randall and a couple of 40s from David Gower and Ian Botham. Derek's whole game was based on confidence. When he didn't have it, he got himself into a terrible tangle of self-doubt and negative thoughts. Mike Brearley encouraged us, his team-mates, to keep telling him how good he was and to build him up into a positive frame of mind.

I was out for 13, caught at slip off the debutant fast bowler Rodney Hogg. He took 6-74 and looked a fine prospect, but a first innings lead of 170 was huge, and from there Australia were always up against it. They fought like hell, though. Kim Hughes was a good stroke-player and made a hundred full of quality shots, and the captain dug out a really gritty ton of his own.

It left us 170 to win. I was run out for 16 by Derek Randall who went on to score another 74 and see us home by seven wickets. Australia weren't going to win 6-0…

`13` and `16`

\* \* \*

## Second Test, Australia versus England, WACA, Perth, 15-20 December, 1978

*Seventy-sixth cap*

We played Western Australia in a warm-up and bowled them out for 52 and 78. We won easily, but I'd scored only four and 13. We were getting some poor to indifferent pitches to play on, which was unusual for a tour in Australia. If you are in good form and a good frame of mind it can be easier to deal with adverse batting conditions. When you're not thinking straight and not batting well, then indifferent or awkward batting surfaces become a nightmare, and I wasn't thinking straight at all.

For the Test, the WACA was a sea of rich, green grass and you don't see that very often in Australia. A grassy pitch meant plenty of movement for the seamers and a lush outfield meant it would be slow and hard to get full value for your strokes. It wasn't a surprise when Australia put us in to bat. Rodney Hogg had us at 5-2 in quick time, sending back Graham Gooch for one and Derek Randall for nought. Mike Brearley and I negated the new ball but it was hard work scoring runs, and that didn't change until Mike was out for 17 and David Gower came in.

David made the pitch look flat and the bowling easy. His timing was gorgeous and his shots easy on the eye, and while I struggled along at one end, David stroked a hundred in just over three-and-a-half hours. His touch and timing were beautiful to watch. I was so enamoured of his innings that at one of our middle conversations I actually said, 'I wish I could bat like you.' His innings won us the match.

I helped in a different way by sealing one end and scoring 77, but my innings took a long, long time. The former Australian captain Lindsay Hassett, a fine batsman himself, paid me a back-handed compliment when he called my seven hours of patience and concentration: 'an exceptional innings by someone who could not find the middle of the bat'. 309 all out was pretty good in the conditions, and Rodney Hogg took five more wickets for 65 runs.

We thought the Australians would get nowhere near us because we had top-class seamers just right for this pitch and we didn't rate most of their batsmen, and so it proved. Bob Willis took five wickets and we had a lead of 119. Not insurmountable, but if we didn't collapse in our second innings, we would win.

I was out lbw to Rodney Hogg again for 23. Graham Gooch went the same way for 43 and Derek Randall scored a positive 45. A total of 208 wasn't huge, but when you added our first innings lead, Australia required 328 to win. Scores and totals are relative to the surface you are playing on, and it would have taken an outstanding batting performance to get anywhere near three hundred. It took us 47 eight-ball overs to polish them off for a win by 166 runs.

77 and 23

* * *

*During your long vigil at the WACA, a telegram addressed to you arrives in the dressing room. It's from an Australian MP called Jack Birney. It says: 'You have done more harm to Australian cricket than the Boston Strangler did to the reputation of door-to-door salesmen.'*

*Even you have to smile at that one.*

*The year of 1978 ends with a flight to Sydney for more cricket, another Test match you do not want to play. Your mind is still elsewhere, still in Yorkshire.*

*The committee hold a special meeting in Harrogate, where the Reform Group put their case. You send a six-page letter outlining your position. The motions of no confidence in the committee and for your reinstatement as captain are defeated. You have one more month to accept their offer of a playing contract.*

# CHAPTER FOURTEEN

# 1979

*An endless series of groundhog days – hotel, ground, play, hotel, dinner, sleep, airport, flight, hotel, ground, play, hotel, dinner, sleep, ground, play, hotel, dinner – on and on, day after day, one blending into the other, your head not in the game, your mind elsewhere, your feet not moving, your bat with no middle, as Lindsay Hassett kindly pointed out...*

\* \* \*

## Third Test, Australia versus England, MCG, Melbourne, 29 December 1978 – 3 January 1979

### *Seventy-seventh cap*

The pitch looked awful and played awful. We were thinking, 'What happened to the normal hard, dry Aussie pitches with bounce?' This one had patchy green grass and bare, dark areas, so winning the toss would be a crucial factor. Our captain called wrong and Australia couldn't wait to bat first. Their players needed a bit of good fortune as the media and public were on their backs, not willing to accept defeat to the Poms. World Series Cricket was making it worse too, all of the star Australian players turning out for Kerry and competing for crowd attendances, TV viewers and newspaper coverage.

Graeme Wood, a tough left-handed opener, played the key innings, batting six hours on a pitch that was up and down to score a round hundred. Graham Yallop scrapped well alongside him, and a final total of 258 all out left us wondering what a good score was on a deck like this. It wasn't a surface we were looking forward to having a bat on!

Sure enough, Rodney Hogg had us three for two wickets before anyone could blink. He bowled me for one and got Mike Brearley lbw for one. Gooch, Gower and Botham all made 20s, but soon it was England all out 143, and Australia with a lead of 115. That is big on any surface, but on a result pitch which was deteriorating rapidly, it was probably worth double that. Rodney Hogg again finished with five wickets. What a find he was – only in the team because Lillee and Thomson were playing for Kerry Packer, but taking his chance and making himself a star almost overnight. He was pretty sharp and bowled very straight. He seamed the ball, and although he didn't try to swing it, if the new ball happened to do a bit in the air, it was a nice bonus. His biggest asset was that he made you play. You had to get forward because the ball kept low, but that was tricky because Hoggy had enough pace to make getting on the front foot difficult. He was very similar to the great Brian Statham of Lancashire and England who believed, 'If you miss, I hit…'

With the pitch getting worse, we were able to bowl Australia out again for just 167, our spinners John Emburey and Geoff Miller to the fore, but that left us chasing 283 to win. It would be the highest score of the Test match on a dire fourth day surface. Everyone in the dressing room was apprehensive, with good reason. We started badly, losing Brearley and Randall to Dymock and Hogg respectively, and that was our chances pretty much gone.

I grafted for 38 before I was lbw to a low ball from Alan Hurst. I would have been better off batting with a shovel instead of a bat. All out 179, and an Australian win by 103 runs. Rodney Hogg took 5-36, for a match analysis of 10-66. In three Tests, he had collected 27 wickets. Wow! Absolutely amazing.

 1 and 38

\* \* \*

## Fourth Test, Australia versus England, SCG, Sydney, 6-11 January, 1979

*Seventy-eighth cap*

The series was passing me by. I knew it, but I couldn't seem to do anything about it. My head wasn't right, and when you feel that way, you will not survive long at the highest levels of sport. It affects you physically as well as mentally. Your feet don't move as well, and you begin to question the way that you play. Objectively I knew what was happening, but I didn't have the mental strength or the willpower to pull myself out of it as I had done so many times before. At the top level it is all about dealing with adversity and being able to carry on.

Australia had got a foothold in the series with the win at Melbourne, and it took a terrific innings from Derek Randall to close the door on them once again. We batted first, got skittled for 152 and conceded a first innings lead of 142. It got a lot worse when I was out lbw first ball of our second innings to that man Rodney Hogg. It wasn't even a great delivery. It was his loosener that surprised me as I got forward too early and the ball just broke back in slow motion.

Fortunately, Mike Brearley played his best innings of the series, making 53. When Derek walked in to join Mike he was on a pair, but under some serious pressure he changed the course of the Test match. Every interval or drinks break, the priority was to keep encouraging him and telling him how well he was batting. It was vital to keep him buoyed up, confident and positive. It was swelteringly hot and took an enormous physical effort from him to bat on and on. He stayed for almost ten hours and made 150, an absolutely brilliant, ultimately match-winning innings.

It left Australia 205 to chase. This Aussie batting unit wasn't great and they buckled far too easily. It helped us that Rick Darling and Graeme Wood got in another tangle that ended with Wood being run out. They opened together in four Test matches and in each match one of them was run out. We got to calling them the Kamikaze Kids – they would go for suicide runs.

The only batsmen who looked good against our spinners was the young Allan Border, who added 45 not out to his unbeaten 60 in the first innings. Even at this early stage it was easy to admire his footwork, and he would become a great batsman all around the world against all types of bowling. Despite Allan's efforts, seven wickets for our spin twins Emburey and Miller gave us the win by 93 runs. We had retained the Ashes in Australia for the first time since Len Hutton's tour in 1954–55.

 8 and 0

* * *

*You fly to Tasmania for a three-day game against the State side. John Hampshire is in Hobart, coaching and playing, but you do not speak. John makes a duck and 46 not out. You make 90 not out, your highest score of the tour. As the deadline for your contract offer approaches, you send a telegram to the Yorkshire committee accepting their terms. It does not put your mind at rest. Nothing does, nothing can as the tour grinds on, this unloved, unwatched series just never seeming to end…*

\* \* \*

## Fifth Test, Australia versus England, Adelaide Oval, Adelaide, 27 January – 1 February, 1979

### *Seventy-ninth cap*

Another day, another Test, another failure for me, and our team bowled out quickly once again. It was a crazy batting series. This time we were 27-5 before anyone could blink. I nicked off to slip from the bowling of Alan Hurst, out for six. Ian Botham mounted a rescue job with 74, but we were all out by tea for 169.

Before Australia had a run on the board, Bob Willis hit Rick Darling under the heart and he collapsed at the crease. He'd swallowed his tongue and his chewing gum got stuck in his throat as he blacked out. Rick was lucky that John Emburey thumped him on the chest to clear his airway, and the umpire Max O'Connell gave him mouth-to-mouth resuscitation. He was carried off unconscious on a stretcher.

Maybe that incident shook up the Aussie dressing room, or perhaps they would have succumbed again anyway. We were a very good pressure bowling team that could make run-scoring very difficult. Whatever the reason, we rolled them over for 164. At times, we'd batted poorly, but they were worse than us. This was the weakest Australian batting team I ever played against. Now it was a one-innings match, and so long as we made a decent score we were confident our bowlers could sort them out again.

I still felt in no kind of form, but got to 49 before I was caught at slip off Alan Hurst again. Lower down the order Geoff Miller made 64, and Bob Taylor, who was not always good with the bat, chose this game to have his best ever knock of 97. England 360 all out was massive, and I don't think any of us believed Australia would get them. Ian Botham and Bob Willis got stuck in with three wickets each, and Australia mustered just 160. A whopping win by 205 runs after being put in to bat was typical of the series overall, and this was turning into a thrashing.

6 and 49

\* \* \*

### Sixth Test, Australia versus England, SCG, Sydney, 10-14 February, 1979

*Eightieth cap*

Both teams had to fulfil their obligations, but with the score at 4-1 and the Ashes long decided, a bit of edge for the contest had gone. The Australian public had lost interest as it was obvious that their team were no match for England, and they do not like losers. Graham Yallop won the toss and, as you would expect, chose to bat on a surface that always helped spinners later on. He fought like hell on a losing ship to score a fantastic 121 runs. Whatever my state of mind, and with my batting in the doldrums, I still had tremendous admiration for his skill, determination and the fact he never quit. With his team outplayed, he showed a fighting spirit all series long. His innings kept them in the game with a total of 198, but only just.

I was out caught slip off Rodney Hogg for 19 and Rod got Derek Randall cheaply too, but the rest of our players all got in and scored a few runs. A total of 308 gave us a lead of 110, which must have been chastening for the home side. Even worse, it was ridiculously easy for our spinners to bowl them out again. They shared nine of the wickets as Australia succumbed for 143, the match almost done in three-and-a-half days. We needed just 33 to win and I got myself out caught at cover off the leg-spinner Jim Higgs for 13. A silly dismissal, but I was still trying like hell to find the rhythm to my batting that had been so frustratingly elusive. My mind was in turmoil and your mind dictates how you bat. I don't blame anyone.

We all have to deal with adversity at some time or other in our lives, and I wasn't able to deal with the politics involved with Yorkshire and my mother dying.

19 and 13

\* \* \*

*You have been a shadow of yourself. A shadow from a once-burning sun.*
*Your worst series ever. Twelve innings, 263 runs at 21.91.*
*You know that you need to do something about it, something –*
*anything – that might drag you out of yourself and the hole that*
*you're in. You stay on for a break in Sydney where Keith Sillett, who*
*you'd met during your time at Waverley Cricket Club and who is the*
*marketing director of the Cathay Pacific airline, suggests a trip to*
*Hong Kong. You can go as Cathay's ambassador.*
*Why not, you think, so you fly out, do some coaching, use your*
*free time to see the sights, do some shopping, lie by the pool. Cathay*
*treat you like a superstar, taking you to dinner, arranging rounds of*
*golf, and then they fly you to Malaysia, to the Rasa Sayang Hotel, a*
*place you've only ever seen on Alan Whicker's TV programme. You*
*love that show, and Alan says that if he could visit just one hotel in*
*the world it would be this one. He is right. It's bliss... nirvana... with*
*its luxury rooms and endless white beaches...*
*At last, miles from home and miles from cricket, you feel the winter*
*begin to slip behind you.*

\* \* \*

*You arrive home the day before Yorkshire's AGM, but this time you*
*do not go. Uncle Algy comes to visit instead, and he tells you exactly*
*what you need to hear:*
*'Keep your mouth shut, Geoffrey. Say nothing and bide your time.*
*Just bat, that is your best answer. You can't win your battles if you*
*don't bat well...'*
*He goes on: 'Raymond Illingworth has said a lot this winter. Sooner*
*or later he will say too much, and when he does, take him for every*
*penny he's got. That will hurt him the most.'*

*You love Uncle Algy, but you have no interest in getting money out of Ray Illingworth. He's right about the batting though. Runs are the answer, the answer to everything. Have been your whole life. Runs are the only thing that can stop the failure, keep the doubt at bay. So you go to see Johnny Lawrence, tell him how you feel, tell him that you have no rhythm, that your technique is wrong and you can't work out why.*

*But Johnny can't put his finger on it either. Not this time...*

*You realise that you need to see yourself bat. You contact the MCC Indoor School at Lord's, speak to head coach Don Wilson, ask him to give you some bowlers and the use of their cameras.*

*It takes three days in London for you to work it out. The broken thumb. That's how it started. In pain, you'd started to grip the bat too hard with your bottom hand, trying to compensate and get some power. That had opened out your chest until you were too square on, and then everything went out of alignment, out of sync.*

*Using Don Wilson's cameras and Don Wilson's bowlers, you turn yourself sideways again, exaggerate the movement of your left hand, arm and shoulder the way you'd teach a kid to play, and at first it feels terrible, wrong, awful... But you stick with it, and after three days, it starts to feel better again...*

*You realise that this is how it always begins... with a weak point, with a tiny fracture, a small thing that affects a bigger thing until it affects everything, and the whole self break down. You are 38 years old. You think to yourself: 'I might never play for England again.' You accept that truth. You go back to Yorkshire. You have a few awkward days with the new manager and the new captain, all of you tip-toeing around one another, trying not to restart the war, but you keep your mouth shut just like Uncle Algy said, you ignore everything else and concentrate on your batting. Concentrate on making runs.*

*It rains and it rains, every day, every game, but you forget about that, forget about the results that are no longer your problem, and you bat: three fifties and then 151 against Derbyshire at Headingley. Decent, but you're still finding yourself again, still waiting for your mind to reach that place of calm, where your body just does the right things without you even thinking, still waiting when the news comes through that you have been chosen for England's World Cup squad...*

*You are amazed and astonished but it's just what you need, and from nowhere you're on a ride that takes you all the way to Lord's, all the way to the World Cup final, and Clive Lloyd's ferocious new West Indies team, bristling with quality batsmen and lightning-quick bowlers...*

*England start the final well, but Viv Richards and Collis King rip the trophy from your hands, smashing the ball all over Lord's to score 286 from their 60 overs. You and Mike Brearley begin England's reply against Andy Roberts, Michael Holding, Colin Croft and Joel Garner. They batter away at you, frightening and fierce, but it's all coming back to you now, all that you had lost, and you add 129 for the first wicket before Mike goes and you soon follow. The rest of the innings slips away against the speed and hostility of Holding and Croft and the unplayable yorkers of Joel Garner.*

*Still, it's just what you needed, playing well in a huge game against world-class bowlers before a full house. You go from London to Harrogate and make 130 not out against Somerset, and from there you go to Chesterfield and make 167 against Derbyshire. You even have a bowl and get a couple of wickets. You are selected for the First Test at Edgbaston and report for nets with England the next day but as you're getting changed you feel so knackered that you turn to Mike and say, 'Captain, do I have to practice?'*

*There's a stunned silence.*

*No-one can believe what they're hearing, but Mike laughs and sends you back to the hotel. Thirty-eight years old and for the first time in your life, you do not want to go to nets...*

\* \* \*

## First Test, England versus India, Edgbaston, Birmingham, 12-16 July, 1979

*Eighty-first cap*

My rest paid off, and by the end of the first day England were 318 for three, with me on 113 not out and David Gower 43. From thinking I'd never play another Test to this... it seemed crazy.

India had brought to England one great seam bowler in Kapil Dev and three of that famous spin quartet in Bishan Bedi, Srinivas

Venkataraghavan and Bhagwath Chandrasekhar. Kapil was similar in pace and ability to our Ian Botham. Tall and athletic, he had a huge shoulder turn, so that at the moment of delivery, as a batsman you were looking at the back of his left shoulder. This enabled him to bowl fizzing outswing and out seam, the most dangerous wicket-taking deliveries. Bishan Bedi was injured for the start of the series but Chandra was a handful right away. He bounded in off a longish run-up and bowled a mixture of top spinners and googlies that sometimes bounced alarmingly. It was vital to judge his length and pick each delivery, because he was quicker than a normal spinner and you had no time to adjust before he was on to you.

Fortunately the pitch was really good and on the second morning I was able to go on to 155 before Kapil got me lbw with a nip backer. With that hundred, I completed a century on what was at the time all six of the English Test match grounds. David Gower was once again at his very best, scoring 200 not out. Most cricketers know that wrist-spinners usually don't bowl as well to left-handers, but maybe David didn't allow Chandra to bowl at him. He was superb.

Our 633-5 declared must have looked like a mountain to India, even on this pitch. Once again our seamers bowled with great heart and discipline, working hard as a unit to bowl them out for 297, and to then turn around and go again when Mike enforced the follow on. Ian Botham with five wickets and Mike Hendrick four saw us home to an innings victory. They built pressure superbly well and gave the Indian batters nothing to hit. All over in four days, with an average of 94 overs a day bowled, and nearly 300 runs scored. An excellent cricket match for players and spectators.

**151** and **DNB**

\* \* \*

*It continues as you go to Worksop to play for Yorkshire against Nottinghamshire, where you miss out in the first innings but carry your bat through the second for 175 not out. Everything that was wrong is now right. All of the doubts and the fears are receding. Uncle Algy's voice stays in your head. Shut up and bat, let the runs make everything alright again, make everything alright in this strange and capricious game that you play.*

\* \* \*

## Second Test, England versus India, Lord's, London, 2-7 August, 1979

*Eighty-second cap*

A Test at the Mecca of cricket during high summer... there's nothing better, and after three days everything seemed to be going our way again, with India shot out for 96 by the first afternoon and us piling up another huge score, 419-9 declared. I got 32 before Karsan Ghavri, Kapil's opening partner, used the slope and took one of his left-arm seamers across me to induce the edge. No-one reached three figures, but all of the batters chipped in.

In England, the weather changes games. We lost nine hours to rain, and India mounted a terrific rearguard action, digging in and taking very few risks. Sunil Gavaskar blunted the new ball with fifty, and then Dilip Vengsarkar and Gundappa Viswanath made hundreds. Vishy played against type. He was a lovely, wristy batsman who liked to play his shots and would often give you a chance, but not here. Dilip took an immediate liking to Lord's. Tall and correct, he would make hundreds at HQ on India's next two visits. Three in a row at Lord's – there are a lot of us batsmen who would like that on our CVs. India batted through, and by the end had earned a pretty comfortable draw.

**32** and **DNB**

\* \* \*

## Third Test, England versus India, Headingley, Leeds, 16-21 August, 1979

*Eighty-third cap*

Eighteen hours of play were lost to rain. To give an idea of what it was like, Ian Botham had just gone into bat on the first afternoon when the rain came and he didn't get to face another ball until four days later. As there was no chance of a result, Ian decided to have some fun and smacked the ball to all parts, scoring 99 before lunch. He had no idea he only needed a single to achieve the magical hundred runs in a session, and he blocked the last four balls of the final over. I was caught first slip for 31 off a Kapil Dev out seamer.

`31` *and* `DNB`

\* \* \*

*You make 95 at Cheltenham against Gloucestershire but get out leg before to the non-spinning spinner John Childs. How the hell did that happen? It still annoys you today if you think about it (which you do...). After the Headingley Test match wash-out comes the Bank Holiday Roses match. John Hampshire throws the ball to you. You bowl your medium-slow inswingers still wearing your cap, and to the delight of the crowd take 4-41 in 14.2 overs, your best-ever figures. Your favourite moment comes when your old mate Jack Simmons misses a pull shot and is so plum leg before that he walks off without bothering to look at the umpire... Flat Jack will never hear the end of that one...*

*Warming up in the nets after the rest day, not out overnight, you top edge an attempted sweep into your face and your left eye begins to swell. It's a big problem because it means you can't get your contact lens in. You battle on, the ball barely in focus, and miss out on another hundred when you're last man out for 94...*

*This strange and unexpected summer...*

\* \* \*

# Fourth Test, England versus India,
## The Oval, London, 30 August – 4 September, 1979

*Eighty-fourth cap*

A good surface, but England struggled and should have done better than 305 all out. Yes, there was some early movement, with Kapil Dev at his best. I still remember his first ball of the day to me. He was bowling from the Pavilion End, and it swung out, drew me forward, pitched on a perfect length and kept on moving out. How I didn't nick it, I will never know. He got me lbw for 35 during his second spell. Graham Gooch batted most of the day for 79 before getting out straight away next morning, and Peter Willey got a gutsy half-century. Then India were made to work by our excellent seam attack. Willis, Botham and Hendrick were more penetrating than even Kapil had been, and we bowled them out for 202.

By Saturday evening we had taken control at 177-3, and with the rest day to come, we could contemplate a probable victory. The pitch was getting drier and encouraging a bit of turn. I had played pretty well, and felt very comfortable to be 83 not out, with a chance of another Test century to come.

On Monday morning, I went to the nets on the outfield at the Vauxhall End to prepare and suddenly I seized up with a back spasm. Never had one before or since, but it was agony. My movement was so restricted that I had to waddle back to the dressing room. Our physio Bernard Thomas injected me with painkillers and taped up my back and ribs, and out I went to continue my innings. Willey, Botham and Brearley went quickly and suddenly India fancied their chances.

My Yorkshire colleague and friend David Bairstow, playing in his first Test match, was up for the challenge, spanking 59. I struggled along at the other end, staying back as much as possible because the stiff muscles made it so awkward to bend. I found Karsan Ghavri the most difficult to face. Left-arm over going across me, and I couldn't get forward, so I got further and further over to off stump to counter the angle, and played him off the back foot. Eventually, I got too far across and was bowled behind my pads for 125. I was reasonably pleased, as I had scored another 42 runs in dire circumstances. It enabled Mike to declare our score at 334-8 and leave ourselves more than eight hours to bowl India out. Having dismissed them four times for less than 300, it seemed academic, but this summer was certainly strange… Their target, a nominal one we thought, stood at 434.

There was no way that I could field, so I sat on the dressing room balcony and watched as Sunil Gavaskar and Chetan Chauhan batted on and on, past lunch on the fifth day and deep into the afternoon before Bob Willis finally broke the partnership at 213. Chauhan gone for 80, but Gavaskar continued on his way majestically, passing three figures for the 20th time in Test cricket and bringing that seemingly impossible target into view. His concentration was so good, his strokeplay so certain it was impossible for me not to sit back and admire this exhibition of batting. He was joined by Dilip Vengsarkar, who glided past fifty, and suddenly Mike was setting defensive fields to try and stop the flow of runs.

From nowhere, they had us by the throat. When Vengsarkar was dismissed the score stood at 366-2, eight wickets in hand and 72 more needed for a remarkable win. It should have been a doddle for India, but as the saying goes, it's never over until the fat lady sings. For some reason they panicked and sent Kapil Dev in to try and bash quick runs. He was out for nought, wickets tumbled, Gavaskar, who had sealed up one end, was out for a fabulous 221, and it all started to unravel. England defended for their lives as an absolutely compelling game came down to the wire. In the end, we were relieved that India fell seven runs short with two wickets still remaining. It's the nature of cricket that a draw can be such a thrilling outcome.

My season was finished, as I needed weeks of medical treatment for my back.

**35** and **125**

\* \* \*

*Your season is over. Your long, strange season that begins in despair and confusion ends here with another century. For Yorkshire, you make 1,160 runs at an average of 116.00. You top the first-class averages with 1,538 runs at 100.53. You are the first player in history to average more than a hundred twice in an English season. At 38 years old, written off and sacked, you are still the greatest English batsman in the land.*

*Under the management of Raymond Illingworth and the captaincy of John Hampshire, Yorkshire finish seventh in the County Championship, lose in the quarter final of the Gillette Cup, lose in the semi-final of the Benson & Hedges Cup and finish fifth in the John Player Sunday League.*

*The Yorkshire captaincy brought you so much pain. Now it has gone, you wonder why you spent so long hanging onto it.*

*World Series Cricket is finished. The Australian Cricket Board and Kerry Packer are losing money hand over fist, so they get around a table. Money talks. Kerry gets his TV rights and in return he packs up his circus for good. Cricket's war fizzles out in the boardrooms of Australia. Tony Greig retires from all cricket and takes up Kerry's offer of a job for life as a Channel Nine TV commentator. Australia's Packer players are allowed back for the 1979–80 season. Greg Chappell is reappointed captain. A three-Test series against England is hurriedly arranged.*

*The war is over, but the game has changed. Kerry Packer has changed it with his coloured clothing and his floodlit day-night matches. Now Kerry's company PBL Marketing has a ten-year deal to promote the game, so this tour of Australia will begin with a triangular tournament of one-day cricket under the lights, featuring Australia, England and West Indies.*

*The old game is still full of surprises, and so are you. Alec Bedser is the tour manager. He comes to you and says that you are not cut out for this pyjama cricket and razzamatazz. You still want to find your form, though, and you make a hundred in a 50-over warm-up against New South Wales Country Districts at Newcastle, and when Ian Botham says you only let him face one over of leg-spinner Kerry O'Keeffe's spell, you tell him he was lucky to get one…*

*Ian extracts his revenge on the coach journey from Newcastle to Sydney. As the bus approaches the hotel, a couple of the lads pin you to your seat and pull off your clothes, and to cheers and laughter, Ian arrives with a can of shaving foam and covers your nipples, nose and privates, then runs into the hotel with your clothes.*

*Maybe this new spirit is catching, maybe you are more relaxed now. You crack a hundred against Tasmania, who have Richard Hadlee guesting for them, and when Geoff Miller picks up an injury, you open the batting in the second ODI against Australia in Melbourne. Dennis Lillee and Jeff Thomson are waiting for you, and so is Rodney Hogg, but you make 68 and England win.*

*You stay in the team for the next game at Sydney, and under the lights you smash 105, going to a hundred with a screaming cover drive from the bowling of Dennis Lillee. They hand you the player of the match award and it feels like a dream... Mike Brearley says, 'The amazing thing was, Boycott never had to slog at all...'*

\* \* \*

### First Test, Australia versus England, WACA, Perth, 14-19 December, 1979

*Eighty-fifth cap*

It takes a heck of a bowler to play a four-ball innings that goes down in history and changes a match, but that is one of the things that this Perth Test will be remembered for. Well, that and the tale of two batsmen who managed to score 99...

As usual, the WACA pitch had plenty of pace, bounce and movement to encourage the quick bowlers and keep us batsmen on our toes. Ian Botham was once again magnificent, and he took the top off the Australian innings, snaring the big wickets of Allan Border, Australia's rising star, and the returning Greg Chappell. It fell to Kim Hughes to keep things together, and he was unlucky to be dismissed one short of a deserved century. Rod Marsh had stuck around with him, but his wicket brought Dennis Lillee to the crease.

Dennis had become involved in a company making cricket bats out of aluminium. It was meant to be a cheap sort of bat for schoolkids to use, but Dennis came out to bat holding one. It was called a 'ComBat' and had a sticker of a rifle on the back! Both sides were flat, and when it made contact with the ball it gave off a horrible clanging sound. Dennis had faced four deliveries when Ian Botham complained to our captain that the aluminium bat was damaging the ball.

I don't know whether that was true or whether Ian just wanted to get under Dennis's skin and irritate him, but if his plan was to upset

Dennis, then it worked. The umpire told Dennis he had to change his bat, and there were a lot of heated words exchanged. Dennis was furious, so angry that he hurled the aluminium bat somewhere over mid-off and stormed towards the pavilion with steam coming out of his ears!

The twelfth man ran on to give him a normal bat, and by this time there was total mayhem, with the crowd getting behind Dennis and shouting abuse at Mike. Now, Mike had already run into trouble with the home press and fans during the triangular tournament, when, in the first game against West Indies, he'd put all of our fielders out on the boundary rope for the last ball to stop the Windies getting the boundary they needed to win. It was within the Laws at the time, but it ultimately led to the first fielding restrictions coming in the following year.

Mike was unrepentant, and as he'd grown a big beard, the papers began using the nickname 'the Ayatollah.' The Perth fans took it up, howling and shouting at him on Dennis's behalf. It was almost ten minutes before the game restarted, and then shortly afterwards we all trooped off again for the close, Dennis still fuming at what had happened.

In the dressing room, I told Mike I thought it was one of the stupidest things he had ever done. I didn't give a monkey's about the bat, but getting their world-class fast bowler angry and fired up before he was about to bowl at us was only going to make him bowl faster and better. I thought it was a huge mistake. We should have been able to bowl Lillee out with the ball in any condition, as he wasn't much of a batsman.

Next morning, Australia were dismissed right away, and you could tell that the crowd were eagerly awaiting the main event. England had waved a red flag in front of the bull and now the locals were anticipating that bull sticking it to England. As Derek Randall and I walked out to bat, Dennis was pacing out his run, and most of the crowd were counting his steps with him.

Derek, as usual lacking a bit of confidence, said to me, 'He'll get me out, Fiery,' and sure enough Dennis came roaring in and had Derek fencing, caught in the slips without scoring. Then I was given out lbw to a nip backer I thought was a bit high and maybe missing leg stump, also for a duck. Can you imagine the pandemonium, noise and jubilation from the spectators as their superman stuck it to us? It was like being in the Colosseum in Rome when the lions were set on the Christians. The crowd loved seeing their hero get his revenge. He soon had David Gower, too, and with Geoff Dymock accounting for Peter Willey, the Aussies had broken the back of our batting at 41-4. The atmosphere was electric. With Geoff Miller next in, followed by Mike Brearley, it seemed as though the match would be won and lost during a crazy row over a metal cricket bat. But Mike had other ideas, and played one of his best innings, scoring 64 to keep us within 16 of the Australia total.

The Aussie batters soon had us back under pressure. The openers added almost a hundred and then Allan Border struck a magnificent 115 from number three to take the match away from us. When we batted again at the end of the fourth day, a target of 354 on a wearing pitch with big cracks opening up was going to be far too many for us. A draw was the best we could hope for, but they struck an early blow when Derek Randall was out cheaply that night.

We scrapped and fought through the final day, and yet wickets kept going down. As we reached the last hour, the new ball was due and I was still hanging in there, batting with the tail and trying to farm as much of the strike as possible. It was going to be a difficult task. As much as I love Derek Underwood, the truth is that he was terrified of pace. Facing a barrage of quick bowlers through his career had left him shell-shocked. Bob Willis was so bad that he once got halfway to the middle during a game at Edgbaston before he realised he had set off without his bat. Any skipper might as well declare when these two were due in.

Derek had stuck around for half an hour and 24 deliveries in the first innings and we needed that again, but he went third ball, caught at slip off Geoff Dymock. That brought Bob in as last man. He survived his first couple, which left me with the strike against Lillee, new cherry in his hand and my score on 97. It was the first series in which Australia switched to playing six ball overs instead of their traditional eight, so when I eased the fourth delivery through the vacant cover area, I called for what I thought would be an easy three runs, as the boundaries at Perth were huge.

That would take me to a century, but just as important, it would get me to the non-striker's end, and leave Bob to negotiate only two deliveries from Lillee. Then I could take most of the next over from Dymock. I got halfway down the pitch for the third run and saw that Bob hadn't moved and was shouting at me to get back!

Dennis saw what was happening and used his brain. He bowled me a rapid bouncer that went miles over my head and then a fast, full one down the leg side. I couldn't get a bat on either. Between overs, I went down the wicket to ask Bob why he didn't run. He said he didn't want to face Lillee, as Dennis would get him out. The first ball from Geoff Dymock, Bob dangles an open-face bat and gives an easy catch to first slip... Game over and I was left stranded on 99 not out.

I was just the fourth Englishman to carry his bat through a completed innings in a Test match, and all of the other three – Bobby Abel, Pelham Warner and Leonard Hutton – made centuries. Actually, Len did it twice... Not much comfort in that!

**0** and **99 not out**

\* \* \*

*There is a two-week break between Test matches to finish Kerry's triangular one-day tournament, and once again, you are free and fearless... 68 against West Indies, 86 not out in a win against Australia (where you bat through the smoke and noise of the Rod Stewart concert next door), 35 and 63 against the West Indies in the tournament Finals... And you love it, love showing Thomson, Lillee and Hogg, Holding, Roberts, Garner and Croft that at 39 years of age you are still pretty good against fast bowling.*

# CHAPTER FIFTEEN

# 1980

*The tour party flies to Brisbane for a game against the State side, but you stay back to rest up and play golf. On the 13th hole at Royal Sydney, you're clambering out of a deep bunker when you slip in the sand and fall back down the face. You land heavily, dislocate a finger and hurt your neck. You yank the finger back into place and go to see Bernie Thomas. Bernie says the finger will be sore but fine. He says he thinks you have a whiplash.*

*You wrap a scarf around your neck to stop it stiffening up. You go to the eve of Test match dinner. The lads think it's hilarious, tying their napkins around their necks and taking the piss, but you tell Mike that you're doubtful for the game. Mike doesn't like that. Mike tells you, 'You're in, you're in…'*

*You ask Bernie Thomas. Bernie says: 'Geoff, I'm sorry but I think you should be playing. I know you're in pain but even injured you are worth at least 20 per cent more than anyone else in the side.'*

*Mike Brearley tells you to take a fitness test in the morning.*

*The morning is damp and wet, so you go to the indoor nets where you face Graham Stevenson and John Lever. Bob Willis and Ian Botham, Mike's lieutenants, stand at the back and watch. Your neck is stiff and sore and you can barely turn your head to see the direction of the ball. Bob and Ian ask Graham and John whether they think you can play. They leave without asking you. They find Mike and tell him you're fit. You find Mike and tell him that you can't play.*

*…You know you shouldn't be playing, know you shouldn't play because small things lead to more small things and more small things lead to bigger things and soon the whole self is affected…This is what is on your mind. This is what you cannot say.*

*Instead, you and Mike have a row outside the dressing room. You play.*

\* \* \*

## Second Test, Australia versus England, SCG, Sydney, 4-8 January, 1980

### *Eighty-sixth cap*

The entire ground was saturated after days of rain, and the pitch itself was very wet. Apparently, the groundstaff had been given New Year's Day off and the pitch was left unprotected. With a huge match coming up, it was mind-boggling that the SCG was unsupervised. The weather remained poor, there was no sun to dry things out and so the pitch was re-covered and left to sweat for another few days while the rain tippled down. The Australian captain did media interviews and admitted the match would be a lottery, because whoever won the toss would bowl first and win the match. The Australians did not want to start, and I didn't blame them as batting would be no fun.

Amazingly, our captain was upbeat. Mike had only one thought – win the toss and let Derek Underwood bowl Australia out cheaply on a wet pitch. He couldn't contain himself. I think his decision to help get the game started was based partly on us losing in Perth plus, although I can't prove it, I believe that he had come to the same view as me, that our batting wasn't good enough to make runs against their bowling attack on a normal pitch. Mike was almost gleeful about the prospect of getting the Aussies in on a wet surface. He was prepared to gamble.

I knew that batting on a soggy pitch against their quicks would be nasty. The ball jumps or flies alarmingly from that Bulli soil when it's tacky. Sometimes it is impossible to bat, and history shows a number of very low-scoring matches where batsmen have been in physical danger. Many of us were hoping we could come back next day when the pitch and surrounds might have dried out a bit, but the authorities had let spectators into the ground and were keen to get the game on.

Sure enough, Mike lost the toss. Graham Gooch and Derek Randall were out to balls that jumped off a length from Dennis Lillee, and I thought it best to look to score before I got something unplayable, and was bowled by a late inswinger from Dymock. A few lusty blows from Ian Botham got the scoreboard moving, but at the close we were 90-7 and Mike's gamble had backfired.

We were all out next morning for 123, and then we fought and scrapped hard to keep Australia down to 145. Ian Botham took four and Derek Underwood a couple as the pitch began to dry out and lose its demons. We went back in and I lasted an hour, but the neck wasn't right at all. The highlight of our second innings came from David Gower, who made 98 not out, another fluent, exquisite knock as everyone else struggled. Last man Bob Willis again couldn't hang on while David got his hundred. Bob had no idea how to defend or even play with the full face of his bat.

The rest day followed and it was beautiful. That pitch dried right out and the Aussies got the benefit, Greg Chappell seeing them home with a 98 not out of his own.

I had a much bigger problem that affected my tour. In the second innings, Lenny Pascoe was bowling quick and he got one to lift and smash into my hand. Trying not to let on is fine, but it was bloody painful. There are a lot of very sensitive nerves in the fingers. I got another from Geoff Dymock that lifted from nowhere and although I did my best to fend it off, it lobbed to gully. Getting out always hurts, but even worse was the small crack in the bone of my thumb, caused when it was trapped against the bat handle.

Bernard Thomas had this new ultrasound gadget he used on me under water and then he gave it to me to use in my room. The more I did, the worse it seemed to get. The management were pestering me to play in the final few matches of the triangular ODI series, as England had lost a couple without me while I was injured. I got fed up being stuck in my room and my thumb not healing so I stopped using Bernard's new-fangled machine. Amazingly, my thumb improved remarkably quickly. When I got home, my physio Paddy Armour said if you use too much ultrasound it makes the bone sore. Thanks Bernard!

8 and 18

\* \* \*

*You bat well against West Indies in those finals, you score 35 and 63, but they are too fast, too strong with all that power and pace, and Joel Garner bringing the ball down from nine feet right into the blockhole... West Indies win 2-0.*

***

## Third Test, Australia versus England, MCG, Melbourne, 1-6 February, 1980

*Eighty-seventh cap*

One of the good things to come from the tour was the blossoming of my opening partnership with Graham Gooch. I knew that he respected me, and he was always watching how I prepared and how I batted out in the middle. Graham would leave no stone unturned when it came to improving as a player, and it showed. He got better and better as his career went on. He hadn't always been an opening batsman, but he was perfect for the role, very good against fast bowling, and someone who could get after the opposition when he got in.

We played very well on the first morning, scoring a hundred runs by the lunch interval. Graham went after the off-spinner Ashley Mallett, hitting him over the top several times, and he had a touch of luck when Dymock dropped a sitter at mid-off from one mishit. Just what we needed. At lunch, Greg Chappell was furious with his players and gave them a real old tongue-lashing. I was not surprised, because if they didn't get a grip, this match could quickly get away from them.

It did the trick. I tried to drive Geoff Dymock, the ball slid off the face squarer than I anticipated and Ashley Mallett held on well in the gully. Dennis Lillee had been off the field feeling unwell, but came back after lunch to bowl off a shorter run. He used all his skill and craftsmanship to pressure our batsman. Close to the stumps and then wider, with a bit of in and out movement but never giving runs away. With Lenny Pascoe fast and aggressive at the other end, they made mincemeat of our batsmen, taking seven wickets for not many runs.

Graham carried on driving the ball very straight until he reached 99, one short of his maiden Test ton. When the fielders came in to save a single and that one run didn't materialise, he succumbed by hitting the ball straight at mid-on and running himself out. It was a silly thing to do, born out of frustration, nerves and the desperation to get a first Test hundred.

231

After he had settled down from his disappointment, I had a quiet word with him.

I told him he had all day to score one run, so next time just hang in there until the bowlers give an easy ball to score off. When you get into the nineties, you are the one in control, you are the boss, and you should never look to merely complete a hundred. Think of scoring a lot more runs than just a century.

On the rest day, I played a few holes of golf with the American crooner Johnny Mathis to give newspaper publicity for his Melbourne concert, and he arranged tickets for some of the team. He was always one of my favourite singers.

When the cricket resumed, it was another very hot, energy-sapping day and Australia rightly and deliberately kept us in the field, exhausting us, grinding us down while all of their batsmen got runs. They batted for 179 overs and made 477. With a deficit of 171 and on a pitch displaying some erratic bounce, we had little chance of winning.

Lillee got me early with a clever bit of bowling. He went wide of the crease and his nip-backer hit a crack and jagged a lot further than I expected to bowl me. Wayne Larkins got one that kept really low from Pascoe, David Gower tried a pull shot off Lillee, which wasn't smart with so many balls not bouncing, and was bowled. Peter Willey, on a pair, made two before being strangled down the leg side by Lillee. Pascoe did for our captain, and while Goochie batted nicely for a half century, he got out just before the close of play. All top six batsmen back in the dressing room, and we were still 14 runs behind.

On the last morning, Ian Botham only had our tail to bat with, but relished the freedom to do as he pleased in the face of inevitable defeat. He blocked the good balls and whacked anything off line, which, with the field up, went to the boundary. He finished with 119 not out but Australia still won comfortably.

They had beaten us easily in all the three Tests and it was a good job we weren't playing for the Ashes, as it would have been a whitewash.

**44** and **7**

\* \* \*

*You fly from Australia to India for the one-off Golden Jubilee Test to be played at the Wankhede stadium, Bombay. You fly ten hours and 5,000 miles to play cricket for five days. Five days that celebrate 50 years of the formation of the BCCI. Then back on the plane, back in the air for another nine hours...*

\* \* \*

## Jubilee Test, India versus England, Wankhede Stadium, Bombay, 15-19 February, 1980

### *Eighty-eighth cap*

We arrived at the ground to find a pitch that looked more like an English green top than the usual dry and bare Indian surfaces. We couldn't work out why they prepared something that played right to our strength, which was seam and swing bowlers. John Lever, Graham Stevenson and Ian Botham were queuing up to have a go on it.

India won the toss and batted but as I expected they had to work hard, with lots of playing and missing as the ball moved around. Sunil Gavaskar was by far their best technician and even he must have got frustrated hunting for the ball because, quite out of character, he slogged John Lever for a six over wide long-on. There were a few seconds of stunned silence from us players and the crowd.

Sunny got to 49, which was top score, and everyone chipped in, even as Both was carving through them and taking six wickets. India managed a respectable 242, and if you want to know how much the ball was moving around, Bob Taylor equalled the world record for catches in an innings by a wicket-keeper with seven!

If we thought it would be a bit easier for us, we were wrong. There was plenty of bounce and carry, and it took a lot of skill just to survive. Karsan Ghavri picked up Graham Gooch and Wayne Larkins early, I was Roger Binny's only wicket for 22, and Kapil got both Gower and Brearley leg before. Not for the first time that winter, our batting was in a complete mess at 58-5.

We were saved by an extraordinary moment of sportsmanship and a superb partnership between the unstoppable Botham and

233

Bob Taylor. They had added 85 together when Bob was given out caught behind after a loud appeal. He told the Indian players that he hadn't hit it and India's captain Gundappa Viswanath, who was fielding at slip, said that he agreed with Bob. He asked the umpire if India could withdraw their appeal, and the umpire allowed them to. That changed the course of the game, as Ian and Bob went on to a record-breaking sixth wicket partnership of 171. It took a lot of courage and integrity from Vishy to give Bob a life in a low-scoring match with the result on the line. It is easy to be generous and change an appeal when it won't affect the outcome, but nearly everyone I know would have just left the decision with the umpire and accepted it as the rub of the green. Not Vishy.

Bob went on to make 43, supporting Ian as he dominated the bowling and the match, making 114 to go with his six wickets. And he was far from finished. With his ton giving us a decent lead of 54, he grabbed the ball and went tearing through the Indian batting a second time, essentially winning the match on his own. Seven more wickets gave him match figures of 13-106 to go alongside his ton, one of the great all-round performances.

There should have been a rest day, but that was forfeited because there was going to be an eclipse of the sun, and so on the fourth morning Graham Gooch and I knocked off the 96 runs required to win without losing a wicket.

**22** *and* **43 not out**

\* \* \*

*Mike Brearley retires from Test cricket to captain Middlesex and pursue a career as a psychoanalyst. You don't blame him. Despite Kerry Packer and his circus and what everyone thinks, cricket is not suddenly awash with money. For the three Tests in Australia and the trip to India you receive £6,500 plus £200 for every previous tour, which for you comes to £1,400. After a 25 per cent tax exemption for earnings made abroad you clear £6,000, which is the average annual salary in Great Britain in 1980. Yorkshire pay you £4,000 and you earn £1000 for each home Test match appearance. You are halfway through a five-year equipment deal with Slazenger that earns you £9,000 a year, so you are hardly on the breadline, but you are about to turn 40 years old and your career will be over soon.*

*The average executive earns £26,000. Eight first division footballers earn more than £50,000. Bjorn Borg, the world's number one tennis player, wins $100,000 in 1980 and has racquet and clothing deals worth a further $675,000. Tom Watson, the world's number one golfer, becomes the first player to win $500,000 in a season and has long term off-course deals with RAM clubs and investment bankers EF Hutton that double his earnings.*

*And you have no idea what you will do once you finish, no idea, because you can't think about that, not yet, not while you can still play... But you are not rich, not rich like the footballers and the golfers and the tennis players and the average executives. You'll have to do something more with your life. Kerry Packer did not change that...*

\* \* \*

*In the summer of 1980 and the spring of 1981, at home and then away, England will play ten Test matches against the West Indies. They are the best team in the world, perhaps the best team of all-time, certainly the best fast bowling unit ever. It's no place for Mike Brearley, no place for a 38-year-old with a Test batting average of 23...*

*...And on that subject, what the hell are YOU thinking of, soon to turn 40 and still walking out there, into that quartet of fast bowlers...*

*Mike recommends Ian Botham as the new captain of England. Alec Bedser agrees and appoints him for the home series with West Indies. You think Mike is swayed by his friendship with Ian. Ian is still a kid, 24 years old, a free spirit, full of life, easily distracted. 'Guy The Gorilla' you'd nicknamed him. At the nets in Perth he got bored and slogged every ball into the street until there were none left and that was the end of practice. That's Ian all over. He loves pranks and jokes, he's like a pied piper to the younger players, and under Mike's captaincy, he had the freedom to be himself. But making him captain against the world's greatest cricket team? It won't work.*

*At the pre-match dinner for the first Test you eat and then discuss the West Indies bowlers. Andy Roberts and his two bouncers – the fast medium one that cons you to hook, and the top-speed one that comes next, that has flattened Colin Cowdrey and knocked Ian Botham's teeth out. Michael Holding, Whispering Death, with that endless run, head swaying from side to side as he comes in, hypnotic and deadly. Colin Croft, who goes wide on the crease and follows you with hot leather as you try and sway out of the way. Joel Garner, who gives you nothing to hit, not ever...*

*You say to Ian: 'You play with Joel at Somerset, where do we score off him?'*

*'You don't, Fiery...'*

*'Well when Viv faces him in the nets, where does he score?'*

*'He doesn't score off him. Nobody does...'*

*'On that note,' you say, 'I'm going to bed. I don't need any more negative thoughts or I won't get to sleep...'*

*You leave. You go back to your room. You think about Michael Holding, Andy Roberts, Colin Croft and Joel Garner. You think about Malcolm Marshall, this new kid they've got who is very quick and skiddy with a fast arm and lots of skill... You think about Sylvester Clarke and Wayne Daniel, who cannot get near this team but who would walk into any other Test side in the world... You sleep, eventually. You do not dream about cricket.*

\* \* \*

## First Test, England versus West Indies, Trent Bridge Nottingham, 5-10 June 1980

### *Eighty-ninth cap*

Trent Bridge was overcast and dark, with a dry pitch. Unappetising. Ian won the toss and decided to bat. Holding bowled an early bouncer at Goochie and the ball went way over the keeper's head at a rapid pace, bounced twice and hit the sightscreen. There were a few raised eyebrows between Graham and I... We had an interesting first hour as the ball whistled through. We didn't see any half volleys or many balls in our half of the pitch. When Clive Lloyd decided to change the bowling, we took the opportunity to meet in the middle and have a chat.

Graham said: 'We are alright now, Fiery, he's bringing on the second string... Garner and Marshall...'

Joel got me caught behind for 36. The team scrapped and fought hard, with Bob Woolmer and our new captain making some runs. These English type of conditions with seam movement were tough but probably gave us our best chance of winning. On flat batting pitches, their pace would still get them 20 wickets, whereas our fast medium, no matter how good, would not carry any threat if it was straight up and down.

Unfortunately they also had a world-class batting line up, a bit better than ours, and it gave them a priceless 45 run lead. Second innings, Andy Roberts bowled me off an inside edge for 75. All out 252 left West Indies with plenty of time and 208 runs to win. Desmond Haynes and Viv Richards broke the back of the chase, and although our bowlers created a mini-collapse, West Indies got home by two wickets.

**36** and **75**

\* \* \*

## Second Test, England versus West Indies, Lord's, London, 19-24 June, 1980

*Ninetieth cap*

Yorkshire had no Championship cricket between the Tests, and for someone like me, who loved playing and needed to bat, a week without cricket was a nightmare. Nets are not the same.

Ian won a good toss on what looked a decent pitch. Then it rained, the start was delayed, and we had to hang around in the dressing room twiddling our thumbs. All the early morning exercises and warm-ups were wasted. I never got used to sitting in the dressing room and I don't know any batsman who likes it. When we finally started, I was out quickly, caught behind off Holding. He was the main destroyer, finishing up with six wickets. Graham Gooch held our innings together with a terrific century, but we were all out for 269. We never seemed capable of scoring more than around 250/260 runs and this was as good a pitch you will ever get at Lord's. It just wasn't enough. By the middle of Saturday afternoon, West Indies were miles ahead and Desmond Haynes and Viv Richards were toying with our bowling. A full house was basking in the lovely warm sunshine, but we were tired and a bit despondent because we knew we were doomed for another defeat, this time a massive one.

Suddenly, out of nowhere, Ian says to me: 'Fiery, come and have a bowl.'

'Fuck off...''Come on, come and have a bowl!'

'Don't be stupid. How am I going to bowl at those two when you, Willis, Hendo and Unders can't get them out?'

Ian insisted, so I had to take the ball, set my field and mark out my run. As I did, the crowd started cheering. By this time, both Dessie and Viv had got centuries and I'm wondering where they are going to whack me and how many I'm going to go for, so I turned my cap back to front and hoped for the best.

I bowled around the wicket and the crowd cheered every dot ball. I suppose the England supporters had nothing else to shout about. Desmond Haynes played forward almost before I had let the ball go and blocked every one. I got the most amazing applause as I completed a maiden. Relief for me.

After someone had bowled at the other end, Ian said, 'Come and have another over, Fiery.'

'Don't be silly...

'Listen,' Ian said, 'they are terrified of you.'

'You are kidding...'

'No. Viv just told me Dessie has asked Viv to come down his end because he says he doesn't want you to get him out, and Viv has told me he's not going down that end unless he has to...'

Crazy! The best batsman in the world and his mate, who was close to the best, queuing up not to face my rubbish bowling. Mind you, deep down they knew if they got out to me, I would be ringing them up as my bunny! Neither of them would want to be reminded of that.

Ian had me bowl a spell of 7-2-14-0. A bit of relief while Haynes and Richards scored big centuries and West Indies declared with over 500 on the board, leaving us with a nasty hour to bat at the end of the third evening.

Their fast bowlers had enjoyed the best part of two days with their feet up, and they knew that with the rest day coming, they could put everything into this 60-minute session. Knock two or three of us over, and it would be a case of mopping up come Monday morning.

Michael Holding was like lightning. Everyone was around the bat. Everyone! Desmond Haynes was camped at short square-leg, almost in my trouser pocket and grinning like a Cheshire cat. Clive Lloyd came and sat on his haunches in a very close silly mid-off position. I played a couple of missiles from out of my throat absolutely dead at my feet. I was good friends with Desmond and Clive, and normally I would have bent down, picked it up and tossed it back, but this wasn't a friendly moment. I thought, 'If your guy is trying to knock my f...ing block off, you can bloody well pick it up yourselves!' So I stood absolutely still and made Clive get off his haunches, take a couple of steps and retrieve the ball. Clive laughed, as he knew what I was thinking.

Let me tell you that we were right in the line of fire and it was some test, but Goochie and I got through it to be not out at the close of play. Monday it rained, and on the last day Graham scored 47 while I was not out on 49 when the match was abandoned. We were lucky to get away with a draw.

**8** *and* **49 not out**

\* \* \*

*You're desperate for some cricket before the next Test, but Yorkshire play twice on juicy pitches and you are out early each time. You need something, anything, but Yorkshire have no academy or ground staff and they don't own Headingley, so you can't have a practice pitch or any decent bowlers.*

*In desperation, you telephone Jack Bond, Lancashire's Cricket Manager. He tells you that the Lancashire first team are practising on Monday and Tuesday, and you are welcome to join them. You make the long drive over the Pennines, there and back each day, just for some cricket. Lancashire cut a pitch on the practice ground and give you 45 minutes of batting against their first team attack.*

*Jack Bond comes over and says, 'I can't give you any more because I have my own team to look after,' but you are more than grateful. What a gesture from your greatest rivals. This is the esteem that you are held in.*

* * *

## Third Test, England versus West Indies,
## Old Trafford, Manchester, 10-15 July, 1980

*Ninety-first cap*

On the first morning the pitch looked bowler-friendly and it was murky overhead, so when Clive Lloyd won the toss, he put us in. His fast bowlers relished the conditions and bowled us out before tea for 150. Half the runs scored off the bat came from the left-hander Brian Rose as the rest of us were blown away.

Viv Richards made a half-century and Clive Lloyd took the game away from us with a splendid hundred. It was another uphill struggle, but rain again came to the rescue. Almost two days were lost. We could focus on saving the match, and that's what we did. All of our batsmen contributed, with me scoring 86 before Holding trapped me lbw.

**5** and **86**

* * *

*You first wear a helmet in the World Cup final of 1979. Mike Brearley began it all with the skull cap he designed in 1977, and then when Andy Roberts broke David Hookes' jaw during a World Series Cricket Super Test, Kerry Packer began importing helmets for his players, and now, in the face of Lillee, Thomson, Pascoe and Hogg, Roberts, Holding, Croft, Marshall and Garner, almost every frontline batsman is using one.*

*You realise that if you don't put a helmet on, it'll be like a red rag to a bull. The West Indies bowlers will take it as a challenge. You don't even practise in it, you just put it on in the Lord's dressing room before the England innings in the World Cup Final and make 57. You drop it again for the Tests with India, but when you get to Australia you wear one again, this time one with a plastic visor that gets steamed up in the heat and makes you breathe downwards to keep it clear.*

*The West Indies use the ball as a weapon. Colin Croft is the most dangerous of all. He says he wants to hit batsmen, wants to hurt them... Hit them. Hurt them. Make them scared to come back and face him again. He bowls from a wide angle with an action that forces the ball back in towards the batsman, following him, chasing him, getting bigger and bigger, at the head... Your head...*

*When the ball whistles past, you hear the crowd gasp and roar but it doesn't bother you. Getting out of the way is second nature. You keep your eye on the ball, your hands and bat out of the way... Second nature, and you wouldn't want it any other way. This war, this attrition, this danger is a part of the game, it gives the bowlers teeth, it makes you feel alive when you face it...*

*Alive in a way that nothing else does...*

\* \* \*

## Fourth Test, England versus West Indies, The Oval, London, 24-29 July, 1980

*Ninety-second cap*

England won the toss and batted on a pitch that looked to have pace and bounce. Just what you didn't want against Holding, Marshall, Croft and Garner. Colin Croft hadn't played at Manchester, but here he was a handful. I'd made three when he hit me over the right eye with a vicious short ball that followed me as I tried to sway out of the way. The ball hit the helmet, which jammed back and opened a cut above my eye. There was blood everywhere. The physio came out, took one look and said I needed stitches, so I had to retire hurt.

They put the stitches in, and I used ice to control the swelling and eventually sat down in the dressing room relaxing with a cup of tea. No sooner had I sat down than Ian came along and said, 'Pad up Fiery, you're in next...'

'Why's that?'

'Because you're better at playing them than us.'

'Thanks, captain.'

Luckily, I was able to rest well into the afternoon as Graham Gooch and Brian Rose played really well and put on 155. That gave me the chance to clear my head and let the eye settle down, but as soon as I took guard I knew I would get Croft to face, and sure enough he bombarded me from around the wicket. He was a wicked bowler who loved hitting and hurting batsmen. I had no problem with that, and any good captain would have made me face the guy who had hit me to see if there was any psychological damage. Bowler and captain were testing me to see if I would flinch and get myself out. I didn't and at the end of that first day we were 236 for only three down. It was our best batting day so far.

Next morning I stupidly ran myself out for 53 hitting the ball straight to Gordon Greenidge at mid-on who threw the stumps down. Mike Gatting and Peter Willey helped our total up to the dizzy heights of 370. Once a team can put a decent score on the board, the opposition come under a bit of pressure, and by the close of play we had got the openers Haynes and Greenidge out cheaply.

Saturday was a wash-out and Sunday was a rest day. We resumed on Monday and our seamers bowled West Indies out for 265. But just when we were feeling like we'd had a great day, the West Indies quicks got in a few overs before the close and completely knocked the stuffing out of us. In no time, we were 20-4. It was total panic as myself, Gooch, Larkins and nightwatchman Emburey were blown away.

Next day, it looked done and dusted by lunch as those great fast bowlers reduced us to 92-9. Even allowing for our first innings lead, there was so much time left that a West Indies win was almost a certainty. Last man Bob Willis went in to join Peter Willey. We knew Bob was a hopeless batsman, so players started to get their fielding gear on. But somehow he survived his first few deliveries, and although he was playing and missing a lot, he got a bit more confident and managed to hang around to score 24 priceless runs and allow Peter to make his maiden Test century. They added 117 for the last wicket and took up so much time that Ian was able to declare just before the close with the captains agreeing on a draw. Somehow, we had survived another close encounter.

53 and 5

* * *

*You remain in London and go to Madame Tussaud's, where you are measured so that they can make your waxwork image. When they ask you where you want to be put in the exhibition, you tell them, 'Next to Sophia Loren...'*

*Meanwhile, it rains and it rains...*

\* \* \*

### Fifth Test, England versus West Indies, Headingley, Leeds, 7-12 August, 1980

*Ninety-third cap*

Preparation was non-existent and we sat around in the dressing room weather-watching. No practice, no play and eventually, on the second day, a delayed start. The covers had been on the pitch and made it sweat. As a batsman, you pray you win the toss and bowl. It wasn't our day. Clive Lloyd called correctly and stuck us straight in.

Once more, we would spend most of the game up against it. West Indies were just better in all departments, shooting us out for 143, and then, despite a good performance from our bowlers, taking a lead of 100-plus. The fourth day was another wash-out, so we went into the last day of the series knowing that all we had to play for was a draw. West Indies were bound to come at us hard again, and so it proved.

Croft and Holding had a real good go at me from around the wicket. A number of balls from Croft in particular were deliberately aimed at my ribs, heart and throat. A very smart and intimidating tactic. Since helmets came in, most batsmen felt more comfortable facing fast bowlers. I can honestly say my best and most important piece of equipment was my chest pad, which helped me have confidence to stay high on the back foot to try and get over the ball and play it down and if it bounced or got big and awkward, I could let it hit me. Graham made 55 and myself 47, and our opening stand of 92, plus the 14 hours lost to rain, meant we escaped again with a draw.

It had been mentally draining batting against those fast bowlers all summer. It felt like I did more ducking and weaving than I did playing shots. I was physically fit but I was in my 40th year. Nobody in their right mind should be fending off fast bowling at that age. And never in the history of Test cricket had any team been lucky enough to have four together. I would like to have had a go against them when I was at my best, but as you get older your reflexes are not as quick.

**4** and **47**

\* \* \*

*This is how it goes against the West Indies: They bowl 12 overs per hour, or 24 per session. If you face half the balls that is 72 deliveries. Half of those are bouncers or short-pitched and you can't hit them. That leaves 36. Eighteen deliveries per hour that you might score from...*

*Even so, you face 1,145 deliveries in the series, over 500 more than any other England player, and average 40, more than any England batsman except Brian Rose, who plays only three matches.*

*Malcolm Marshall says of you, 'As a batsman, he commands the respect of every bowler in the world... The [team] conversation never strayed far from Boycott...'*

*But you call what you just did survival, not batting. You spend the series camped on the back foot, so before the one-off Centenary Test against Australia, you go home, to Ackworth CC, and let the lads there bowl you back into form. You go to Old Trafford for the Roses match and make 135, and then somehow get out caught and bowled to David Lloyd's lollipop left-arm spin. After a summer of Holding, Roberts, Marshall, Garner and Croft, it at least makes you smile...*

\* \* \*

### Centenary Test, England versus Australia, Lord's, London, 28 August – 2 September, 1980

*Ninety-fourth cap*

A special occasion to celebrate the centenary of the first Test match played in England. Australia won the toss and batted well on a good, dry surface. Graeme Wood scored a hundred and Kim Hughes made it look easy with his century.

Then more rain in a summer when it never seemed to stop. We didn't get to bat properly until the Monday. DK Lillee knocked over Graham Gooch and Bill Athey, before David Gower and me stopped the rot with a partnership of 96. On the few occasions I batted with David, I loved it. Right and left hand seemed to work well, and he was good at rotating the strike and running singles.

Then Lillee came back from the Pavilion End, bowled David for 47 and got me with a beauty that went up the slope off the ridge for 62. Lenny Pascoe polished off the next five in 32 balls for England to be all out for 205. Suddenly we were up the creek without the proverbial paddle. We had succumbed tamely and yet the pitch was very good. Yes, it always gives a bit of help to the seamers because of the slope, but ours was a very poor effort. I hadn't seen the dismissals as I was upset at getting out and had gone for a walk behind the Pavilion to get over my disappointment. I was playing well and thought I was on for a hundred.

Aussie came out and smacked us around, and were able to declare leaving us 370 runs to make in 350 minutes. The way we batted first innings we had no chance.

Just as I'm padding up Ian came to me and said: 'Don't get out Fiery or they'll bowl us out again.'

Dickie Bird told me later on that Dennis Lillee was marking his run-up at the Pavilion End and said to him: 'Hey Birdie, if I get your mate Boycott out, I'll get the rest and we'll all be up that road by tea time.'

'Tha won't get him out. He's in good nick,' Dickie replied.

'If I do, I'll get the rest easy...'

Dickie was right. I was in good touch and good rhythm. The Australians must have been watching Michael Holding and Colin Croft go around the wicket and give me a going over so they tried the same tactic, with Lenny Pascoe bombarding me from the Pavilion End. Lenny was a huge, burly, in-your-face fast bowler who loved banging it in short. He liked hitting the pitch in his half more than the batsman's and would finish his follow through as near to you as possible.

This went on for a while until Dickie Bird said: 'Right that's enough. You've had a good go at him Lenny, so now just the odd one.'

Lenny wasn't happy, and captain Greg Chappell raced from first slip to get involved.

Greg told Dickie he didn't agree that Pascoe had bowled too many. Dickie said: 'I do.'

Greg: 'Well, I disagree…'

Dickie said: 'I'm the umpire and if you want, I'll give you an official warning,' and off he walked to inform his partner at square-leg. No answer to that.

We saved the match and I finished with 128 not out. As Jim Laker said on BBC television, 'I bet Geoffrey Boycott wishes the season was just starting not just ending.'

**62** *and* **128 not out**

\* \* \*

*That is your wish, and not just because you go to Scarborough to play Derbyshire and make 154 not out… You are nearer to the end than the beginning now, you know it, feel it, and yet you don't want it to end, can't think about it ending… Not now. Not yet. Your life is changing, though. You move away from Fitzwilliam and the place you've lived in all your life to a gorgeous old farmhouse with a garden in Woolley near Wakefield. The hundred against Australia at Lord's is your 19th in Tests. You go past Len Hutton's total of 6,971 runs for England. Only Hammond and Cowdrey are ahead of you now.*

*Mike Brearley leads Middlesex to the County Championship title and the Gillette Cup. Yorkshire finish sixth in the County Championship, lose in the semi-final of the Gillette Cup, in the group stage of the Benson & Hedges Cup and finish second-bottom of the John Player Sunday League. John Hampshire resigns as captain. Chris Old is appointed in his place. Ray Illingworth remains as manager.*

*You ask yourself hard questions about the forthcoming tour of West Indies. You are 40 years old. How smart is it to be opening the innings against the greatest quartet of fast bowlers in history? The pitches will be quicker. Your reaction times will be slower. Holding and Croft will attack you from around the wicket. There will be no limit on the number of short deliveries. Scoring opportunities will be further limited. England are almost certainly going to lose. You will need courage, determination, a strong mindset, patience and concentration, and even then, after a couple of hours' batting you may only have 15 or 20 runs to your name.*

*You ask yourself, 'Is it worth it, just for that?'*

*But you already know the answer...*

*You fly to Johannesburg and practise at the Wanderers cricket club, where your friend Peter Stringer organises hordes of young, keen fast bowlers who come at you from around the wicket and bang it in from 20 yards to imitate the attack you will face in the West Indies. It is difficult and uncomfortable, tough and dangerous, but the more you do it, the easier it gets...*

*While you are in Johannesburg, your friend Peter Cooke asks about the possibility of a team of England players coming to South Africa for a short unofficial tour in the winter of 1981. He talks names and sponsors. He talks big money for a one-month engagement. He says he will fly to Trinidad to watch England play West Indies and tell you more.*

# CHAPTER SIXTEEN

# 1981

*You fly to Trinidad. Ian gives stirring speeches. He says he will take the fight to West Indies. It's a heroic attitude, you think, but so was the Charge of the Light Brigade, and they all died.*

*England lose Bob Willis to injury before the Test matches begin. He flies home and is replaced by Robin Jackman of Surrey. Now it's bazookas against pop guns.*

*The series begins in Port of Spain. The local fans are angry that the Trinidad wicket-keeper Deryck Murray has been dropped in favour of David Murray from Barbados. The West Indies Cricket Board receive threats of retribution. They install security lights at the Queen's Park Oval and employ a security patrol, but the night before the Test, the lights fail and the security guards don't turn up. Protestors enter the ground, slash the covers open with knives, dig holes in the pitch and soak the bowlers' run-ups.*

\* \* \*

### First Test, West Indies versus England,
### Port of Spain, Trinidad, 13-18 February, 1981

*Ninety-fifth cap*

The ground staff had to fill the holes in the pitch and dry the run-ups, so the game started half a day late. Some of the crowd got restless and started throwing bottles on the field, which held things up even more. Ian eventually won the toss and put them in, but nothing, not our bowlers, the vandals or the bottles, could stop West Indies. Gordon Greenidge and Desmond Haynes put on 144 for the first wicket, and from that powerful platform they batted on into the third day to total 426 before we had to face the music.

At the end of the second day's play, Ian had a press conference and said words to the effect of, 'on this wicket we would struggle to get a result in ten days,' and 'if we lose now, heads will roll.' I thought he was judging the pitch on our bowling against their batting, and it was naive to think it would play the same when their attack bowled on it. I had played seven matches in Port of Spain over three tours and it usually broke up and had some uneven bounce.

Graham Gooch and I put on 45 quick runs before lunch, and then straight after the break I got over-confident trying to drive Colin Croft and was caught at slip for 30. Big mistake, as all batsmen are vulnerable after a break. On top of that, Croft was so awkward from wide of the crease that I should have taken a little more time to line him up. Sure enough, that West Indies attack made the pitch look far more dangerous than our bowlers had, blowing us away for 178 and enforcing the follow-on, Ian's words hollow now.

As the last day began, we were 65-2 in our second innings with me 29 not out and David Gower on 21. Although nobody said it out loud, I knew I had to bat all day for us to have any chance of the draw. Kenny Barrington took me to one side and said, 'Talk to the guys at the other end. Keep them going. Do a good job for yourself and you will be doing a good job for the team. Oh and don't get out...'

I took an off stump guard to Croft, and Holding went around the wicket to David, which cramped him for room and stopped his off side shots. The occasional ball did keep low, and it was extra awkward when you were being made to jump around and duck and weave on the back foot and then you got a shooter.

We toughed it out for a while, but Gower went for 27 and then Geoff Miller followed, which meant I was joined by our captain. After Ian had an extravagant play and miss, I reminded him we were trying to save the match.

Ian said: 'Keep talking to me...' So I would come down after every over and urge him to stay in and bat time, not runs.

We'd been batting for an hour or so when I said to him: 'The new ball is due in a few overs and we must be together when West Indies take it. We are almost certain to lose one of us to the new conker but it is absolutely vital the other is there to talk to our tail-enders and give them a bit of confidence. Without one of us, these will blow them away because they are terrified...'

No sooner had we had our chat than Clive Lloyd brought on Viv Richards to bowl his little off-spinners and speed up getting that new ball. What happens? Ian's brains go out the window, he tries to hit a Viv lollipop into the city centre and holes out to Michael Holding at mid-off. Lack of concentration. Ego. Bragging rights between friends... Whatever caused it, Viv went berserk and his team-mates were hugging and congratulating each other, while I couldn't believe the stupidity of the shot.

Sure enough, the ninth delivery with the new ball from Michael Holding leapt at my throat, hit me on the left glove and sped in an arc to gully. Even after five-and-a-quarter hours at the crease, I don't think I could have done much about it. I reckoned it hit one of the re-earthed patches caused by the vandals, but it didn't matter now. I was out for 70. One flash of irresponsibility by Ian and one lethal ball to me had sealed England's fate. Those great fast bowlers could see the finishing line, and soon enough it was an innings defeat.

Whose head was going to roll we wondered? Not Ian's of course, as he told the press, 'That's the way I play.'

I seem to have heard that excuse before and since.

**30** and **70**

\* \* \*

*Turmoil on the field and turmoil off of it...*

*As he promised, Peter Cooke comes to Trinidad. The idea of an unofficial tour to South Africa takes shape – one month next winter before England go to India with England. Peter has a sponsor, Holiday Inns of South Africa. They are offering a fee of £50,000 each as long as you, Ian Botham and some other big names are in the squad.*

*£50,000 is a fortune.*

*It'd take you over two years to make that playing with Yorkshire and England.*

*A day after the Trinidad Test finishes, you, Ian Botham, David Gower, Graham Gooch, John Emburey and Graham Dilley sign letters of intent that Peter takes back to South Africa.*

*You fly to Guyana for the second Test, which is cancelled when the Guyanese government revoke Robin Jackman's visa and serve him with a deportation order because he has played and coached in South Africa in breach of the Gleneagles Agreement. You endure a 10-hour journey to Barbados via Trinidad, where prime ministers, presidents and government officials fly in to decide whether the tour will be allowed to continue.*

*You hang around in Barbados. A lot of the media expect the tour to be abandoned. Some of the players want to go home. Graham Dilley says he wonders what would happen if anyone knew about the letters you six have signed. Ian Botham and Graham Stevenson come to your hotel room. Ian tells you that if the tour is off, he and Graham would like to go to South Africa for the rest of the winter to play and coach, and wonder if you could use your contacts to fix it up for them. You tell them that if and when the cancellation is official, you will make some calls.*

*You wonder what the hell will happen if it is cancelled, but after a few more days of discussions, the island governments decide that the tour will continue, and you forget about South Africa.*

*You arrive at the Kensington Oval. You go and look at the pitch. It's covered in live green grass. You say to the curator, Tommy Pierce, 'What is this then? Where has all this green come from?'*

*Tommy tells you, 'They want results...'*

*You hate it, hate this pitch, this green, green pitch, because you know what it means, know what it will be like to face Andy Roberts, Michael Holding, Colin Croft and Joel Garner on it.*

*It will be a nightmare.*

*You tell Tommy: 'Your fast bowlers don't need any more help...'*

\* \* \*

### Third Test, West Indies versus England, Bridgetown, Barbados, 13-18 March, 1981

*Ninety-sixth cap*

Ian won the toss and put West Indies in to bat again. Twice in consecutive Tests, and that can't have happened before in the Caribbean. Nobody could blame him on this occasion. As a batsman, you have a chance if there is pace and bounce off a hard surface or some seam movement from a grassy pitch, but if there is pace, bounce and movement all together you have no chance.

This was a pitch you could have nightmares about.

251

Robin Jackman made his debut and had a dream start, with Gordon Greenidge caught at slip off his fifth ball. Then Graham Dilley got Viv Richards for a duck. We had West Indies on the rack at 65-4 when Larry Gomes edged behind and David Bairstow dropped him. Gomes had 13 at the time and it was a costly miss. Larry went on to fifty, but more importantly stayed with Clive Lloyd while Clive got stuck into our seamers and smacked them around. They didn't have the pace to force him off his front foot, and his driving was so intimidating and powerful our bowlers were in danger of getting hit by a rocket in their follow through.

Clive made exactly 100 out of a pretty modest score of 265, but totals are relative to the surface you are playing on, and this was not a good one.

So it was that on the morning of day two, I walked out with Graham to open the England innings on that green, green pitch, and faced one of the most famous overs ever bowled.

Andy Roberts took the first from the Southern End. Graham wanted to face, and he thick-edged a couple through the vacant area between slips and gully for four and a two.

Then Michael Holding marked out his run from the Pavilion End to bowl at me.

\* \* \*

*The over that you are about to face will become a mythic thing. It will live on. The TV footage that survives does not quite do it justice. First of all, the Kensington Oval is fuller than any ground looks like it should be. There are 15,00 people inside, and 15,000 more who will say that they were. There are people sliding through a gully under one of the stands. There are people jumping over the pitch-side fence. There are people climbing onto the roof of the Hall & Griffith Stand and perching like birds on the raked tin. Every seat, every row, every aisle of every stand is full. The noise is unreal. The air itself seems to vibrate.*

*There are two things that you don't yet know. The first is that Tommy Pierce has told Michael Holding that you hate this pitch. The second is that Clive Lloyd has asked Michael Holding which end he wants to bowl from. It's the first time in Michael's career that he has done so. Michael tells Clive: 'Whichever end Andy doesn't want...'*

*Maybe these things mean nothing. Maybe they have no effect at all. But for whatever reason, when Michael begins his run, everything feels right. He is instantly in rhythm, his feet falling exactly how they should, his head swaying softly as he runs, and when he bowls it feels as though he just lets it go, but instantly, with no warm-up, no loosener, he is at full pace. It comes from nowhere, happening before you know it's happening...*

*The first delivery is not quite full, not quite short and it smacks into the glove of your top hand as you ride the bounce. The ball lands in front of Viv Richards at slip. You turn away towards short leg. Your chest is out, your shoulders are back, your head is up, you look like a great military general staring at enemy lines.*

*You wear a short-sleeved shirt, your chest pad underneath, an arm guard held in place by a roll of tubigrip, the blue helmet with its clear plastic visor. On his long walk back, Michael Holding thinks, 'Wow, that felt good...' He thinks about the next ball he will bowl. He knows that he has to keep a tight line to you. He knows that he has to make you play, but he knows how hard that is to do.*

*The second delivery is an almost carbon copy of the first. In the fraction of a second available to you, you do play, and you miss. The third delivery is on the same line again, but this time it lands on the seam and jags back into you, smacking you on the thigh. It hurts.*

*Michael has a long, slow walk back to his mark, and each time, the crowd seem to be drawn further into what is happening. The atmosphere is sharp and expectant. It's a guessing game now. You wonder when the short one is coming. Michael knows that you are wondering. The fourth ball leaps from that green, green pitch at sensational speed and you glove it down to gully. The fifth is just a little shorter. It smacks into that green, green pitch again and this time rears up at your throat, but somehow, you get a glove up and play it down to Joel Garner in the gully again.*

*One ball to go. Holding is bowling very, very fast, but the scary thing is, it seems effortless, as if he can bowl even faster if he wants to.*

*As he walks back, Michael is thinking: 'I have just bowled five of the best deliveries I can, and Boycott is still here...' He wonders if he can bowl another over as good as this one. He wonders what ball he should bowl next. He turns at the top of his mark, and decides.*

*He comes in again, and bowls fuller on a tight line, incredibly fast, and all he sees is the ball pass your pad. He is in a daze, in the zone. He hears the crazy noise that the crowd make. He does not see the off stump explode from the ground. He does not see you turn and walk off. He does not see the people sliding off the roof, the people running onto the ground.*

* * *

I remember my friend Desmond Haynes at short leg jumping up in the air with delight, and as I left for the dressing room, the whole stadium was erupting. West Indians everywhere were leaping up and down with uncontrolled excitement. Spectators precariously perched on roof-tops were bouncing up and down, and people came onto the field hugging each other in ecstasy. The whole stadium was dancing wildly and going crazy before my eyes. It must have been great theatre, and I might have enjoyed it if I hadn't been the one that was out. Mikey has since described how surprised he was that line, length and pace all came together so perfectly for a first over. I never threw my kit around whenever or however I was out, so I just got undressed and sat quietly to contemplate my dismissal. Silence is best, because words are of no comfort. It is soul-destroying. Don't let anyone tell you differently.

* * *

*In Frank Keating's book about the tour, Another Bloody Day In Paradise, hailed as a classic when it is published later in 1981, his account of the Holding over begins its journey towards mythic status. Frank writes: 'Boycott looked round and palely down at the remains of his wicket and then, as the din assailed his ears, his mouth gaped and he tottered as if he'd been visited by the Devil himself; and then, slowly, he walked away, erect and brave, and beaten. That single over, magnificent and cruel at the same time, had, as it soon turned out, won the Test.'*

*You cannot stop thinking about your dismissal, your failure, going over and over that final delivery, trying to work out how you missed it. After play, you go back to the hotel, you eat, you think, you sleep. You do not dream about cricket.*

*At 7.30am you are woken by a knock on the door. It is AC Smith, tour manager. He tells you that Ken Barrington has died of a heart attack during the night.*

\* \* \*

It was a terrible shock, the last thing anyone would expect on a cricket tour, especially a guy who had just been laughing and joking with us all, and who had been bowling wrist-spinners to me in the nets for days on end. Kenny had been in the team when I made my debut, all those years ago in 1964. Now I was here at the end. There was a minute's silence out on the field before we started, and one or two players were in tears, but then you have no choice but to continue the match. Tough.

From then on, it was the Viv Richards show. Our one genuine fast bowler, Graham Dilley, seemed to be affected by Kenny's death and never bowled with any pace. Robin Jackman kept on running in but Viv was on the front foot almost before he had let the ball go, and he smashed everything. Viv hit one back at Jackers so violently that he didn't have time to get his hands down to the ball – it hit his boot and still rocketed for four runs. Talk about pop guns. Clive Lloyd batted on and on until West Indies were so far ahead we couldn't have scored all of those 523 to win if he had allowed us two more innings.

Graham Gooch, who had been very close to Kenny, scored a brave and magnificent 116, and David Gower got a half-century. The rest of us were dismissed in haste for only 46 runs off the bat.

**0** and **1**

\* \* \*

*You don't care that you are 40 years old. You don't care that the pitch was one from a nightmare. You don't care that Michael Holding is 27 years old and has just delivered the fastest over of his life. All you care about is the failure, the failure and the way it makes you feel, that feeling that you have feared and loathed all of your life.*

*There are 11 ways that a batsman can be dismissed. Of those, six – retired out, timed out, obstructing the field, hit wicket, handled the ball and hit the ball twice – are glancing rare. Of the other five – run-out, stumped, caught, lbw, and bowled – by far the most common is caught. More than 60 per cent of your innings end in that way. Being clean bowled is different...*

*By the time you face Michael Holding in Barbados, you have batted 168 times in Test matches and have been out bowled 27 times. That is 16 per cent of the total, below the mean average for a top-order batsman of around 20 per cent. You have faced almost 30,000 deliveries, which means that any one delivery has about a 0.5 per cent chance of dismissing you. The chance of it bowling you is 16 per cent of that 0.5 per cent, or 0.08 per cent.*

*To you, being bowled means failure at its most absolute. You cannot accept it, not without understanding it, and so you find the BBC crew and ask them if you can see their highlights footage, which is about to be shipped back to England. At the Holiday Inn in Bridgetown, you watch the Holding over again and again in slow motion, watch it until you are satisfied that you understand what happened on that electric Bridgetown morning.*

*Here is what you see:*

\* \* \*

Four out of the first five balls had reared up from just short of a length into my throat. I had missed one and gloved three just in front of slip and gully. The bounce was alarming and at that pace, the law of averages says sooner or later I am not going to be able to keep the ball down. Why? Because when a ball is chest height you should be able to get above it and with soft hands play the ball down. Problems arise when the ball gets up around your shoulder or your neck. Then it becomes impossible to get high enough over the top of the ball to play it down safely. If it hits the splice of the bat or your gloves, you have no control and it will lob for a catch.

All this was going through my mind. I was trying to think on my feet how to play it better and not get gloved out. I remembered seeing Bob Simpson batting at Perth when that was the bounciest pitch in the world. When a fast bowler hit the deck short of a length he didn't attempt to get in line and defend the ball. Instead he swayed to the leg side and let the ball bounce over his stumps. When people first saw him do it they thought maybe he was a bit wary of fast bowling. Not on your life! He didn't want to get out defending a high bouncing ball, so he trusted the bounce to go over the top of the stumps. I was fascinated by his thinking and execution. When I tried it for that sixth ball I didn't get far enough over when Michael bowled a touch fuller. My thinking was good, but execution poor.

* * *

*You fly to Montserrat to play the Leeward Islands, where you make 72 and 15, and then to Antigua for the fourth Test and another meeting with Michael Holding. This is what the game does. It makes you face again what has just defeated you.*

*This capricious game.*

*When you land, you pick up a copy of the local paper. Colin Croft has given an interview and said, 'I hate all batsmen and I love to see blood.'*

*You bring the paper with you to the High Commission in St John's, where there is a reception for both teams to mark Antigua's first ever Test match. You march up to Colin and ask him, 'What's this all about?'*

*'I like to hit batsmen' he says.*

*Graham Stevenson overhears. 'You'll not hit me, Crofty...'*

*'I get you, you easy to hit...'*

*'Well then you'll have to bowl at the square-leg umpire, because I'll be hiding behind him. I've got a wife and two kids at home...'*

*I say to Crofty 'What about if your mum was batting'*

*'I hit her too...'*

* * *

### Fourth Test, West Indies versus England, St John's Recreation Ground, Antigua, 27 March – 1 April, 1981

*Ninety-seventh cap*

I had nine days to wrestle with having to face the same fast bowlers again. I knew the eyes of the world would be watching to see how

I fared against Mikey after his over in Barbados. When fast bowlers get on top of a batsman it can create psychological damage and leave scars. It was going to be a test of my mental strength as much as my batting technique.

My moment of truth came quickly, as Ian won the toss and this time chose to bat. Graham Gooch and I played beautifully, putting on 60 for the first wicket. I drove Roberts for four, steered Mikey for four through the covers, then off drove him for four, as well as clipping Croft off my legs for four. As Mikey walked back to his mark, he said: 'Nice pitch, Geoffrey....'

Then Graham ran himself out. He drove Croft into the empty spaces at long-on and wanted three. I tried to shout no, but he was insistent. He told me later he was sure he could make it.

I hadn't missed a ball and was feeling in great touch, but you are never in with that lot. Colin Croft went around the wicket and bombarded me with short stuff. It was a legitimate attack to the body, and I don't blame him for making batting uncomfortable. He was probably thinking about his newspaper article. I played a few well from neck height until one just flicked my thumb and I was out caught behind for 38.

Peter Willey got a really gutsy century. I loved his matter of fact, no-nonsense approach. Whatever the quicks threw at him, he just got stuck in and never backed off. Crofty started giving him a working over with short stuff, following through to eyeball him from a short distance away. Pete just stood and glared with his right hand on his hip. Then Crofty bounced him outside off stump and Pete whacked it up and over square point for six. He waved his hand at Crofty as if to say, 'F... off!' He deserved his century, but again it only got us to 271 all out.

All eyes were now on Viv. As the world's greatest batsman and the local boy who lived a stone's throw from the ground, he was the main reason that Antigua had been recognised with its first Test match. The stage was set, and the fans were packed in to see the great man score a hundred. As usual, he was up for the challenge. He smashed Ian through the off side for four right away, and raced to 29 with seven boundaries. Viv and I usually chatted at the end of an over if we passed each other:

'I wanna impress them here, Boycs,' he said.

He was pumped up and determined to dominate. We thought we'd escaped when Paul Downton caught him down the leg side, but the umpire had his arm out for a Graham Dilley no ball! Jesus…

There was no stopping Viv after that. He hooked a Dilley bouncer out of the ground then sauntered down the pitch with that little smile playing on his face, getting as near to Graham as he could. He wanted to confront the bowler whose fastest and best ball he had dispatched out of the park. Viv's hero was the heavyweight boxer Joe Frazier, who had courage, aggression and a compulsion to go forward and meet his opponent head on. Joe never took a backward step, and neither did Viv. In those few moments, it was all said without a word.

From then on he was on the front foot looking to drive, but using those lightning reflexes to rock back and smash anything short. Viv drove through mid-off for his century, and as he did so the police ran on just ahead of hordes of people wanting to hug their man and celebrate with him. The police provided his safety net as they surrounded and protected him. Four hours, 19 fours and one six, plus a piece of history.

The new ball was due, and Ian asked me to bowl a couple of overs in the hope I might disturb Viv's concentration. I turned my cap around and marked out my run, the crowd shouting and laughing, but Viv told me he was prepared to block forever rather than get out to me. I informed him that England's best batsman, Jack Hobbs, used to make a point of giving his wicket away to the most deserving bowler once he had reached a century and I reckoned I was the most deserving case…

Viv said: 'Can't do that, Boycs… I need another fifty for 4,000 Test runs, and I'm going to get 200…'

What the Gods give they can also take away… Next morning, he cracked Graham Dilley's first ball for four, but then he attempted a massive, ugly pull off the fourth and spooned it up in the air. He was so angry with himself, and walked off smacking his bat against his pad. We'd taken a beating, and couldn't even get the tail-enders out. Garner and Holding put on 104 runs. Perhaps Mikey wanted to show me how it was done, as he made 58 not out… Clive Lloyd finally called them in at 468-9, and Graham and I had a couple of overs to survive that night. We made it through. The next day was the rest day, and it rained so hard, the fourth day's play was a wash out.

It meant that if we could bat through the final day, we could escape this battering with a draw. Could we? Yes, we could because Graham and I played so well and had an opening partnership of 144. No mistakes and no lives, just good, solid backs-to-the-wall batting. Graham was out for 83, but I went on to 104 not out to ensure the draw.

After Barbados, I was so proud I had the mental strength and ability to come through that ordeal with a hundred in the very next Test match.

**38** and **104 not out**

\* \* \*

*You fly to Jamaica, where you are met at the airport with an armed guard. More than 800 people have died in the violence surrounding the election of October 1980, in which the JLP win a majority. There have been strikes, fires, attacks on police stations. It is an ideological war between the former Prime Minister Michael Manley, whose PNP has ties to Cuba and Russia, and the JLP, which is closer to the US, Canada and the UK. Your hotel has armed police in the corridors. You are escorted to and from the ground each day... You play in turmoil again.*

\* \* \*

### Fifth Test, West Indies versus England, Sabina Park, Jamaica, 10-15 April, 1981

*Ninety-eighth cap*

West Indies won the toss and put us in, mainly because if there was anything in the pitch it would be the first morning and Clive wanted to give his fast bowlers any help possible. They didn't play spinners so were not interested in a pitch breaking up later in the match. Their intention was to batter the opposition into submission in the first innings, then bat and make a big total before cleaning them up with pace again. It usually worked.

I once told Viv if I ever came back on this earth I would want to play for West Indies. He was a bit surprised but when I explained, he laughed. I wouldn't have to face four fast bowlers, and as they usually won in four days, I would get a day off on the beach...

Goochie and I gave England a good platform with 93 before I was out caught behind off Joel Garner. Graham went on to score a magnificent 153 but even with a good start and a big hundred we were still all out for 285. We could never score big enough totals to put them under pressure. Their pace just wore us down.

Gordon Greenidge and Desmond Haynes put on over a hundred and the middle order of Larry Gomes and Clive Lloyd piled the runs up. They closed on 442, another huge lead, Clive's plan working perfectly.

Graham and I were out quickly, Mikey Holding got Bill Athey and we were rocking once again. But just as we were under huge pressure, we got a slice of luck when Malcolm Marshall had to go off with strained rib muscles. David Gower kept his discipline and concentration for over seven hours, interspersed with that sublime timing, to finish with a superb 154 not out and get us a draw.

Did I regret making myself available for the tour? No, but watching Graham Gooch at the age of 28 and David Gower at 24, I sometimes wished I could have had a go at this West Indies team when I was their age. I was at my best then, with much sharper reflexes. As I'd got older, my determination, concentration and desire never diminished and my technique always stood the test of time, but nature has a way of slowing us all down. That's life. To do what I had done at 40 was an achievement in itself.

**40** and **12**

\* \* \*

*From the heat and violence of Jamaica to the cold and rain of England, the endless cycles of this capricious game you play. There are not many runs waiting for you in the damp of May, nothing doing under the captaincy of Chris Old. It's your last innings before the first Ashes Test when you finally pass three figures, 124 against Nottinghamshire at Bradford...*

*And Yorkshire cannot win a game under Raymond Illingworth and Chris Old, drawing five and losing two of the first seven Championship games, losing in the first round of the Gillette Cup and the quarter final of the Benson & Hedges Cup, winning only one of the first five games in the John Player Sunday League...*

*The Committee can't blame you for that...or can they?*

*From Kingston, Jamaica to Nottingham, England. From Michael Holding, Andy Roberts, Joel Garner, Colin Croft and Malcolm Marshall to Dennis Lillee, Rodney Hogg, Terry Alderman and Geoff Lawson. A series that will go down in history for its sheer unlikeliness begins in relentless symmetry...*

\* \* \*

## First Test, England versus Australia, Trent Bridge, Nottingham, 18-21 June, 1981

*Ninety-ninth cap*

1981 is remembered as a great Test match summer. I don't believe it was, and for a lot of it as a player it didn't feel that way. For most of the time, especially early in the series, England were losing, and we batsmen had an examination of our technique that frazzled our brains. Much of the cricket was forgettable as bowlers dominated and the balance between bat and ball was lost.

One look at the Trent Bridge pitch and the weather told me it would be a low-scoring match, one that favoured the seamers and could not last five days. Australia won the toss and bowled us out for 185 in just 57 overs. All the wickets went to Dennis Lillee, Terry Alderman and Rodney Hogg, and only Mike Gatting was able to put together a decent innings of 52.

We had top seam bowlers too in Bob Willis, Ian Botham, Mike Hendrick and Graham Dilley and were able to bowl Australia out for 179. Allan Border scored 63 but the rest struggled. Rodney Marsh threw his bat at a Bob Willis short ball and top edged it miles in the air down to me on the fine leg boundary. I was so near the crowd and could feel all eyes on me as I waited and waited for this thing to descend. When it is a big skier you have too much time to think and dread dropping it. It eventually came down and stuck in my hands and out of sheer delight and relief I threw it way up in the air. It was now a one-innings match, but Lillee and Alderman were too good for us. Five each as they took only 36 overs to bowl us out for 125. We all knew Lillee was a great bowler, smart, clever, a craftsman at the top of his profession, but we had never seen this Alderman guy or heard much about him. It was his debut in international cricket, and he was perfect for English conditions. An athletic sideways action that made the ball swing and seam out and nip back at a lively pace, it was awkward to get forward to him. He delivered the ball from so close to the stumps that he didn't give you any angles to score, and he bowled straight, so if you missed, you knew you would be a candidate for lbw. What an inspired choice by the Australian selectors. We scrapped and fought all the way, getting six Aussies out, but they got home by four wickets.

**27** and **4**

\* \* \*

*You are selected for your one hundredth Test match, just the second player of the 490 to have represented England to reach that magical number. Colin Cowdrey is the only other. He played 114 times, a number you would most likely have passed already had you not exiled yourself. It has taken 17 years, nearly half of your life.*

*Grace, Fry, Rhodes, Hobbs, Sutcliffe, Hammond, Hutton, Trueman, Compton... 481 others... you stand above them all now...*

\* \* \*

### Second Test, England versus Australia, Lord's, London, 2-7 July, 1981

*One hundredth cap*

My hundredth Test match for England, and MCC presented me with a gorgeous decanter engraved with the Lord's pavilion.

Australia put us in again and we spent the best part of two days compiling a not very special total of 311. Aussie made it hard work as we had to contend with the Lord's slope and the ball moving off the seam. Only Peter Willey with 82 and Mike Gatting with 59 did any good. I got 17 and our captain made a three-ball duck.

Ian at least broke the Australians' opening stand with their score on 62, getting John Dyson for a turgid seven, and suddenly we went bang, bang, bang, Graeme Wood, Graham Yallop and Trevor Chappell fell quickly to leave them 81-4. But Allan Border was a tough nut, and he shepherded the tail, which wagged pretty badly from our point of view. Even now, I can't believe Dennis Lillee made 40 not out, and from nowhere, Australia took a 34-run lead.

At one down in the series, our first aim was to avoid going further behind. Early wickets were the danger, but a partnership of 123 between me and David Gower steadied us down. We weren't parted until just before lunch on the final day, when I was out for 60. David went on to get 89, but the day was best remembered for Ian Botham's second duck of the game. He was bowled sweeping at Ray Bright and returned to the pavilion with the great old ground in silence.

The real drama came after the match had petered out, when it transpired that Alec Bedser had asked to see Ian. Exactly what was said only two people know for sure, but it appears that when Alec told Ian that the selectors had decided to remove the captaincy from him, Ian said he would resign and Alec allowed him to. Alec Bedser was always a decent man and Ian was a great cricketer, so why humiliate and embarrass him with a statement that he had been sacked? Much better for all parties if he could resign without that stigma.

I had no inkling it was going to happen. Ian had been captain for 12 games, drawn eight and lost four. Not great, but we had been playing one of the best teams, if not the best team, of all time for ten of those, and these Aussies weren't bad, either. I think what swayed the selectors was Ian's form. Our great all-rounder seemed to have lost his magic, especially with the bat. His value to us as a player was immeasurable, far above that of his captaincy. He was handed the job too young, and I wish that the selectors had made him captain far later in his career.

**17** and **60**

*Yorkshire are changing captains too, not officially, but every time Chris Old is off playing for England or out with one of his ailments, it's David Bairstow, or John Hampshire or even Neil Hartley, who isn't even capped, taking over. It's bloody chaos, Yorkshire are not winning, and things are prickly between you and Illy once again. You feel that cold wind beginning to blow...*

*The England selectors have a brainwave and ask Mike Brearley to return as captain. It seems like a gamble to you, because Mike's batting will load even more pressure on the rest of you to get runs, but then maybe it is inspired too, because Mike is close to Ian, and he soon has him laughing and joking again, soon brings back the smile to Guy The Gorilla's face, soon has those cares and worries lifting from his mighty shoulders... Suddenly the dressing room feels like a different place, all of the tension and the fear and the defeatism dissipating... This is Mike's true skill, finding his way into heads and hearts, repairing them, making them ready again... Ready for anything.*

* * *

## Third Test, England versus Australia, Headingley, Leeds, 16-21 July, 1981

### One-hundred-and-first cap

I could play another hundred Tests and not be part of a match like this one. Just like everyone else, I watched on and was completely mesmerised by what was happening.

Australia won the toss and took two days to score 401 runs, which just about made sure they couldn't lose. The ball seamed around as it usually did at Headingley, so 401 was a terrific score and it put us under pressure. Ian Botham bowled 40 overs for his six wickets and although that was a little confidence boost for Ian, I don't remember any of us celebrating. We knew batting would be a real test for us. And so it proved, as Lillee, Alderman and Geoff Lawson bowled us out for 174.

I got too far over trying to cover the corridor of uncertainty, and had my leg stump knocked out by a Lawson nip-backer for 12. Ian was the only one of us to put a score together. He had to graft for a fine half century, and I truly believe that innings did him more good than his six wickets or any encouraging words from his team-mates or friends.

Australia hadn't bowled much and were easily fresh enough to enforce the follow-on, which they did just before the close on Saturday. They struck right away, Dennis Lillee removing Goochie for nought. We went into the rest day 227 runs behind, a massive lead anywhere in the world, but at Headingley, with the ball nipping around... That rest day seemed to last for an eternity, with us knowing we were staring at another heavy defeat. I look back and wonder what our selectors were thinking having brought Mike Brearley back. Where could they go from here?

Monday morning was overcast and perfect for bowling seam up. Two days to save the match. Deep down we all knew we had no chance. Our players had booked out of their hotel expecting the game to end sometime in the afternoon. I was staying at home and arrived early to have a good, long net practice. The crowd was poor for an Ashes Test as Yorkshire folk don't like to watch the Aussies beating England.

I grafted on, but at the other end wickets kept going down steadily. After lunch, at 105-5, Ian joined me. We were in a hopeless position, and not long after the break I was given out lbw for 46 to a nip back ball from Alderman. Because of the movement he was getting, I was batting out of my crease and getting a big stride forward. Surely that far forward couldn't be out? If there had been DRS, I would definitely have used it! Barry Meyer was a good umpire and a top bloke, but every time I saw him after that I reminded him that it couldn't possibly be out.

Then Bob Taylor went for one and Ian was left with our tail-enders. When you are losing and getting beaten up so comprehensively, there is nothing to say, and our dressing room was very quiet. At tea, Ian asked our captain how he wanted him to play. Mike shrugged as if to say however you wish, thinking that it was just a matter of time before we packed our bags and went home with our tails between our legs. That was perfect for Ian. No pressure. It freed his mind and gave him a licence to enjoy himself knowing it wouldn't matter if or how he got out. With the weight of captaincy and his team struggling he hadn't been able to bat like that for over a year.

What happened next is history. As Ian expressed himself, hitting the ball on the up and flashing it to all parts, his confidence lifted sky high. Everything he tried came off, with extravagant strokes and even the edges from his big heaves flying to the boundary. The Aussies must have felt that this can't last, it's just a bit of valiant resistance and he will hole out sooner or later. But as luck and talent were going his way, Ian got more outrageous. The two destroyers, Lillee and Alderman, were bowling with more men on the boundary than a spinner has when he is getting tonked! Ian ran up and down the pitch laughing and bouncing his way to a century off only 87 balls. In the dressing room we were like everyone else who saw that innings. Astonished. Laughing. Enjoying the spectacle. You couldn't take your eyes off what was happening.

Graham Dilley joined in at the other end scoring a very important 56 and even Chris Old made 29. You could sense the Aussies had lost control as Ian beat them into submission. By close of play, Ian was 145 not out from 148 balls with 27 boundaries and one six. England had gone from six for one to 351-9 – 345 runs in a day. Was this the same pitch and the same seamers who had tormented us England batsmen? Amazing and magical are the only words to describe it.

When we all came back down to earth, we understood that we were still only 124 runs ahead with one wicket left, and that was Bob Willis. Next morning, only five more runs were added and the reality was Australia only needed 130 for victory. Nobody was thinking of winning the match. We were going to get stuck in, get as many wickets as we could and restore a bit of our lost pride.

As everything was going for Ian, Mike opened the bowling with him, and he got Graeme Wood out cheaply caught behind, but after that not much happened. There was no rush for Australia. They had all day to get the runs. The fifty came up and it looked as if they were going to get home comfortably until Mike gave Bob Willis a go at the Kirkstall Lane end. Fast bowlers usually bowled from that end because it was slightly downhill.

Suddenly all hell broke loose as Big Bob found rhythm, length and line. Trevor Chappell was caught behind, and nine balls later Kim Hughes nicked one to second slip, where Ian caught it. Graham Yallop only lasted three balls before he got a lifter and now Bob was racing in. What a sight he was. Fast, nasty and accurate, with bounce. Chris Old got the big wicket of Allan Border, bowled for nought. Then John Dyson got a lifter and was caught behind. Jesus, we hadn't time to catch our breath and they were six down for nothing.

I began to think, 'Can we really bowl them out for under 130?'

No, surely not.

But like every fast bowler, once Bob found that spark it was as if someone had switched a light on. They don't need anyone to talk to them. They get in the zone and the ball comes out of their hand like a missile, everything in perfect unison. He was repeatedly hitting that awkward spot just short of a length, and the pitch did the rest as the ball reared alarmingly. You could see the Aussies didn't fancy it.

Rod Marsh came in and tried to alter the dynamics by attacking, just as Ian had done the day before. He attempted a hook off Bob, top edged it, and it skied to fine leg where Graham Dilley took a splendid catch. Geoff Lawson lasted two balls, caught behind off Bob, and they were 75-8. Is this really happening? We have 45 runs to play with for an unbelievable win.

Just when we thought we had done the impossible, Ray Bright and Dennis Lillee started to score runs and we couldn't stop them. The hundred came up. I was at fine leg starting to think, 'Are we going to get so near and yet finish up so far away? These two can't bat!'

Lillee was staying leg side and slicing or scooping runs in an awkward but effective way, until he spooned one off Bob towards mid-on. It was going to fall short but Mike Gatting dived forward to take a superb catch inches off the grass. One run later, Bob yorked Bright and it was all over. We had won by 18 runs. I raced from fine leg to grab two stumps and sprinted off the field towards the dressing room as the crowd rushed on to the field. We were ecstatic, and had achieved the most improbable victory ever. Bob Willis had the magic figures of 8-43 in 15.1 overs of pure theatre.

I gave one of the stumps to Ian. The Aussies didn't want any stumps as they had lost a Test match they were winning easily for four days. Bad luck!

**12** and **46**

\* \* \*

# Fourth Test, England versus Australia, Edgbaston, Birmingham, 30 July – 2 August, 1981

*One-hundred-and-second cap*

Australia had two weeks to absorb the shock of losing that Test match. It must have been like a boxer winning every round and having your opponent on the ropes ready to be counted out when he slips you a sucker punch you never saw coming. It had to stay with them for days and some probably wrestled with it at night too. Amazingly, this game began to play out in the same kind of way. Mike Brearley won the toss and decided to bat on another bowler-friendly pitch. He played his best innings of the series top-scoring with 48 in another poor England first innings. All out for 189, and another five wickets for that Terry Alderman.

Australia chipped out 258 and took a first innings lead of 69. In low-scoring games, any kind of lead can be priceless. Towards the end of the second day, Mike was out cheaply and David Gower and I were fighting like hell to save another Test match.

Early next morning I got one that turned and bounced from Ray Bright and was caught behind. Bright went on to take five wickets and England were all out for 219.

Another batting nightmare had left Australia only 151 to win. How can this keep happening to us? Australia should have been the ones with a hangover from Headingley. Chris Old got Graeme Wood out lbw that evening, but lightning can't strike twice. With only 151 to score, surely Australia can't cock it up again? But that is cricket. So often it puts you straight back into a position that has just caused you heartache and nightmares. Out we came for what would surely be the final day's play. Bob Willis got John Dyson quickly and followed up with the wicket of Kim Hughes, but then the lefties Border and Yallop dug in and began to put runs on the board.

Aussies do their scores and numbers back to front in cricket, and 87 is their Devil's number. They are superstitious about it because it is 13 short of a hundred. Unlucky it was, as John Emburey forced the breakthrough we needed, Yallop caught at slip, inevitably by Ian. Shortly afterwards, Embers got one to turn and bounce and glove Allan Border. Wow! At 105-5, we were here again. Five top batsmen gone and 45 runs still needed. Game on.

I remember so clearly that I was fielding at fine-leg under the Tom Dollery Stand. It was an emotional morning and the crowd could sense the possibilities. At the back of everyone's mind was the collapse at Headingley. It must have started to get in the Aussie players' minds too. I shouted to our captain, who was at first slip: 'Get the Gorilla on!'

Ian was next to Mike at second slip. He heard me and started laughing and nodding in agreement. The crowd behind me had heard too, and they began clapping and cheering for him.

Next over, Ian was on at the City end.

For me, Ian, along with Fred Trueman, was the best bowler at tail-enders I played with. He was a big unit, and got his power from wide shoulders and a strong backside, with a trim waist that allowed him to get great rotation to bowl out swing and out seam. His natural pace was sharp, but at tail-enders he would race in with venom and spear it into their ribs. It was intimidation, and most didn't fancy getting hurt so they would stay a little leg-side or back away. Once he had set them up, he would pitch the ball right up, and if they were not in line it would be difficult to stop. In came the Gorilla, and down they went:

Rod Marsh, bowled for 4.

Ray Bright, lbw first ball, 0.

Dennis Lillee, caught behind, 3. Martin Kent, bowled for 10. Terry Alderman, bowled third ball, 0.

Ian had five wickets for one run in 28 deliveries. It was one of the finest 45 minutes of cricket you could wish to experience.

Australia all out 121. England had won by 29 runs and we were 2-1 up in the series.

Absolutely staggering.

13 and 29

\* \* \*

*This series… This capricious and wonderful game.*

*England is dreaming, England is on fire with it, the Ashes alive again in hearts and minds, but for you it is a time of struggle. One fifty in the series, and not even the sniff of a hundred.*

*You have made 7,618 runs in Test match cricket. You are seven runs short of overtaking Colin Cowdrey as England's all-time leading run-scorer. You are 414 runs short of Garry Sobers' world record of 8,032 runs.*

*But only if you're in the team.*

*You lack rhythm in your batting and have been short on runs since March. You are on the United Nations blacklist for having coached and played in South Africa after the Gleneagles Agreement. You will soon be 41 years old, and at 41, there will be no way back once you are dropped.*

*You go to see Mike Brearley. You tell him that you are concerned, you are worried about your form, your lack of runs. Mike puts an arm around you, the arm he put around Ian too. He soothes you, talks to you, encourages you towards a less anxious, less cautious frame of mind.*

\* \* \*

### Fifth Test, England versus Australia, Old Trafford, Manchester, 13-17 August, 1981

*One-hundred-and-third cap*

Batting first, England were soon in trouble with Graham Gooch and I out to Lillee and Alderman. I was thinking, 'Is this nightmare ever going to end?' I was gone for 10. We ended the first day on 175-9, but after the miracle of Headingley came the miracle of Old Trafford, with Big Bob Willis wielding his bat for 11 runs, and hanging around while Paul Allott, on debut, got his highest first-class score of 52! I don't know who was more surprised, Bob or Paul, but it gave us all a big lift.

A few hours later, our total of 231 looked even better as we shot Australia out for 130. Thirty-one overs was all it took to finally end their quest for the Ashes. We added another 70 to our lead before

271

the close. Next morning Terry Alderman got me lbw for 37, but Chris Tavaré was like a limpet as he blocked up one end for the best part of seven hours, wearing the Aussies down for his 78.

The stage was set for Ian. A full house on a Saturday afternoon, and the Aussies right up against it. He'd got a duck in the first innings, but after his batting at Headingley and his bowling at Edgbaston his confidence was through the roof. Lillee tried bouncing him and Ian took him on, winning the battle by putting him out of the park. Runs came and so did the swagger. The crowd were behind him, and once a player like Ian gets momentum there is no stopping him. He thinks he can hit anything you send down at him, and he did just that, taking the match away from Australia with a magnificent hundred struck from 86 deliveries and including six sixes.

Ian did so much damage to them psychologically that even when he was finally out for 118 golden runs, Alan Knott and John Emburey scored a half century each and put the final nails in the coffin. All out for 404 meant Australia would need 506 to win.

Yes the pitch was playing good by now, but no team in history had made that many to win a Test. Australia made a fist of it with hundreds from Graham Yallop and Allan Border, who was handicapped by a fractured finger, but it was a win for us by 103 runs. The Ashes retained.

**10** and **37**

\* \* \*

*You have passed Colin Cowdrey. You have scored more runs for England than anyone else ever has. You are 367 runs behind Garry Sobers and his world record of 8,032, but you are not scoring many now. Does it cross your mind that the final Test at The Oval could be your last? Summers end at The Oval. Careers end there. Same every year. What happens at The Oval tends to stick in the minds of the selectors.*

*There is only one answer to the worries and the doubts. There has only ever been one answer. You know what it is.*

\* \* \*

## Sixth Test, England versus Australia,
## The Oval, London, 27 August – 1 September, 1981

### *One-hundred-and-fourth cap*

As usual at The Oval, it was a good, firm, dry, bouncy pitch. Mike put Australia in, which I think had more to do with the traumas they had suffered in the last three Tests than the condition of the surface. Maybe he thought there was psychological damage to their batsmen, and if there was any freshness in the pitch he wanted our bowlers to get stuck into them early. As it was, they didn't crumble, but after another hundred for Allan Border they didn't really capitalise, either. A total of 352 was good but not special.

I had a new partner in Wayne Larkins, who made a tidy 34. Left-arm fast bowler Mike Whitney bombarded me with lots of short stuff. He had plenty of pace but didn't move it much, and that's not a recipe for having a long Test match career. Without the extravagant movement of previous pitches, I found it easier to play Alderman off the back foot. The only problem I encountered was a fast short ball from Lillee that followed me and smacked me on the chin. In that moment I found out I could take a punch!

I was fine, and Dennis bowled beautifully all day. He had such great skill, and he was superb once again in taking 7-89. What a competitor he had been since we first encountered one another a decade ago. I held the innings together, but was finally seventh out to Dennis for 137. My overriding feeling was one of relief to have got some proper runs at last. Our innings closed on 314, still 38 behind thanks to the brilliance of Dennis Lillee.

Allan Border had emerged as Australia's best player during the series and he delivered once again, making 84 to go with his ton in the first innings. Dirk Welham, a young kid playing his first Test, batted nicely until he was on 99, then out of the blue he played too early at Mike Hendrick and spooned an easy catch to me at mid-off. I dropped it, and Dirk became the 12th Australian to score a century on debut since 1893.

They declared overnight, giving themselves a whole day to bowl us out for a consolation win. I missed Lillee's fourth ball and was plumb lbw. Don't know how. Mike Brearley and Mike Gatting made half centuries and Alan Knott got us through to the draw with 70 not out.

Terry Alderman got the plaudits for taking 42 wickets in his debut series, but Dennis was right behind him on 39. Australia had two tremendous bowlers on seamer-friendly pitches, but England had Ian Botham. In the end, Ian was the difference, and a summer that had begun with him as low as he could get ended with him as a national hero. He deserved all of the acclaim and fame that came his way.

`137` and `0`

\* \* \*

*You go to North Marine Road for the Scarborough Festival week, where Yorkshire will play in the Fenner Trophy, have a game against a Barbados XI and then a County Championship match with Northamptonshire. But Raymond Illingworth leaves you out of the team for the Fenner Trophy, and when you give a television interview to promote your new book, you say that you will be seeking 'a showdown' with the management.*

*The interview enrages Raymond, who arrives on the morning of the Championship game and says that he is suspending you. Word spreads through the crowd of 5,000, who begin to whistle and boo. Some of them enter the field of play and the start of the match is delayed. Sid Fielden begins collecting signatures from the members demanding a vote of no confidence in Raymond Illingworth. After 75 minutes of play, you pack up and leave the ground. The report in the Times the following day reads: 'Most of the spectators rose to their feet and applauded him as he passed out of the gates in full view of the players.'*

*Chris Old conducts a dressing room poll asking the players three questions: Do you want Geoff Boycott as captain next season? Do you want Geoff Boycott in the team next season? Do you want Ray Illingworth to continue as team manager?*

*It is a naive move from an inexperienced captain, made worse when the committee make the results public. It smacks of a petty vendetta by the faction of the club who are against you. Committee member Eric Baines resigns in disgust. Sid Fielden is elected in his place. The Yorkshire Reform Group gathers strength. Wisden's editor's notes call the poll 'an absurdity'. It says that the players who voted against you are not fit to tie your bootlaces. Yorkshire set up a sub-committee to investigate, but by the time they come to interview you, you have left for the tour of India.*

*Peter Cooke remains in contact through the summer of 1981. By late September he is ready to offer contracts for a brief tour of South Africa beginning immediately after the tour of India. Stuart Banner, a representative of Holiday Inns South Africa, flies to England. Holiday Inns will pay £500,000 for 14 players plus the physio Bernie Thomas. Stuart Banner wants to judge how committed each player is, so he meets with Graham Gooch, Alan Knott, Graham Dilley and Mike Gatting at a London hotel, and speaks to Ian Botham, David Gower and Bob Willis on the telephone. Mike Gatting withdraws, but Graham Gooch tells Stuart that his friend John Emburey is keen to make the trip. Stuart returns to South Africa confident that the tour can go ahead.*

*Mike Brearley does not want to tour India, and retires from international cricket for the second time. Keith Fletcher is appointed in his place. Keith is 37 years old and hasn't played Test cricket for four years. You think this is a mistake. You fly to Hong Kong in your role as Cathay Pacific's ambassador, but as soon as you land you are taking telephone calls from TCCB Chairman George Mann, Secretary Donald Carr and Robin Marlar of the Sunday Times telling you that the Indian government are making noises about not admitting you for the tour. They are asking that you agree not to visit South Africa again, and that you publically condemn Apartheid.*

*You refuse. On the issue of Apartheid, you have made clear many times your opposition to it. In your new book about the West Indies Tests, In The Fast Lane, you again denounce it unambiguously. But you are not prepared to give up your right to travel where you wish. You tell George Mann, Donald Carr and Robin Marlar that you will not lie to suit the TCCB and the Indian Government, especially when companies like British Airways fly to South Africa and India, and the Indian government don't ask BA to stop, or Barclays Bank, or any of the other companies that trade freely with both countries. It seems that only cricketers aren't allowed to exercise that right. Then Robin*

*Marlar refers the Indian government to the passages about Apartheid in your book, and they grant your visa.*

*When, later in the tour, you are introduced to Mrs Ghandi, India's Prime Minister, you present her with a copy of In The Fast Lane.*

*She laughs as she accepts it. She tells you: 'You caused me so much trouble before this tour.'*

*You arrive in India worried. You're worried about the rowing and fighting at Yorkshire, worried about your health because you had your spleen removed as a young boy, worried about the South Africa thing, worried about Keith Fletcher and his plan that you should play in just two of the three warm-up games...*

*So you play at Pune on a good pitch and make 101 not out. You do not play at Nagpur on a terrible pitch where Derek Underwood takes 11 wickets. You play at Baroda on a slow pitch and make 66 and 73 not out.*

*You worry about the hotels outside of the big cities, one of which Keith Fletcher calls 'a spacious cow shed'. You worry about the food that you dare eat. You go to Bombay for the first Test.*

\* \* \*

## First Test, India versus England, Wankhede Stadium, Bombay, 27 November – 1 December, 1981

### *One-hundred-and-fifth cap*

As a batting unit I felt we were underdone, and that was dangerous playing India in India. So many touring teams underestimated them in home conditions. History showed they were tough to beat, and now they were led by their best ever batsman Sunil Gavaskar, a truly great technician with a smart cricket brain.

The pitch didn't look as if it would last. India got first go, and were all out for 179, a score that was quickly put in context by our first innings of 166. Before the series began, Keith Fletcher and I had spoken about his plan to play five frontline bowlers, which I felt would weaken the batting too much. Those match-winning bowlers he'd put his faith in, plus the keeper, scored 18 runs between them. As I told Keith, my experience of Test cricket was that batsmen put you in a position to win, and bowlers take the wickets to win. But without enough runs it doesn't matter how good the bowlers are.

As the pitch got worse, India made a good score of 227 in their second innings, with their great all-rounder Kapil Dev whacking a priceless 46. We needed the highest score of the match, 241, to win, and that was miles too many. Kapil and Madan Lal went almost unchanged and in 27 overs of mayhem bowled us out for 102. It was a chastening experience, and their spinners weren't even required.

I thought at the time that losing the first Test and having to play catch-up cricket in India would be a mountain to climb. And it was!

**60** and **3**

\* \* \*

*The Robin Jackman affair and the questions over your visa to tour India cause concern among the players interested in touring South Africa. They worry about bans and sanctions from the TCCB. They worry about endangering their county contracts. They want more money and more security if the tour is to go ahead.*

*Peter Venison of Holiday Inns South Africa flies to Bombay. He increases the offer to a three-year deal, £45,000 per player for the first year, increasing by five per cent in the second and third years if any ban is imposed. There will be no tax due in South Africa, and the funds will be paid over in full before the tour begins. All travel and hotel expenses for players and their families will be met. The tour will finish in time to return home for the county season.*

*The 13 players must sign their deals by 18 January 1982. Peter Venison agrees to come back to India to collect the contracts.*

*Tinned ham sandwiches and spam for lunch. The heat and the travel, the poor hotels, the five-foot beds and the boring nights. They all add up, they all weigh on you, weigh on you with all of the worries and the cares that you have...*

*This capricious game. Capricious and endless, although you are closer to the end now. Closer than you know...*

\* \* \*

## Second Test, India versus England,
## KSCA Stadium, Bangalore, 9-14 December, 1981

*One-hundred-and-sixth cap*

My favourite Indian cricket ground. I had a good feeling about it as soon as I walked onto the field for practice. We got the chance to bat first on a very good surface and scored 400, but it took us two days. India were masters at rearranging the field and slowing the over rate down. A total of 94 overs of spin were bowled in our innings, yet only 79 overs a day were completed. Even the West Indies fast bowlers managed as many as that.

Their spinners frustrated the hell out of our batsmen. If they couldn't win, they made damn sure we couldn't score quickly enough to leave our bowlers enough time to bowl them out twice. When they came to bat, India knew we had to make all the running and simply occupied the crease. They had a master craftsman in Sunil Gavaskar, and he batted us out of any chance of a win by himself. He scored 172 in over 12 hours, and the only time I thought he made a mistake was when John Lever hit him on the back leg while he was in the seventies. It looked plumb, but then you always felt badly done by without neutral umpires. Oh for DRS.

We had a few hours to bat on the last day and I was bowled Joshi for 50 to go with my 36 in the first innings.

**36** and **50**

* * *

*Ian Botham pulls out of the South Africa tour. He has new and valuable commercial deals with Nike and Shredded Wheat. His solicitor Alan Herd calls Peter Venison and tells him the news. David Gower follows. As far as you're concerned, it's over. Other players get cold feet. When Peter Venison calls again two weeks later to say that the sponsors will accept Ian's absence as long as no-one else drops out, you tell him that David Gower has opted out too.*

*You go to Jammu, in the north, where at the hotel, the beds are filled with damp. Raman Subba Row, tour manager, will not complain because he doesn't want to upset the hosts, so instead he organises*

*fan heaters to try to dry them out. You fall out with Raman when he
tells you it's okay for the players to get pneumonia from the damp
beds. Tinned ham sandwiches and another game.*

*It is Christmas. You fly to Delhi. You go to the hotel. You have
dinner. You go to your room. You think about the bowlers you will
face. You think about Kapil Dev and Madan Lal, Dilip Doshi and
Ravi Shastri, Kirti Azad and Sandeep Patel. You think about Garry
Sobers and his 8,032 runs. You go to sleep.*

*You do not dream about cricket.*

\* \* \*

## Third Test, India versus England,
## Feroz Shah Kotla Stadium, Delhi, 23-28 December, 1981

*One-hundred-and-seventh cap*

At around 4.20pm on the first day, I hit a leg-side boundary off
Dilip Doshi to pass Garry Sobers' world record for the most Test
runs. I was thrilled to bits, but in my interview with the media at
the end of the day, I was very clear that it didn't make me a better
batsman than Garry Sobers. For me Garfield St Aubrun Sobers was
and remains the best batsman I ever saw, and a smashing guy. I
never heard of him doing a bad turn to anyone and he played
cricket in a wonderful, sporting way. In later years when I did lots
of TV commentary in the West Indies, he was a good friend.

I said I didn't play for records, but if you play well for long enough
records just come along. Sunil Gavaskar joked with me, saying that
I should keep the record warm for him as he expected to pass me
in about two years' time. And he did!

England made 476 with Chris Tavaré scoring 149 but again, India
were better than us. They replied with a no-hurry 487 of which
Gundappa Viswanath scored 107. The game fizzled into another
draw with me and Graham batting out time.

**105** and **34 not out**

\* \* \*

*It's as if you just held on long enough before it all falls apart. The English newspapers arrive, and the back pages are plastered with the news that Keith Fletcher told you and Chris Tavaré to get a move on while you were batting together in Delhi.*

*You are incensed because it is not true. You are incensed because it gives your enemies at Yorkshire more ammunition. You are incensed because you hear that the Yorkshire committee want to pay you up and sack you...*

*You find Peter Smith of the Daily Mail and Pat Gibson of the Daily Express. You tell them that Keith Fletcher said nothing to you about speeding up. You ask if they made the quotes up or used journalistic licence to get a headline. They play you their interview tape. On it, you hear Keith Fletcher tell the journalists exactly what they reported, word for word.*

*You ask for a meeting with Keith Fletcher and Raman Subba Row. Keith tells you he was misquoted. You play him the tape. Keith waffles away, so you play it again and again until he admits that he didn't mean it in the way it sounds, and that he was going to speak to you and Chris but then he didn't. You demand a retraction and a public apology. Ramon Subba Row says no. You insist. You get one. It's plastered all over the papers again. Raman Subba Row does not like it. He thinks that the captain of England making an apology reflects on him. The damage is done. Your relationship with Keith Fletcher and Raman Subba Row deteriorates. Keith Fletcher can't look you in the eye. Raman Subba Row is angry and vengeful.*

*Soon after the Delhi Test, you wake up feeling feverish and quickly become ill. The hotel doctor gives you some tablets and tells you to seek further help. Bernie Thomas and Raman Subba Row have gone to visit the Taj Mahal so you contact a doctor at the British High Commission, who runs some tests, tells you that you have a viral infection and recommends that you spend a few days at the mini-hospital inside the High Commission. But when Raman Subba Row returns from the Taj Mahal he tells you that you are flying to Calcutta that night with the rest of the team whether you want to or not.*

*You get the message. You understand now what Raman Subba Row is all about.*

# CHAPTER SEVENTEEN

# 1982

## Fourth Test, India versus England,
## Eden Gardens, Calcutta, 1-6 January, 1982

*One-hundred-and-eighth cap*

I hardly had the strength to practise in the nets. I would bat for a few minutes and then have to rest before going back for a few more minutes. I felt dreadful when we started the Test match and I got worse as the game progressed. England batted, and I was out caught behind off Kapil Dev for 18. I went straight back to bed at the hotel and didn't field. I had no appetite and couldn't eat for three days. The diarrhoea came back and I spent days and nights laying on the bed and rushing to and from the toilet. The room was nice but very dark and it was exhausting and depressing having to spend so much time in that small space hoping to feel better. I was requested to get up and bat for our second innings but was out lbw to Madan Lal for only six runs. Then straight back to bed. I was fed up, and insisted on the manager getting me a doctor. I told him I desperately wanted to go back to Delhi to see the British doctor at the High Commission. I even telephoned him to ask if he would take me in as his patient and I offered to pay my own air-fare. But Subba Row would not hear of it and insisted that once the Test was over, I would have to go to Madras with Botham and Willis and their wives while the rest of the team moved on for a tour match at Jamshedpur. I got the message. It was about getting his own back after insisting on the captain's apology in Delhi.

Subba Row was deliberately unhelpful and bloody-minded. Our relationship as manager and player had got so bad that I felt he didn't give a damn about my welfare.

On the final day of the game, Bernard Thomas took me to one side and advised me to get out of my dark room if I could. He suggested a walk in the fresh air. Well, where can you find fresh air in a city crammed full of 18 million people? The only place that I could think of and that I knew was the golf course at Tollygunge. I took Bernard's advice and went for a walk, trying to buck myself up. The golf shop insisted I have a local guy to go with me and carry a few clubs. I had a couple of hits but I didn't have any energy or inclination to hit more, and had to keep resting on a bench around each hole. I gave up and went back to bed.

As soon as I got back, Subba Row was on the phone summoning me to his room. Had I been playing golf? No, I had been for a walk as Bernard Thomas suggested, in the only place where I wouldn't be pushing through lots of people. The idea that I had the energy to play golf in my physical state was ludicrous, as I had spent most of a five-day Test match in and out of bed with diarrhoea. If I didn't have the energy to field how was I going to have the energy to play golf? I apologised if my actions were misunderstood but I was not golfing and I believed I had the assistant manager's blessing.

Keith Fletcher was present and not best pleased that his England team hadn't been able to force a win. I told him I understood his disappointment but don't take that frustration out on me. I had not done anything secretively or surreptitiously and was just trying to follow Bernard's advice and get well again. I'd had a dreadful time feeling unwell.

The more we talked the less we agreed. Subba Row kept saying I went without his permission and demanded an apology to him and to the team. It was tiresome trying to explain as he wasn't listening and I had had a bellyfull of him and his captain. I was ill and had an unsympathetic manager who was more concerned about getting his own back rather than helping me recover my health. For the way he treated me, I thought he was an asshole and still do. On top of that, I had a captain who had lied and crucified me in public.

I was at my lowest ebb and just wanted to go home, so I went into the players' room and wrote out his apology and a separate apology to the team, and my resignation from the tour.

* * *

*Even the notes of apology turn into a farce when you try to leave them stuck to the fridge in the team room where you know that everyone will see them, but they keep falling off, so you end up having to pin them to the table with a bottle opener.*

*Two weeks ago, you batted your way to history in Delhi. Now you are sick and worried and being escorted to the airport by Raman Subba Row, flying home to an uncertain future.*

*This capricious game.*

*You don't know it yet but you have played your final Test, scored your last run for England.*

*This is how it ends. Not on a cricket field but on a golf course.*

*This is how it ends, 4,000 miles from home, sick and alone.*

*This is how it ends: lbw bowled Madan Lal, 6.*

*Just like almost everyone else who has played this game, it does not end well. It does not end how you would want it to end, how you would dream it.*

*But you do not dream about cricket.*

\* \* \*

## Geoffrey Boycott

**108 Tests, 193 innings, 23 not outs,
8,114 runs at 47.72, 22 x100, 42x 50.**

# Afterword

While Geoffrey Boycott's resignation from the tour of India was acrimonious, it didn't seem at the time to be a terminal blow to his chances of continuing an international career. Although he was now 41 years old, the hundred he made in Delhi as he overtook Garfield Sobers was evidence of his enduring quality with the bat, and he had often thrived on conflict, using it as fuel to drive himself onwards. England's opponents in the summer of 1982 were to be India and Pakistan, teams that he had excelled against in the past.

After his arrival home, he appeared on BBC TV's *Sportsnight* programme, where he was interviewed by David Coleman. He gave a vivid account of his trip to Tollygunge golf club, describing 'a couple of dozen big, black and white vultures, then lovely green parrots that fly past and birds with red bushy tails,' and went on to say, 'to suggest I have played my last Test because I have come home early seems grossly unfair.'

Yet even as he spoke, Peter Cooke was reviving the tour of South Africa. He had a new sponsor, South African Breweries, and began contacting some of the players that had expressed an interest in going. He compiled a squad of 16, with Bob Willis as captain, but Willis dropped out shortly before the tour was due to begin. After an approach was made to Keith Fletcher, who declined, Boycott was, at the last minute, persuaded to change his mind and join the tour. He was asked to captain but turned it down, and the job went to Graham Gooch.

The cricket, which was undistinguished, consisted of three 'Tests' and three one-day matches against a South African XI, none of which England won. When they returned home in April, they were banned from international cricket for three years by the TCCB. Only two of the 15, Graham Gooch and John Emburey, played for England again.

There would be six more rebel tours of South Africa before the country returned to international competition in 1991, one by a Sri Lankan team, two by West Indies sides, two by Australian teams and finally, in 1989–90, another England party. Their fates were very different. Members of the English and Australian teams served bans but returned to the cricket establishment. The West Indies players were ostracised socially and professionally, some lived and died in penury, and fierce arguments continue over the morality of those tours.

What they have in common is a financial imperative. Despite Kerry Packer taking credit for changing the finances of the game, cricketers in general continued to be poorly paid. Here is what Geoffrey wrote for this book when he was describing his motivation for going on the tour:

*'Our trip was never intended to be an alternative to established cricket. We had worked out we could fit this in without breaking our county contracts and without disrupting international cricket. We were not simple enough to believe a match in South Africa wouldn't be controversial and that is why secrecy was paramount. We were not going [there] to help South African cricket or support apartheid or bridge any ideology. Wages in cricket were poor and quite simply it was a professional opportunity to earn money. With people going on holiday to South Africa, businesses trading with that country and British Airways flying regularly back and forth we felt why should cricketers be treated differently? Cricketers didn't earn much so a tour to South Africa was always about money. Nothing else. Much the same as the IPL now. At that time England paid £10,000 for a four-month tour of India and Sri Lanka as against £50,000 for one month in South Africa.'*

As he made clear to the TCCB when he was about to tour India in 1981, Boycott did not see why cricketers or other athletes should be singled out in not trading with South Africa. There were and are many people vehemently opposed to that view, and the sporting boycott is properly credited with placing the horror of Apartheid under an uncomfortable worldwide spotlight and keeping it there until it was consigned to the dustbin of history. Players like Barry Richards and Mike Procter from South Africa lost their international careers because of it. The West Indian rebel Richard 'Danny Germs' Austin became an alcoholic and drug addict, dying homeless and on the streets at the age of 60, in part because he could not cope with being shunned by his own people. David Murray, another of the West Indian tourists, ended up selling trinkets to tourists on the beach in Barbados. How do you measure their lives against those who lived and died under the Apartheid regime? It's impossible.

There is no moral equivalence here. In the end, the players at least had a choice.

1982 was to be another turbulent year for Geoffrey. The events surrounding his sacking and eventual reinstatement by Yorkshire after a popular uprising among the county's members and supporters would make another entertaining book. Yet he returned once again and played on until 1986, when he was 45 years old and still scoring centuries. Cricket was everything to him, I think, and he admitted that for a long time after his retirement he couldn't bear to pick up a bat.

His last ever game of professional cricket came at Scarborough, and he gave the following description of what happened. I don't think that I or anyone else could better it, and of course, the final words of this book should go to him:

*'Something had come to an end, something wonderful. The Yorkshire Committee hadn't told me I was finished, but I sensed in the background certain members of the Committee were working to get rid of me. It would have been nice for me, our members and my supporters to be told that it was to be my final game, and we could have celebrated my last match for the county. Instead, I felt, 'this is it then.' I waited for the ground to clear. Then I wandered around on my own, among all the newspapers and food wrappers and tin cans. It didn't feel like death exactly, but I did think a part of my life was finished.'*

| | Matches | Innings | Runs | Highest Score | Average | 50s | 100s |
|---|---|---|---|---|---|---|---|
| **Countries** | | | | | | | |
| Australia | 38 | 71 | 2945 | 191 | 47.5 | 14 | 7 |
| West Indies | 29 | 53 | 2205 | 128 | 45.93 | 15 | 5 |
| New Zealand | 15 | 25 | 916 | 131 | 38.16 | 6 | 2 |
| India | 13 | 22 | 1084 | 246* | 57.05 | 2 | 4 |
| South Africa | 7 | 12 | 373 | 117 | 37.3 | 2 | 1 |
| Pakistan | 6 | 10 | 591 | 121* | 84.42 | 3 | 3 |
| **Total** | **108** | **193** | **8114** | | | **42** | **22** |
| **Venues** | | | | | | | |
| Lord's | 16 | 29 | 1189 | 128* | 45.73 | 6 | 3 |
| Trent Bridge | 10 | 17 | 663 | 131 | 44.2 | 4 | 2 |
| Headingley | 10 | 16 | 897 | 246* | 59.8 | 0 | 4 |
| Kennington Oval | 8 | 15 | 747 | 137 | 53.36 | 2 | 3 |
| Old Trafford | 7 | 13 | 442 | 128 | 36.83 | 2 | 1 |
| Edgbaston | 6 | 10 | 418 | 155 | 52.25 | 1 | 1 |
| Melbourne Cricket Ground | 5 | 10 | 252 | 76* | 31.5 | 2 | 0 |
| Sydney Cricket Ground | 5 | 9 | 369 | 142* | 46.13 | 2 | 1 |
| Queens Park Oval | 5 | 9 | 620 | 112 | 77.5 | 6 | 1 |
| WACA | 3 | 6 | 319 | 99* | 63.8 | 4 | 0 |
| Sabina Park | 3 | 6 | 142 | 68 | 23.67 | 1 | 0 |
| Adelaide Oval | 3 | 6 | 266 | 119* | 53.2 | 1 | 1 |
| Brisbane Cricket Ground | 3 | 6 | 190 | 63* | 38 | 1 | 0 |
| Kensington Oval | 3 | 5 | 114 | 90 | 22.8 | 1 | 0 |
| Wankhede Stadium | 2 | 4 | 128 | 60 | 42.67 | 1 | 0 |
| Lancaster Park | 2 | 4 | 42 | 26 | 10.5 | 0 | 0 |
| Bourda | 2 | 3 | 161 | 116 | 53.67 | 0 | 1 |
| Wanderers Stadium | 2 | 3 | 85 | 76* | 42.5 | 1 | 0 |
| Niaz Stadium | 1 | 2 | 179 | 100* | 179 | 1 | 1 |
| Arun Jaitley | 1 | 2 | 139 | 105 | 139 | 0 | 1 |
| Antigua Recreation Ground | 1 | 2 | 142 | 104* | 142 | 0 | 1 |
| Basin Reserve | 1 | 2 | 78 | 77 | 39 | 1 | 0 |
| St Georges Park | 1 | 2 | 124 | 117 | 62 | 0 | 1 |
| Newlands | 1 | 2 | 16 | 15 | 16 | 0 | 0 |
| Karachi National Stadium | 1 | 2 | 87 | 56 | 43.5 | 1 | 0 |
| Eden Gardens | 1 | 2 | 24 | 18 | 12 | 0 | 0 |
| KSCA Stadium | 1 | 2 | 86 | 50 | 43 | 1 | 0 |
| Eden Park | 1 | 1 | 54 | 54 | 54 | 1 | 0 |
| Carisbrook | 1 | 1 | 5 | 5 | 5 | 0 | 0 |
| Gaddafi Stadium | 1 | 1 | 63 | 63 | 63 | 1 | 0 |
| Kingsmead | 1 | 1 | 73 | 73 | 73 | 1 | 0 |
| **Total** | **108** | **193** | **8114** | **246*** | **47.72** | **42** | **22** |

# Acknowledgements

Sir Geoffrey would like to acknowledge: Andrew Samson, Lady Rachael Boycott, Jeff Kendrick, Graham Webster.

Jon Hotten like to acknowledge the following books and sources: *Boycott: The Autobiography by Geoffrey Boycott* (Pan); *Opening Up* by Geoffrey Boycott (Arthur Barker); *The Corridor Of Certainty* by Geoffrey Boycott (Simon & Schuster); *In The Fast Lane* by Geoffrey Boycott (Arthur Barker); *Put To The Test* by Geoffrey Boycott (Arthur Barker); *Time To Declare* by Basil D'Oliveira (JM Dent); *I Don't Bruise Easily* by Brian Close (Futura); *Yorkshire And Back* by Raymond Illingworth (Queen Anne Press); *One Man Committee* by Raymond Illingworth and Jack Bannister (Headline); *Another Bloody Day In Paradise* by Frank Keating (Harper Collins); *Ball of Fire* by Fred Trueman (JM Dent); *On Cricket* by Mike Brearley (Constable); *The Return of the Ashes* by Mike Brearley and Dudley Doust (Pelham); *The Ashes Retained* by Mike Brearley and Dudley Doust (Hodder & Stoughton); *The Cricket War* by Gideon Haigh (Wisden), and in particular, *Boycs* by Leo McKinstry (Corgi), which is now published as *Geoff Boycott: A Cricketing Hero* (Willow). Also, ESPNcricinfo; Cricket Archive; and Andy Bull's piece "Holding To Boycott: The Greatest Over Ever?" (the *Guardian*, 2017).

# A documented life

Sir Geoffrey has kept a wide range of letters and documents relating to his career, many of which we are printing here for the first time.

Boycott's school report from the summer of 1956, when he was 15.
Exceptional at cricket, work to do in Latin and French...

## 1st XI CRICKET REPORT

This year five matches had to be cancelled because of heavy rainfall and as a result the First XI has not enjoyed a successful season. We began with eight regular team members: Cartledge, Sell, Morley, Hambleton, Kenningham, Trueman, Wild and Boycott, but were without the valuable services of last year's captain, Moore. Some of last year's members have not done as well as we hoped and many newcomers have been tried without success. At the beginning of the season we were without a regular wicket-keeper but Trueman has admirably fulfilled expectation.

On behalf of the team I would like to express my appreciation to Mr. Tate, Mr. Taylor and Mr. Sale for the time and effort they have spent in coaching the team; and to Mr. Rhodes for his careful preparation of our wickets; to Connolly for his work as secretary; to Sell for acting as treasurer, and, finally, to our scorer, Ackroyd.

### RESULTS.

H.G.S. 58 (Boycott 27): King's School, Pontefract 73. (Boycott 8 for 20)   Lost

H.G.S. 102 (Boycott 59): Castleford G.S. 125.                               Lost.

H.G.S. 114 (Boycott 60, Morley 21*): Ackworth 45 for 7 (Wild 6 for 20) Drawn

H.G.S. 143 for 4 (Boycott 105*) Rain stopped play.

H.G.S. 46: Wath 44 (Wild 5 for 17, Randall 3 for 20)                         Won.

H.G.S. did not bat: Thorne 27 for 3. Rain stopped play.

H.G.S. 55: Mexborough 58 for 7 (Boycott 4 for 22)                          Lost

H.G.S. 129 (Boycott 48, Morley 44): Old Hilmians 50 for 5.               Drawn

AVERAGES (Batting)

|          | Inn's | N.O. | Runs | Highest score | Average |
|----------|-------|------|------|---------------|---------|
| Boycott  | 7     | 1    | 325  | 105*          | 54.2    |
| Morley   | 6     | 3    | 117  | 44            | 39      |
| Trueman  | 6     | 0    | 48   | 25            | 8       |

AVERAGES (Bowling)

|          | Overs | Maidens | Runs | Wickets | Average |
|----------|-------|---------|------|---------|---------|
| Boycott  | 57    | 15      | 122  | 17      | 7.2     |
| Wild     | 59.5  | 20      | 159  | 20      | 7.95    |
| Randall  | 35.2  | 11      | 86   | 8       | 10.75   |

G. Boycott V.S.

## Yorkshire Schools' A.A.A. Championships.

At this year's meeting, held in Leeds on June 14th, the School gained firsts in the Junior and Senior Pole Vaults. Griffiths won the Junior event against keen competition with a vault of 9ft. 11in. (The School record is 9ft.) Snookes was the winner of the Senior section with a vault of 9ft. 3in. (The School record is 9ft. 1¼in.) We congratulate them on their success.

## Yorkshire Senior (Men's) A.A.A. Championships.

### Bradford, May 31st.

This year was the first time that the School had been represented at this Senior meting. In winning the 440 yards from the previous Yorkshire Champion, Moore gave his best performance so far with a time of 50.9 seconds. Once again we congratulate Moore on his achievement and we hope that this will be the first of many successes for him in Senior Athletics.

L.M.T.

28

The young Boycott in outstanding form for Hemsworth Grammar School in 1958. His hundred came against Normanton Grammar.

TELEGRAMS:
LORD'S GROUND LONDON
TELEPHONE NOS.:
PAVILION .. .. .. LORDS 1611-3
TENNIS CO /.. .. .. LORDS 1288
TAVERN .. .. .. LORDS 1724-5
WORKS DEPT. .. .. CUNNINGHAM 6855

Marylebone Cricket Club,

Lord's Ground,

London, N.W.8

1st August, 1964.

Dear Geoff.

I am directed by the M.C.C. Committee to invite you to join the M.C.C. team, which will tour South Africa next winter.

The team will fly from London Airport on October 15th, 1964 and will return on February 19th, 1965. The Committee have agreed that the players' salary for the tour will be £700, plus a kit allowance of £125 and an allowance of £7 per week throughout the tour for incidental expenses. Furthermore, M.C.C. may consider a reward up to a maximum of £150 for discipline and contribution to team spirit on and off the field.

I shall be sending you the Notes and Instructions for the tour together with the contract and copies of the itinerary in the near future.

I should be grateful if you would confirm your acceptance of this invitation as soon as possible.

Yours sincerely,

Secretary, M.C.C.

G. Boycott, Esq.

Boycott's invitation from MCC to play in South Africa
in 1964-65, his first overseas tour.

Marylebone Cricket Club,

Lord's Ground,

London, N.W.8

1st August, 1964.

Dear Geoff:

    I am directed by the M.C.C. Committee to invite you to join the M.C.C. team, which will tour South Africa next winter.

    The team will fly from London Airport on October 15th, 1964 and will return on February 19th, 1965. The Committee have agreed that the players' salary for the tour will be £700, plus a kit allowance of £125 and an allowance of £7 per week throughout the tour for incidental expenses. Furthermore, M.C.C. may consider a reward up to a maximum of £150 for discipline and contribution to team spirit on and off the field.

    I shall be sending you the Notes and Instructions for the tour together with the contract and copies of the itinerary in the near future.

    I should be grateful if you would confirm your acceptance of this invitation as soon as possible.

Yours sincerely,

Secretary, M.C.C.

G. Boycott, Esq.

Confirmation of Boycott's fee for the tour of South Africa in 1964-65

**An Agreement** made the   seventh       day of August  1964, BETWEEN THE MARYLEBONE CRICKET CLUB, LONDON, of the one part, AND    G. Boycott

of   the Yorkshire County Cricket Club                          Cricketer, of the other part **Whereas** it has been arranged by the Marylebone Cricket Club that a Team of Cricketers with Mr. M. J. K. Smith as Captain, and Mr. D. B. Carr as Manager, shall visit South Africa for the purpose of playing a series of Cricket Matches during season 1964/65 upon certain terms and conditions agreed to between the said parties and

**Whereas** the said cricketer has agreed with the Marylebone Cricket Club to go out with the said Team for the purposes and upon the terms and conditions hereafter mentioned.

**Now** it is hereby agreed between the parties hereto as follows :—

1.—The said cricketer shall leave England on 15th October, 1964 by air subject to his being physically fit when leaving England and having obtained certificates to that effect from a Doctor, and a Dentist nominated or agreed to by the Marylebone Cricket Club, such certificates to be forwarded (within one month of date of departure) to the Marylebone Cricket Club. Should any illness or accident befall the said cricketer after the date of the Medical Certificate and before departure, immediate notice is to be given in writing to the Marylebone Cricket Club. In the event of the said cricketer failing to leave England for any reason whatsoever on the date nominated by the Marylebone Cricket Club this Agreement shall be void, save that the cricketer undertakes to continue to be bound by the conditions set out in Clause 6 hereof.

2.—The said cricketer shall play in such of the matches which may be arranged for the M.C.C. Team as the Captain of the M.C.C. team for the time being or the Manager shall from time to time desire and so far as matches and practices are concerned shall conform to the directions of the said Captain or the said Manager, and further the said cricketer shall conform to all the instructions of the Manager especially with regard to social functions and all disciplinary matters off the field and shall generally use his best endeavours to make the tour a success in every possible way.

3.—The said cricketer shall keep himself as far as possible physically fit to play in all matches during the Tour and the said Manager shall be entitled to cancel this Agreement, if, in his opinion, the said cricketer shall have become incapable of continuing to play for the said Team or on account of his misconduct or disobedience or of conduct not conducive to the esprit de corps of the Team and the said Manager, after consultation with the said Captain, may direct that the said cricketer shall return home to the United Kingdom, if for reasons of discipline or for any other reasons, he, the said Manager, considers such a course to be in the best interests of the Marylebone Cricket Club and the said Team as a whole. In either of the events hereinbefore referred to the said cricketer shall be entitled, in addition to the cost of his passage home (and subject to a right of appeal by the said cricketer to the Marylebone Cricket Club on the return of the remainder of the said Team to the United Kingdom) only to such proportion of the amounts hereby agreed to be paid to him as shall represent the time he has been an active member of the said Team and the time which, in the circumstances, would normally be taken by him on his passage home to the United Kingdom immediately following the date of his dismissal.

4.—The said cricketer shall not play in any Team other than the said M.C.C. Team without the consent of the said Captain or said Manager.

5.—The said cricketer shall conform to the ground regulations where matches are being played during the tour whether he is taking part in the match or not and shall not infringe any of those regulations without first obtaining permission of the ground authority.

6.—During the period commencing with the date of this Agreement until the first day of March, 1967, the said cricketer shall not make or concur in making any public pronouncement about cricket or cricketers, or any matter, or incident arising during the said visit (the subject of this Agreement) without prior consent of the said Manager or of the Secretary of the Marylebone Cricket Club. In this clause "public pronouncement" includes any publication of, or contribution to, any book, magazine, periodical or newspaper, any comment or commentary in any wireless or other broadcast, or in any theatre, television or film appearance, and any lecturing or public speaking

The astonishingly formal contract signed by Boycott for his
first overseas tour with MCC, to South Africa in 1964-65.

cricketer shall ~~....~~ misconduct or disobedience or of conduct not conducive to the esprit de corps, the said Manager, after consultation with the said Captain, may direct that the said cricketer shall return home to the United Kingdom, if for reasons of discipline or for any other reasons, he, the said Manager, considers such a course to be in the best interests of the Marylebone Cricket Club and the said Team as a whole. In either of the events hereinbefore referred to the said cricketer shall be entitled, in addition to the cost of his passage home (and subject to a right of appeal by the said cricketer to the Marylebone Cricket Club on the return of the remainder of the said Team to the United Kingdom) only to such proportion of the amounts hereby agreed to be paid to him as shall represent the time he has been an active member of the said Team and the time which, in the circumstances, would normally be taken by him on his passage home to the United Kingdom immediately following the date of his dismissal.

4.—The said cricketer shall not play in any Team other than the said M.C.C. Team without the consent of the said Captain or said Manager.

5.—The said cricketer shall conform to the ground regulations where matches are being played during the tour whether he is taking part in the match or not and shall not infringe any of those regulations without first obtaining permission of the ground authority.

6.—During the period commencing with the date of this Agreement until the first day of March, 1967, the said cricketer shall not make or concur in making any public pronouncement about cricket or cricketers, or any matter, or incident arising during the said visit (the subject of this Agreement) without prior consent of the said Manager or of the Secretary of the Marylebone Cricket Club. In this clause "public pronouncement" includes any publication of, or contribution to, any book, magazine, periodical or newspaper, any comment or commentary in any wireless or other broadcast, or in any theatre, television or film appearance, and any lecturing or public speaking, and any other comment or information made or given in circumstances in which the cricketer knew or ought reasonably to have known that any part or the gist of any part thereof was likely to become or be made public.

7.—The said cricketer shall assign to the Marylebone Cricket Club the copyright in any photograph still or cinematograph which he may take of any match or official function in which the M.C.C. Team takes part. The Marylebone Cricket Club may grant permission for the use of such copyright at their sole discretion. Such permission shall not be unreasonably withheld.

8.—In the event of the said cricketer wishing to sell any goods a list of such goods shall be sent to the Manager of the M.C.C. Team one week before departure with a written undertaking to declare the same to the Customs authorities and to pay duty thereon as required.

9.—The said cricketer shall receive from the Marylebone Cricket Club the following consideration either as salary paid to him or monies paid on his behalf as the case may be (1) The sum of £700 as his remuneration for the above services during the tour; a kit allowance of £125 to be paid to him before leaving England and further, the Marylebone Cricket Club may consider a reward for discipline and contribution to team spirit on the basis hereinafter recommended by the said Captain and Manager, this reward, however, under no circumstances will exceed £100 ... ... ... per week during the progress of the tour to cover charges for drinks, tobacco, and all other expenses; (3) His board and lodgings (exclusive of drinks) in South Africa during the tour; (4) His railway and air fares during the tour; (5) His washing bills up to a reasonable amount and the usual gratuities to servants during the tour.

10.—No expenses will be allowed except as hereinbefore mentioned.

11.—No player shall be allowed to take with him any member of his family without the permission of the M.C.C. Committee.

(Signed)

Geoff Boycott

## M.C.C. WEST INDIES TOUR

Manager
L. E. G. Ames

1967          1968

Captain
M. C. Cowdrey

April 5th

Dear Geoffrey,

I write to thank you for your contribution on the tour and to congratulate you upon your superb batsmanship on so many occasions. I congratulate you too upon your fielding.

As I said to you before we parted, your aim must be two fold – to be the best batsman in the world and (because you are so richly blest with gifts) the nicest man in the world in every way.

With every good wish,

Yours ever,

Colin

gg

---

KIPPIN
BICKLEY
KENT
IMPERIAL 4252

30th August, 1967

Dear Geoff,

Just a line to say how pleased I am that you are opening the innings for me in West Indies.

As I think you know, I am your greatest fan, and I wish you a very happy and successful tour.

Thank you for your charming letter.

As ever,

Colin

If you're coming to London let me know.

gg.

A letter from Cowdrey prior to the West Indies tour of 1967-68. Cowdrey had somewhat controversially replaced Brian Close as skipper, while Boycott was recovering from the fall-out of having being dropped for slow scoring the previous summer. This is followed by a note of appreciation to Boycott from Cowdrey after the tour, acclaiming his "superb batsmanship".

296

Telegrams :
'S GROUND LONDON
Telephone Nos. :

Pavilion        01-289-1611-5
Tennis Cou.     01-289-1288
Tavern-Cater.   01-286-2909
Works Dept.     01-286-6855
Prospects of Play  01-286-8011

*Marylebone Cricket Club,*
*Lord's Ground,*
*London, N.W.8*

Secretary :
S. C. GRIFFITH
Assistant Secretaries :
J. G. DUNBAR    D. B. CARR
J. A. BAILEY

FT/SA/I/P/SB

URGENT - CONFIDENTIAL                    18th September, 1968

Dear Geof

  We were all extremely sad to hear of Mr. Vorster's
announcement concerning the forthcoming M.C.C. tour to
South Africa. No final decision regarding the tour will be
made until we hear officially from the South African Cricket
Association, but it would appear to be almost certain that
it will be cancelled.

  On behalf of the M.C.C. Committee, I can only
express our deep regret to you and all the other players
selected for the tour.

  In view of the likelihood of the South African
tour being abandoned, we have today made a tentative approach
to both India and Pakistan concerning the possibility of a
short tour to those countries of, perhaps, 10 weeks'
duration, commencing after Christmas.

  In the event of such a tour being arranged, M.C.C.
would wish to take the strongest side possible and we would
anticipate offering similar terms to players as those
applying to the South African tour.

  I should be grateful if you would let Mr. Carr, or
myself, know, if necessary by telephone, not later than
next Monday, 23rd September, whether you would be available
for such a tour if it was arranged.

Yours Sincerely

S. Griffith
Secretary, M.C.C.

phoned 24/9/68
SB.
conversation D.B. Carr. NO

G. Boycott, Esq.

The letter from MCC to Boycott about the imminent cancellation of
the tour of South Africa in the winter of 1968. Boycott's handwritten
note in the bottom corner confirms his phone call to Donald
Carr declining the suggested tour of India and Pakistan.

**Marylebone Cricket Club,**
*Lord's Ground,*
*London, N.W.8*

Telegrams
LORD'S GROUND LONDON
Telephone Nos.

Pavilion                01-289-1611-5
Tennis Court            01-289-1288
Tavern-Caterers         01-286-2908
Works Dept.             01-286-6655
Prospects of Play       01-286-8011

Secretary:
S. C. GRIFFITH
Assistant Secretaries
J. G. DUNBAR    D. B. CARR
J. A. BAILEY

ACCOFF/SB

11th August, 1969

Dear Geoff,

We have recently received the accounts from the Clarendon Court Hotel for the New Zealand Test Match at Lord's.

I note that on your account there are two items for drinks for 7/6d. and 4/-s. As you know, the players are responsible for paying for their own drinks, and I should be grateful if you would let me have payment of 11/6d. as soon as possible.

Yours sincerely,

*D.B. Carr*

D.B. Carr
Assistant Secretary, T.C.C.B.

G. Boycott, Esq.

*15/8/69*

---

**Marylebone Cricket Club,**
*Lord's Ground,*
*London, N.W.8*

Telegrams
LORD'S GROUND LONDON
Telephone Nos.

Pavilion                01-289-1611-5
Tennis Court            01-289-1288
Tavern-Caterers         01-286-2908
Works Dept.             01-286-6655
Prospects of Play       01-286-8011

Secretary:
S. C. GRIFFITH
Assistant Secretaries
J. G. DUNBAR    D. B. CARR
J. A. BAILEY

EXP/SB

30th September, 1969

Dear Geoff,

Further to my letter of 11th August, and your reply of 15th August, concerning the items for drinks on your account at the Clarendon Court Hotel during the New Zealand Test Match, I have now clarified the position with Alec Bedser and Ray Illingworth.

The Chairman did not, in fact, give any permission for drinks with meals to be charged to the Board, and I must, therefore, ask you if you would kindly let me have a cheque for 11/6d. to cover the two items concerned.

All best wishes.

Yours sincerely,

*D.B. Carr*

D.B. Carr
Assistant Secretary, T.C.C.B.

G. Boycott, Esq.

13 Oct 1969.  386 Bradford Rd.
Stanningley
Pudsey

Dear Geoff,

Many thanks for your letter of the 10th October.

I agree with all you say in your letter, I had a couple of drinks accounts sent to me for 1/- & 17/- which were for 2 or 3 of us at Dinner and I wrote to D. B. Carr explaining (the same thing as you say in your letter). He wrote back saying Alec said he had never given permission so rather than continue the performance I sent a cheque for the accounts but I also stated that we

had given permission.

Happy this clears the matter up for you Geoff. Its typical M.C.C. but I just got fed up of writing. If I am in a position to do anything next year I shall most certainly see to it.

Yours

P.S.
The golf is fairly good at the moment.

These letters (left) to Boycott from Donald Carr asking for repayment of 11s 6d spent on drinks at the players' hotel during a Test against New Zealand in 1969 illustrate the often petty nature of the TCCB's treatment of international cricketers. On this page is a letter from the England captain Raymond Illingworth, supporting Boycott's account of the evening.

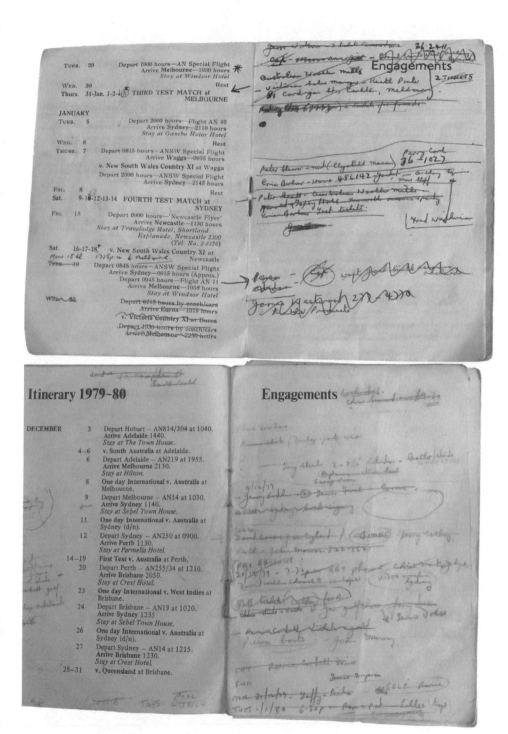

Itineraries issued to the players for the tours of Australia in 1970-71 (top) and 1979-80. Each have been annotated by Boycott as the tours unfolded

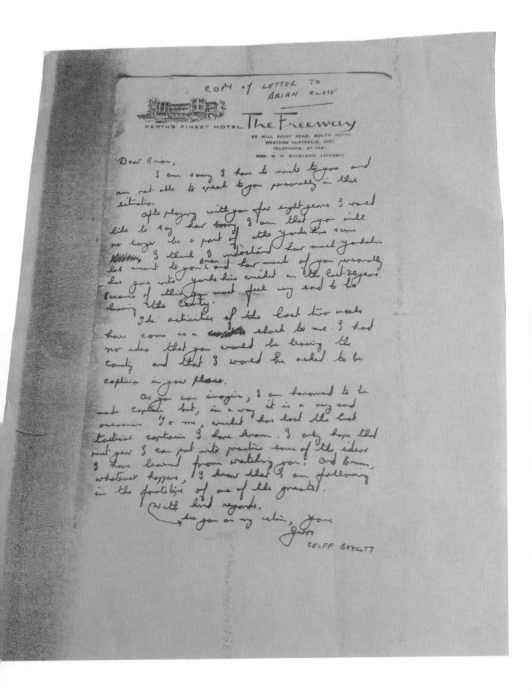

Boycott's copy of the letter he sent in December 1970 from Perth to Brian Close, who had just lost the captaincy of Yorkshire, with Boycott taking over.

CORNHILL INSURANCE TEST SERIES

ENGLAND v. NEW ZEALAND

CONDITION OF ACCEPTANCE AND NOTES AND INSTRUCTIONS
FOR TEST MATCHES

1. ACCEPTANCE

You are requested to inform the Secretary of T.C.C.B.
at Lord's by telephone (01-289 4405) or telegram,
immediately whether:-

(a) You are completely fit
(b) You are available
(c) You require hotel accommodation, and for which
    nights
(d) You accept the invitation on the conditions laid
    down by the T.C.C.B.
(e) You require a blazer, cap, sweater and tie (sizes
    must be given)

2. CRICKETER UNABLE TO ACCEPT INVITATION

If you are unable to accept the enclosed invitation for
any reason you may not play for your County on any date
or dates when the Test Match is taking place, except
with the approval of the Selection Sub-Committee.

3. PRESS, ETC.

By your acceptance of the invitation you undertake that
you will not make or concur in making any public
statement as regards any Test Match of the current
series or any aspect of the series until two years after
the end of the series, without the permission of the
T.C.C.B., or the Chairman of the Selection Sub-Committee,
acting on behalf of the T.C.C.B. This prohibition shall
be read as including writing a book, or writing for the
Press, public speaking, broadcasting or interviews for
television or sound films.

4. ASSEMBLY ON THE GROUND

You are requested to report to the England Captain on
the Test Match ground at Trent Bridge not later than
3.00 p.m. on Wednesday, 5th August, 1978.

Play will commence at 11.30 a.m. on the first, second,
third and fourth days and at 11.00 a.m. on the fifth
day.

The Cricketers and Selectors will dine together on the
evening of Wednesday, 9th August, 1978.

5. REMUNERATION

The fee offered to each cricketer playing will be £1,000
(Captain £150 additional), the fee for those selected but
not playing will be £350, substitute fieldsmen will be
paid at the rate of £25 per day (additional to any fee).
Such payments will be made through your County.

/...

- 2 -

5. Remuneration

The fee offered to each cricketer playing will be £210
(Captain £32 additional), 12th man on duty throughout
the Test Match £116, 12th man on duty first and second
days £74, 12th man on duty third, fourth and fifth days
£42, reserves £42.

6. Accommodation arrangements and expenses

Accommodation has been arranged at

The Bridgford Hotel,
Nottingham.

If staying at this hotel, your hotel account for bed,
breakfast, early morning tea and a newspaper will be paid
by the Ground Authority. You will be responsible for
paying any other expenses incurred by you in the hotel.
If you do not use the accommodation provided, you will
not be entitled to claim hotel or lodging charges.

In special cases, provided that permission has been
granted by the Chairman of the Selection Sub-Committee,
through Mr. D.B. Carr at Lord's and the account approved
by him, you may claim the cost of accommodation on the
night of Tuesday, 26th July, 1977

7. Travelling Expenses

You may claim the cost of a first-class railway fare or,
if travelling by car, 10p per mile for the following
journeys:

(a) From the ground on which you were last engaged, or
    from your home, if not playing immediately prior to
    the Test Match.

(b) To the ground on which you are next engaged, or to
    your home, if you are not so engaged.

Incidental Expenses

You will be given an allowance of £5.00 for each evening
meal, Sunday lunch and a meal on journeys to and from the
match.

You will also be allowed £10.00 for a five-day Test Match
for incidental expenses, including taxis and tips. The
Captain to receive an entertainment allowance of £6.00
per playing day.

Complimentary Tickets

If you are selected to play, or act as 12th man, you will
be issued, when you report to the ground, with two
complimentary tickets, giving free admission to the ground
and to reserved seats, in addition to your own free
admission.

/...

A letter sent to players selected for the New Zealand Tests in the summer of 1977.
Everything is spelled out, including the remuneration for any 'loss of digits'.

302

If you desire to purchase any additional tickets you should apply to the Secretary of Nottinghamshire C.C.C. immediately.

Up to two lunch and tea tickets per day will be available to you for the use of your guests, on request.

If you are travelling by car and wish to bring it into the ground, you should apply to the Secretary of Nottinghamshire C.C.C. for the necessary pass.

10. **Medical Attention**

The T.C.C.B. cannot consider claims for medical expenses unless permission for the treatment has first been obtained from the Chairman of the Selection Sub-Committee, or his nominee as Manager of the team, or the Secretary of the Club on whose ground the Test Match is being played.

11. **Insurance of Cricketers**

The T.C.C.B. will take out an Insurance Policy to cover the risk of an accident to a cricketer (including 12th man and reserves) playing in Test Matches, as follows:

**Accident and Life**

| | | |
|---|---|---|
| Loss of one or more limbs (leg, arm or eye) | | £20,000 |
| Loss of digits: Hands: | Thumb | 25% |
| | Index | 20% |
| | Middle | 12% |
| | Ring | 10% |
| | Little | 8% |
| Toes: | Big | 6% |
| | Others | 3% |
| Temporary Total Disablement | | £75 |

**Life Cover**

Death due to any cause will be covered for the sum of £30,000.

12. **Discipline**

The Chairman of the Selection Sub-Committee or his nominee as Manager of the team shall be responsible for all disciplinary matters during the period of the Test Match.

Under no circumstances will any cricketer, playing in a Test Match be allowed to play in any other match on the Sunday of the Test Match.

/...

Any serious infringement of these Conditions and Notes and Instructions or breach of discipline by a cricketer, selected to play for England during the current season which the Chairman of the Selection Sub-Committee considers outside the scope of his jurisdiction, shall be dealt with by the Discipline Sub-Committee.

13. **Advertising on Cricket Clothing**

In accordance with the agreement reached at the last meeting of the International Cricket Conference, no cricketer may have any visible form of advertising insignia on any cricket clothing or equipment (other than bats) when playing in any Test Match. Pads and boots must be plain white and batting gloves, if not plain white, must be one plain colour. The major manufacturers have been informed of this decision but you are advised to notify your normal suppliers that under no circumstances will you be allowed to wear any advertising insignia on any item of clothing or equipment as specified.

14. **Dress and Turn-out on and off the field**

All cricketers representing England in a Test Match are expected to be smartly turned out both on and off the field. Whilst it is accepted that players may wish to be dressed casually when reporting on the day prior to a Test Match, having been involved in lengthy travel, it is considered most important that they are smartly dressed when arriving at and leaving the ground on each day of the match. Jackets and ties should always be worn on these occasions.

Under no circumstances will track suits be worn for net practice.

15. **Colours**

Each new England cricketer will be issued with:

One blazer. One cap. One tie. One sleeveless sweater. One long-sleeved sweater.

Replacement sweaters, caps and blazers may be issued on the authority of the Chairman of the Selection Sub-Committee, but a new blazer may only be issued to a cricketer, who is still playing for England, after a minimum of eight years.

16. **Prize Money**

The T.C.C.B. have agreed to make the following prize money available for each Test Match in the current series:

To the winners - £2,500
To the losers - £1,500
If the match is drawn - £2,000

*[signature]*
Chairman
T.C.C.B. Selection Sub-Committee

*Copy Mr G. Boycott Captain*

## NEW ZEALAND CRICKET COUNCIL

3RD FLOOR, S.I.M.U. BUILDING, LATIMER SQUARE, CHRISTCHURCH, C.1.
CABLES AND TELEGRAMS "UMPIRE" CHRISTCHURCH.
ADDRESS ALL REPLIES TO R.G. KNOWLES, SECRETARY, P.O. BOX 958, CHRISTCHURCH.
PHONE - DAY 82-964; NIGHT 326-692

ROTHMANS TOUR — ENGLAND TO N.Z. 1978

TEST MATCH PLAYING CONDITIONS

It has been agreed with the England team management that the following conditions will apply.

1. (a) If either team is one up in the series after the penultimate test, the Auckland test to be of 5 days duration.

   (b) If the Auckland Test is a six day test (i.e. in the event of series being nil all or 1 all), the rest day to stand as a rest day.

2. (a) To play on the rest day, play to be abandoned for the day on the 2nd or 3rd day by 1 p.m.

   (b) In the event of both the 1st and 2nd days of any test being washed out completely without a ball ........ the match to become a 4 day match, ........ rest day.

3. If an hour or more of playing time is lost through rain, weather or light (weather interference) an extension of play by 30 minutes on any of the first 4 days of the match shall be allowed on the day the time is lost provided no session of play shall exceed 2 hours 30 minutes and provided the days play shall terminate no later than 6.30 p.m.

*Amended Playing Conditions as agreed by the N.Z.C.C. and G. Boycott Captain. England K. Barrington Manager England.*

*7th Feb. 1978.*

A note from the New Zealand Cricket Council confirming playing conditions for the 1978 series skippered by Boycott and managed by Ken Barrington.

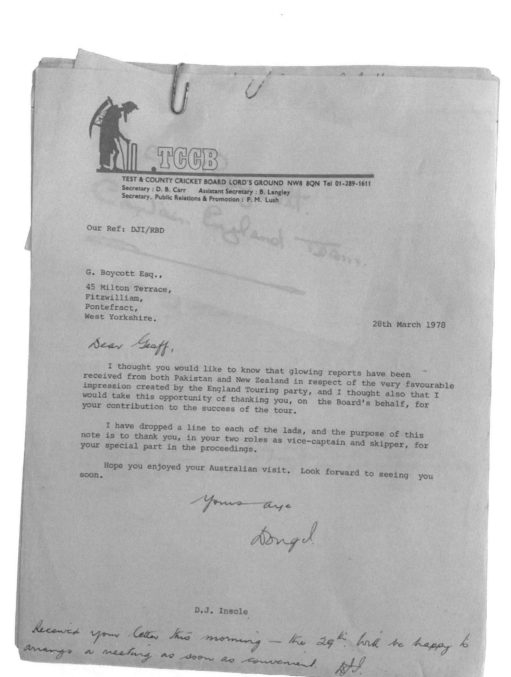

**TCCB**

TEST & COUNTY CRICKET BOARD LORD'S GROUND NW8 8QN Tel 01-289-1611
Secretary : D. B. Carr    Assistant Secretary : B. Langley
Secretary, Public Relations & Promotion : P. M. Lush

Our Ref: DJI/RBD

G. Boycott Esq.,

45 Milton Terrace,
Fitzwilliam,
Pontefract,
West Yorkshire.

28th March 1978

Dear Geoff,

I thought you would like to know that glowing reports have been
received from both Pakistan and New Zealand in respect of the very favourable
impression created by the England Touring party, and I thought also that I
would take this opportunity of thanking you, on the Board's behalf, for
your contribution to the success of the tour.

I have dropped a line to each of the lads, and the purpose of this
note is to thank you, in your two roles as vice-captain and skipper, for
your special part in the proceedings.

Hope you enjoyed your Australian visit. Look forward to seeing you
soon.

Yours aye

Doug

D.J. Insole

Received your letter this morning — the 29th will be happy to
arrange a meeting as soon as convenient. DJI

A letter from Doug Insole, congratulating Boycott on the winter tours of 1977-78, when
he captained England in Pakistan and New Zealand following Mike Brearley's injury.

45 Milton Terrace,
Fitzwilliam,
Nr. Pontefract,
West Yorkshire.

Dear Mr. Carr, Chairman

### Tour Report

I enclose my Tour Report and hope that it may be found to be of interest to the powers that be.

I have refrained from personalised comment as I do not think it is my place to make personal observations and, in any event, the only criticism in this connection which I might have raised would have been in connection with the attitude to practise of only a single member of the party so that perhaps I may be excused naming a name.

I think I have sufficiently emphasized and explained all the points which I feel it worthwhile making except – because I am not sure of the extent of the circulation of the Report – in so far as Pay Differential is concerned.

I have, of course, a personal interest in this although, I suppose not quite as great an interest as those much younger than I am, who are likely to have quite lengthy international cricketing careers.

I do feel that there is a case for meaningful differentials, recognising experience, performance and ability, length of service and number of appearances – and that an appropriate scale, tied to these considerations, might well be in the general interest of providing valuable incentives which could do nothing but good for our national team.

As a suggestion for future tours:-

| | | |
|---|---|---|
| (1) | Basic tour salary | £5000 |
| (2) | For each previous tour | £300 |
| (3) | For each previous test appearance prior to tour | £50 |
| (4) | Nothing extra once tour begins except share of awards and prizes etc. | |

I had wondered about an additional "responsibility" payment to each of the Captain and Vice Captain – but think that this is perhaps unwise.

I am,
Yours sincerely,

GEOFF BOYCOTT

The covering letter sent by Boycott to Donald Carr alonga with his 1978 Tour Report. Note the fees suggested for future tours...

Tel. Morecambe 411077

Flat 3,
Marlow House,
84 Sandylands,
Morecambe, LA3 1DP

24th. November, 1978.

Dear Geoff,

I thought you might like to see the details of Arthur Connell's statement to Members which is designed as background to events of the past six weeks and which will have reached them all today.

Whilst I shall have to look at the who situation realistically and (as you know) I do not pretend that in every way you are whiter than white, I find parts of the statement naive, inaccurate, cynical and downright hypocritical and I intend to say so in a piece to be broadcast on the morning of December 9th.

If the whole thing were not so tragic, it would amuse me to find Fred achieving respectability to the extent of being quoted by the Committee in its own defence! The simple fact is (and I shall say so) that until he joined Packer, Fred was your No. 1 supporter. He took credit for bringing you back into the England fold and was over the moon when you handed him an "exclusive" about that on a plate. Fred is my close friend, but on this topic he and I disagree fundamentally and so do not discuss the subject.

As I have said to you, there are areas in which it is my opinion that you are open to criticism.

In these areas I have said what I felt had to be said and I have said it publicly. But, as in New Zealand this year, if I think you are being criticised for the wrong reasons I shall say so no less publicly or vehemently.

If the meeting goes against you --- and while you have a lot of support you must prepare yourself for it to happen --- I presume you will find it impossible to play under Hampers. If that happens and you feel I can help in any way to sort out an alternative for you, please do not hesitate to call on me. I do not seek to horn in and I am not, in offering my help, seeking a story. The help will be there if you need it. That's all.

I know it must be damn near impossible to do justice to yourself out there with this mess hanging over you but an awful lot of people back home will be rooting hard for you in the Tests. All the luck in the world at Brisbane, and the other games after that.

Yours sincerely,

A letter to Boycott from TMS commentator Don Mosey concerning the captaincy of Yorkshire, sent while Boycott was 10,000 miles away in Brisbane, December 1978. 'Fred' is Fred Trueman, a close friend of Mosey's.

letter left at Lord for Mike Brearley 1979
Wiged by Edgar 915 June.

# The Westmoreland Hotel
## at Lords

Lodge Road
London NW8 7JT
Telephone: 01-722 7722
Cables: Wesmorotel London NW8
Telex: 23101

June 7th

Dear Mr. Brearley

It gives me great pleasure to HEARTILY recommend to you a very promising cricketer who is emerging as one of the game's great all-rounders.

This young man G. Boycott by name has now developed into a bowler of great skill and variety, so much so, that I think his place could be clinched for many years to come.

His deceptive change of pace alarming swing and great accuracy tends to produce many irrational shots from most of the top players playing today.

The habit of bowling with his hat on is reminiscent of that truly great bowler George Herbert Hirst who I am sure he has modelled himself on.

Beware however of rheumatism, fibrositis and superficial post-patella pads (knee-cap)

I hope this young man benefits from your acute handling.

Yours in RESERVE

J.H.

1979, and a moment of levity between Boycott and John Hampshire, who wrote this jokey letter to Mike Brearley recommending "the young man G Boycott" as a promising bowler.